The New Industrial Economics

By the same author

The Economics of Energy (with M. G. Webb)

The New Industrial Economics

An Introduction to Modern Theories of the Firm

Martin Ricketts

Reader in Economics
University of Buckingham

St. Martin's Press
New York

First published in the United States of America in 1987

Printed in Great Britain

ISBN 0-312-00458-3

Library of Congress Cataloging-in-Publication Data

Ricketts, Martin J.
  The new industrial economics.

  Bibliography: p.
  Includes index.
  1. Industrial organization (Economic theory)
I. Title.
HD2326.R53   1987   338.6   86-27918
ISBN 0-312-00458-3

To my mother and father who
will wonder at the capacity of the
academic to make such a fuss about
the transparently obvious.

Contents

Preface

For many years the study of business enterprise has been a relatively neglected facet of economic theory. Most theoretical developments from the mid 1950s onwards involved areas remote from the preoccupations of everyday business life. The internal structure of enterprises was left to organisation theorists, the strategic development of individual firms to business historians, and the analysis of entrepreneurial endeavour to biographers. Indeed economists in the universities and people working in the world of business, at least in the United Kingdom, appeared to have little to say to one another. This was not merely the result of a prejudice against abstract theory on the part of business people. Most of them perhaps, had neither the leisure nor the inclination for reading much economic theory, but in addition their patience would have been tried by an approach which, even allowing for the demands of simplification and abstraction, appeared unrecognisable as a representation of the world in which they lived.

In this book I have attempted to present a review of certain theoretical developments which have become increasingly important during the last decade but which inevitably have their roots further back. These developments all derive from an interest in the problem of information and the transactional difficulties which are encountered in a world where people can never be fully informed. The result is a body of theory which, even when involving a high degree of abstraction, relates to problems of immediate interest to business people. It also provides greater coherence to the business economics which was the product of an era in which economists still communicated with the business world. It is uncanny how close are textbooks such as Edwards' and Townsend's *Business Enterprise*, (the result of a series of seminars at the London School of Economics in the early 1950s) to the spirit and content of modern

transactions cost theory. Their emphasis on entrepreneurial judgement in a world of continuing change would now be called
'Austrian', while their description of the transactional problems
encountered with suppliers or customers and the resulting tendency
towards integration (p. 206) has not been improved upon in the
modern literature. Before the late 1970s however, the transactions
costs view of the world had not been developed systematically, and
it was always possible to characterise business economics as
comprising practical wisdom rather than respectable theory. Once
the information problem began to command attention as the
central problem in economics, however, this attitude changed. The
objective of this book is to show how transactions cost theory
affects our view of business enterprise.

It is important to be clear at the outset that the theory of the firm
expounded here is not a theory of production as conventionally
defined. The entire book is about exchange. The reader will look
in vain for detailed discussions of the properties of production
functions or cost functions; estimates of economies of scale or
minimum efficient scale of plant; elaboration of the 'structure, conduct and performance' paradigm, and many other areas which
make up the core of most established textbooks in industrial
economics. It is no accident that the central tool of analysis used
in this book is not the usual production function diagram, but the
Edgeworth box. This emphasis permeates every chapter. It explains
the content of the opening chapter on costless exchange and the
chapter which succeeds it on transactions costs. It explains the subject matter of chapter 3 on the entrepreneur as an intermediator of
exchange transactions, and of chapter 4 on the policing and enforcement of property rights. Throughout part 2 it is asymmetric
information and the resulting view of the firm as a governance
structure for complex and implicit exchange transactions,
associated with the names of Ronald Coase and Oliver Williamson,
which is at the centre of the stage.

The development of the book as a whole should not be considered as a set of more or less disconnected topics, but as a gradual
elaboration of a particular 'view of the world'. In the first few
chapters the barest outline of the landscape is informally sketched
in, while in part 2 extra colour, missing structural features and
additional detail are superimposed. The reader may like the final
picture or he may hate it, but he should at least be aware that what

he is looking at is intended to be a single item and not a sequence of independent exhibits. A determination to stick to a central theme is also reflected in the choice of empirical work which is cited. Reference is made to some of those studies which impinge most closely on the transactions costs view of the firm. The literature on quasi-vertical, vertical and international integration, for example, is outlined in chapter 7; while that on managerial incentives and the effects of differing property rights structures is reviewed in chapter 8. No attempt has been made to cover comprehensively the existing empirical literature in industrial economics however, as this would have involved an enormous increase in the scope of the book.

If the analytical foundations of the book are neoclassical, they are supplemented by a rhetoric which is distinctly 'Austrian'. This combination of neoclassical analysis and Austrian rhetoric has always seemed to the writer to be of great persuasive power, and it may therefore be appropriate that a health warning should appear in the preface. Historically it seems to have been a combination favoured by many of the writers who developed the transactions costs approach to the firm. Knight used perfectly competitive theory as a benchmark against which to compare the world of profit and uncertainty; Schumpeter is said to have admired Walras above all other economists; Coase, who has a claim to be considered the father of the modern theory of the firm, was also instrumental in developing the neoclassical theory of externalities; and Hayek, for whom the information problem has always been central, produced work in the inter-war years which was formally close to the tradition of neoclassical equilibrium theory.

With exchange transactions as the central issue, the analysis is for the most part individualistic and concentrates on the behaviour of individual economic agents. These agents are also narrowly self-interested. They will shirk as soon as it is in their own perceived interest to do so, and they will rob you if they think they can get away with it. People are not, of course, like this; at least not universally and not all the time. To find the book bearable the reader merely has to believe that it is more likely to be rewarding to analyse the world on the assumption of selfishness then selflessness. Other social scientists including psychologists and sociologists may have alternative methods of approaching the analysis of institutions and I have no interest in asserting the exclusive claims of economics in this area, least of all an economics based entirely on self-interest. I hope the book demonstrates however, that the economic approach and the self-interest assumption are capable of providing a framework for the analysis of business institutions which is both coherent and enlightening.

Thanks are due to many colleagues and friends who have discussed the issues presented in these pages over several years. Norman Barry has been particularly helpful in discussions on the subjectivist tradition in economics. In addition it is necessary to mention my teachers: Stanley Dennison whilst at Newcastle and John Jewkes for whom I worked for two years at the Industrial Policy Group in London were both closely interested in the subject of economic organisation and will find novelty in the book less in the ideas it describes than in the way they are presented, Jack Wiseman at York is responsible for much of the 'Austrian' influence although he will find in these pages that three years as his research assistant left me a somewhat wayward convert, Tony Culyer, my DPhil supervisor, first introduced me to the work of Armen Alchian and the literature on property rights, and Alan Peacock, first at York and then at the University of Buckingham, has been unstinting in his support. In a jointly written book at present under preparation we hope to discuss problems of public policy and of government-industry interreaction. Space constraints have prevented any extended discussion of policy issues in this book.

To Mrs Linda Waterman at the University of Buckingham I owe a great debt of gratitude for deciphering my handwriting, typing the manuscript, checking the spelling, and keeping a watchful eye for split infinitives. To complete this task accurately in conjunction with the other demands of the school of Accountancy, Business and Economics was a notable achievement.

Part I
Basic Concepts

In conditions of perfect knowledge, the theory of the firm is very simple: there are no firms.

Brian J. Loasby

1 The Gains from Trade

1. PRODUCTION AND THE FIRM

The firm is not an easy economic concept to define. Everyone accepts that IBM or ICI or Ford constitute 'firms'. But from an economic as distinct from a purely legal point of view it is necessary to discover what underlying principles enable us to refer to such international giants using the same word as might be used for the local grocer's retail outlet. And if the local grocer's shop is a 'firm' would the same be true of a small hospital run by a charitable foundation, or a church, or even a family? Established textbooks in the principles of economics typically reveal little curiosity about this issue. The firm is simply the fundamental microeconomic unit in the theory of supply. Firms exist and can be recognised by their function, which is to transform inputs of factors of production into outputs of goods and services. With some notable exceptions the implied asymmetry between the theory of demand, with its emphasis on the *individual consumer* as the ultimate microeconomic building block, and the theory of supply, with its emphasis on the firm, is rarely explored.

Conventional theory does, however, provide a clue to the nature of 'the firm'. The process of production usually involves coordinating the activities of different individuals. Suppliers of labour, capital, intermediate inputs, raw materials and land cooperate with one another to produce outputs of goods and services. The institutional setting in which this coordination of activity is attempted may vary enormously, but where economic agents cooperate with one another not through a system of explicit contracts which bind each to every other member of the group, but through a system of bilateral contracts in which each comes to an agreement with a 'single contractual agent', the essential ingredient of 'the firm' is

3

present. It is therefore the nature of the contractual arrangements which bind individuals together which, at least from the point of view of economic theory, constitutes the central preoccupation of the theory of the firm. Much of this book will be concerned to elaborate upon this basic idea and to investigate the insights which flow from it.

2. SCARCITY

Most expositions of elementary economic analysis start with a statement to the effect that economics is concerned with choice. If individuals are confronted by limited resources they must choose between alternatives. Following the definition of Robbins (1932, p. 16), 'Economics is the science which studies human behaviour as a relationship between ends and scarce means which have alternative uses'. As Robbins recognised, this definition is not of very great interest when applied to isolated individuals. A lone individual would have an allocation problem to solve, but a student of such a person's activities would find it difficult to go further than asserting the proposition that out of all the perceived available courses of action, the isolated decision maker chooses the alternative which he most prefers.

As part of a community of individuals, however, each person is confronted with a more complex problem. Each individual will usually find that his best strategy is not to cut himself off from all communication with his fellows, but rather to co-ordinate his activity with that of other people. Making the best use of scarce resources will therefore involve forming agreements with others, and economics then becomes the study of the social mechanisms which facilitate such agreements. Hidden in this statement, however, are two rather different preoccupations.

First, it is possible to ask in any given situation what particular allocation (or allocations) of resources, what set of agreements, would be best in the sense that no individual or set of individuals within the entire community could gain by opting out and substituting alternative feasible arrangements. Economists express this idea in the technical language of game theory as identifying allocations of resources which are in 'the core' of a market exchange game.[1] Suppose there were a community of four individuals. Each we may assume *could* live the life of a recluse, but none wishes to do so if cooperation with the others is capable of adding to his or her perceived satisfaction. The four meet and discuss various proposals which will make them all better off. No one will accept a deal which reduces their well-being below that of an isolated recluse, and similarly no final agreement would hold if any two or possibly three out of four could benefit by coming to some alternative arrangements between themselves. A set of agreements which it is in no single individual's or group of individual's interests to renounce in favour of an available alternative, is said to be in 'the core'. Allocations of resources that are 'core' allocations represent in one sense a 'solution' to the resource allocation problem.

A second and rather different question, concerns the *process* by which agreements are formulated. If the tastes and preferences of our four individuals are known to the economist, and if their skills and endowments of resources including tools and equipment as well as natural resources, raw materials and land are likewise clearly defined, it should be possible in principle to list all the conceivable options available. Working out allocations of resources which are in 'the core' becomes a matter of mere 'calculation'. All the necessary information which is formally required to uncover a 'solution' is present, and the rest can be accomplished by a sufficiently devoted mathematician or adequately powerful computer. But this tells us nothing about the methods adopted by our four individuals to solve their resource allocation problem. Imagine, for example, that by some fluke of history the four people meet on an otherwise uninhabited island (the sole survivors from four separate shipwrecks). Each person will have little idea of the skills possessed by his associates. Indeed each may be in some doubt about his own capabilities in the new and unfamiliar environment. The potential of the island to sustain life, the characteristics and uses of the available resources, the best methods of using these resources for various purposes (making clothes, building shelter, finding food, etc.) are all a matter of guesswork and hunch. Setting up the problem in this way makes it clear that what our four individuals lack most is not a calculator, but *information*.

Facing the appalling problems of survival the four islanders are likely to agree to cooperate with one another. These agreements will not represent a 'solution' to the problem of resource allocation in any ideal sense, since no one can possibly know what the ideal way of proceeding entails. Instead, agreements between the four represent stages in a process of discovery.[2] As time advances experience will reveal something of the relative talents of the individuals and the properties and potential of the available resources. Arrangements between the individuals are continually modified in the light of past experience and of expectations about the future. In this framework it is still possible to argue that the subject matter of economics is the allocation of scarce means between competing uses, but it is clear that the nature of the economic problem when opportunities are not fully known is quite different from the problem conceived of as making the best of available resources in the context of perfect information.

3. THE ALLOCATION PROBLEM

At this stage it will prove useful to develop the theme further by reference to a simple example of the sort frequently encountered in basic textbooks on the principles of economics. We continue to assume that the world consists of four individuals who possess differing endowments of resources. Conventional analysis then proceeds on the assumption that the limited resources available to each individual permit them to produce various known combinations of goods and services. Suppose for simplicity that people desire only two goods (x and y). With the resources at his disposal person A can produce any combination of x and y in the area $aa'o$ illustrated in Figure 1.1. Given that both x and y confer benefits on person A it is inconceivable that he would choose to produce at any point inside the line aa'. This line aa' is called person A's production possibility curve. Its downward slope reflects the fact that the production of *more* of any one good requires resources to be diverted from the production of the other. The steepness of the curve indicates the amount of y which has to be sacrificed to produce an extra unit of x. In the case of person A one more unit of x entails the sacrifice of four units of y. Thus the slope of the production possibility curve indicates the *marginal opportunity cost* of an extra unit of x. If person A produces more x its marginal cost will be $4y$. Note that the cost of x can be interpreted as a physical and objective measure (the amount of y forgone) only

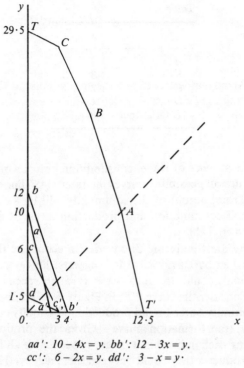

aa': $10 - 4x = y$. bb': $12 - 3x = y$.
cc': $6 - 2x = y$. dd': $3 - x = y$.

Figure 1.1

because we have assumed that all the options available to A are known to him with complete certainty.

Each of the other people (labelled B, C and D) will also face constraints on their ability to produce. The constraints are represented by the lines bb', cc' and dc' in Figure 1.1. Notice that some individuals are luckier than others. All points on person B's production possibility curve are unattainable by any other person. Notice also that the marginal costs of production differ for each person. Person D for example is relatively poor but in terms of y sacrificed he is the cheapest producer of x.

As solitary individuals each person will have to pick a point on his or her production possibility curve. Suppose for example that x and y were not substitutable in consumption and that everyone consumed these goods in fixed proportions (say equal quantities of

Table 1.1

	x	y
A	2	2
B	3	3
C	2	2
D	1	1
Total output	8	8

each). In the absence of trade, consumption points would be given where production possibility curves intersect a 45° line through the origin. The total output of the community will by 8x and 8y and the individual consumption and production levels of each person are recorded in Table 1.1.

One of the most enduring discoveries in economic theory, first fully established by David Ricardo, suggests, however, that these four individuals could do much better through specialisation and exchange. Consider the curve *TT'* in Figure 1.1. This is referred to as the 'community outer-bound production possibility curve' or the 'community transformation curve'. Given the production constraints facing each individual it is easy to see that if all four people produced product x they could between them achieve 12.5 units of output. If now some y is to be produced it will entail the sacrifice of some x and it seems reasonable to allocate the person to y production who can produce it at least cost. This person is A, for whom each unit of y will entail the sacrifice of only 0.25 units of x. Person A has the greatest 'comparative advantage' in y production of the four individuals. If A specialises in y production and persons B, C and D specialise in x production, the community in total will achieve an output of 10 units of x and 10 units of y (point A). Further y production can only be achieved by using another person in addition to A. The person who can produce further y at least marginal cost is now person B for whom the marginal cost of y is 0.33x. Complete specialisation of both A *and* B in y production and of C and D in x production would enable the community to achieve 6 units of x and 22 units of y (point B). Yet further y production must now involve person C, for whom the marginal cost is 0.5x, and so forth.

Given the rather extreme assumptions we have made about

Table 1.2

	A	B	C	D	Total
Units of x and y	2.5	3.5	2.5	1.5	10.0

consumption patterns it is clear that point A will represent the best production point. Specialisation has resulted in an increase of community output of 2 units of x and 2 units of y. No alternative arrangements exist which would permit the achievement of any points further out along the 45° line. We would expect therefore that any agreement between the four individuals would involve A specialising in y production and B, C and D specialising in x production.

This still leaves open the question of how the benefits of specialisation are to be distributed. We might for example envisage one of the transactors making the following suggestion. 'Since our joint efforts will result in a total increase in output of $2x$ and $2y$ above that achievable by our original uncoordinated activity, let us each share equally in this benefit. Final consumption levels would then be as recorded in Table 1.2. All individuals achieve a consumption level 0.5 units higher than those recorded in Table 1.1.

This attempted solution will not work, however. To see why, it is necessary to consider all the trading options available to the various transactors. There is nothing to stop A and B, for example, from getting together and agreeing to collaborate without the others. Similarly, persons C and D might come to a separate agreement. The total output or 'payoff' achievable by all the conceivable 'coalitions' of people is recorded in Table 1.3.[3] The reader should take an entry at random and check that its meaning is clear. If persons C and D collaborated they could achieve a combined output of 4 units of x and 4 units of y as is illustrated in Figure 1.2. D would specialise in x production thus yielding 3 units of x, while C would produce 1 unit of x and 4 units of y. In total they therefore produce 4 units of each commodity.

Now consider the position of persons A and D. If they accept the deal offered in Table 1.2 they will join in an agreement which involves all four transactors with a total payoff to the 'coalition' of

Table 1.3

'Coalition'	'Payoff' (units of x and y achievable)	'Coalition'	'Payoff' (units of x and y achievable)
A	2.00	BC	5.25
B	3.00	BD	5.25
C	2.00	CD	4.00
D	1.00	ABC	7.60
		ABD	7.60
AB	5.20	BCD	7.50
AC	4.40	ACD	6.80
AD	4.40	ABCD	10.00

10 units of x and 10 of y. Out of this, A will receive 2.5 units of each commodity and D will receive 1.5 units of each. But from Table 1.3 we see that simply by ignoring the others and striking a deal between themselves, A and D could receive a combined payoff of 4.4 units of each commodity instead of the 4.0 of Table 1.2. It follows that the 'allocation' of Table 1.2 is not in 'the core'. Persons A and D could both be better off by renouncing the allocation of Table 1.2 and agreeing an alternative between themselves.

To illustrate the case of an allocation which *is* in 'the core' consider the entries of Table 1.4. Comparing the entries in Table 1.4 with those in Table 1.3 it will be confirmed that no coalition of individuals could do better by striking a separate bargain between

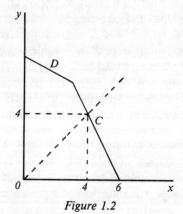

Figure 1.2

Table 1.4

	A	B	C	D	Total
Units of x and y	2.40	3.10	2.30	2.20	10.00

themselves. An allliance of B, C and D for example could produce a payoff of 7.5, but their combined allocation in Table 1.4 is 7.6. A similar calculation can be performed for every other possible coalition. Thus the allocation of Table 1.4 is in 'the core' of the exchange game.

An agreement to specialise in accordance with comparative advantage and then to allocate the output as described in Table 1.4 is therefore one 'solution' to the economic problem of making the best out of scarce resources. It is not, however, a unique solution, as the reader can verify by checking the entries of Table 1.5 against those in Table 1.3. The three allocations recorded in Table 1.5 are also in 'the core'.

Table 1.5

	A	B	C	D	Total
Units of x and y	2.50	3.00	2.25	2.25	10.00
Units of x and y	2.00	3.20	2.40	2.40	10.00
Units of x and y	2.22	3.11	2.33	2.33	10.00

4. THE COORDINATION PROBLEM

In the section above, attention was focused primarily on calculating a 'solution' to the allocation problem under certain specific conditions. Little was said explicitly about the *mechanism* by which a solution might be achieved. Specialisation implies the existence of a coordinating mechanism by which one person's activities are made compatible with the actions of others. In the example of section 3 this mechanism consisted of a bargaining process. The four individuals could be seen as initially forming provisional agreements. If it then transpired that alternative more beneficial arrangements were possible for some individual or set of individuals (the provisional agreements did not represent a 'core' allocation) then the parties could 'recontract'. The process of recontracting would continue until it was in no one's interest to renounce the existing provisional agreement. At this point the agreement would be finalised.[4] The provisional agreement summarised in Table 1.2 for example was renounced by persons *A* and *D*. If at the end of further negotiations the agreement summarised in the first line of Table 1.5 were hit upon, this would hold and the process of recontracting would cease.

The recontracting process just described does present some awkward dilemmas for the theorist, however. For if this process means anything, it must imply that the individuals involved possess incomplete information about the production possibilities and preferences of others. For if information were perfect there would be no purpose in conducting 'negotiations'. All the potential 'core allocations' or 'solutions' could be computed mathematically, as indeed we computed some in Tables 1.4 and 1.5. The big problem would then be that of choosing between a number of possible known solutions rather than discovering *some* particular solution or other. Choice between multiple solutions raises extremely difficult issues since a move from one possibility to another involves some people becoming better off and others worse off (compare lines 1 and 2 of Table 1.5). Which of the many possible options available might eventually be agreed upon is therefore not easy to determine, and it is at least conceivable that no agreement would be forthcoming. Faced with this problem economic theorists have developed an ingenious escape route. It is possible to show that as the number of contractors in a market increases, then under certain conditions the set of 'core' allocations diminishes in size. Indeed, in the limit, with an infinite number of contractors the 'core' shrinks to a single allocation.[5] No longer is there a problem of choosing between multiple solutions since only a single determinate solution exists.

For a theorist working with the full-information assumption and anxious to show the existence of a unique solution to the allocation problem, a shrinking core is no doubt a matter of some satisfaction. It is difficult to suppress the feeling, however, that where search is a costly activity the smaller the core the more tiresome and protracted is the process of finding it. In a world in which information is discovered through the process of negotiation there would not appear to be the same compelling reasons to expect any particular outcome to occur. Indeed, it is not even clear that the final agreement will represent a core allocation. After some provisional contracts have been made the parties search around for a better deal. Nothing is finalised until each contractor finds that he cannot improve on his allocation. But this raises the question of how long people are prepared to search for coalitions which improve on their present position. As the number of contractors increases so the number of potential coalitions increases exponentially and the number of core allocations declines. Any commitment to try all conceivable possibilities could be likely to imply never coming to a final agreed solution.

If the process of forming contracts with one another involves the use of scarce resources, then the 'best' use of these scarce resources cannot be said to reside entirely in the discovery of a 'core' allocation. A more crucial question concerns how scarce resources are used in the process of contracting itself. Conventional expositions of the recontracting process and the discovery of an allocation of resources which is in the core of the exchange game are therefore suspect. Either the process described is itself a user of scarce resources, in which case it cannot be inferred that search will continue indefinitely until a solution is found, or the process does not use scarce resources, in which case it is merely an unnecessary story to cloak the 'full-information' assumption.

5. TATONNEMENT

The bargaining framework outlined in section 3 deriving from the work of Edgeworth is not the usual approach to elementary treatments of economics. It is more conventional to concentrate on the role of markets and the price system as a device for co-ordinating activity. Suppose, for example, that all contractors were able to exchange x for y at a ratio of 1 for 1. For every person the market price of x is one y and vice versa. Returning to Figure 1.1 it is seen that person A must sacrifice only 0.25 units of x in production to obtain a unit of y whereas in the market the price of y is $1x$. With the marginal cost to person A of y production so much less than the prevailing price, it will be in his interest to specialise in y production and exchange in the market. By this means he can

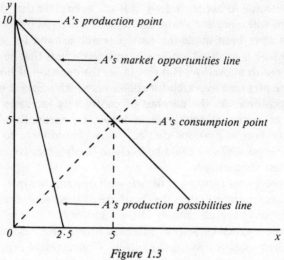

Figure 1.3

achieve a *production* level of 10 units of *y* and a *consumption* level of 5 units of each commodity (see Figure 1.3).

But the marginal cost of *y* production is less than the assumed prevailing market price for both persons *B* and *C* as well. Only person *D* will find it to his advantage to specialise in *x* production since for him the marginal cost of *y* exceeds the market price (the marginal cost of *x* on the other hand is less than its market price). Faced, therefore, with this ratio of exchange, the four individuals will be induced to specialise according to their area of comparative advantage and between them they will produce at point *C* in Figure 1.1.

Given the special nature of consumers' preferences, however, it is clear that with production of 28 units of *y* and only 3 units of *x* there will be enormous excess demand for *x*. Equilibrium in the market requires quantities demanded and supplied at the prevailing price to be the same. Clearly a higher price of *x* relative to *y* is required to induce persons *B* and *C* to change their area of specialisation. Point *A* will be achieved if the price ratio is set between 3*y* for 1*x* and 4*y* for 1*x*. A single ratio of exchange applying to all transactors will result in a market equilibrium at point *A*.

This market 'solution' to the resource allocation problem turns out to be closely related to the concept of the 'core' mentioned in the last section. Suppose, for example, that the ratio of exchange were $3y$ for $1x$. These market opportunities clearly do not affect person B since they are exactly the same as the opportunities which confront him in production. He will continue to consume 3 units of each commodity. Person A on the other hand will specialise in y production (10 units) and exchange 7.5 units of y for 2.5 units of x thus achieving 2.5 units of each. Both persons C and D will specialise in x (3 units each) and exchange 1.75 units for 2.25 units of y thus achieving 2.25 units of each. Comparing these results with Table 1.5 the reader can verify that they correspond with the entries on the first line. A market ratio of exchange of $3y$ per $1x$ will produce an allocation of resources in the conditions specified, equivalent to the first 'core' allocation of Table 1.5. As an exercise the reader should verify that a market rate of exchange of $4y$ per $1x$ will produce a result equivalent to the 'core' allocation recorded on the *second* line of Table 1.5. Indeed, it can be rigorously proved that any competitive equilibrium will imply an allocation which is in the 'core'.[6] A given ratio of exchange applying to all contractors of $3.5y$ per $1x$ will produce the third allocation of Table 1.5.

This theory of competitive equilibrium, however, suffers from similar difficulties to the exchange theory of Edgeworth discussed above. In its most general form the theory indicates that there will exist, under specified conditions, a set of relative prices such that individual responses to these *given* prices will be compatible with equilibrium in every market. The question which the theory does not attempt to answer is precisely *how* this equilibrium set of prices is to be discovered. As Shackle (1972) puts it 'what (general equilibrium) theory neglects is the epistemic problem, the problem of how the necessary knowledge on which reason can base itself is to be gained' (p. 447). Like the recontracting process of Edgeworth the theory of competitive market equilibrium has an equivalent story to tell. In this case it is supposed that an 'auctioneer' sets prices and that people form provisional agreements at these given prices. If it transpires that excess demands or supplies exist the provisional agreements lapse and the auctioneer modifies prices in an attempt to eliminate any disequilibria. This process is termed the 'tatonnement' process and is associated primarily with the name of Leon Walras.[7]

The major problem with the Walrasian auction is not simply that it does not represent an accurate representation of reality. Resource allocation is not conducted by means of Walrasian auctions and, more to the point, the reason why is not difficult to understand. Such a process would be enormously costly. Indeed such is the complexity characteristic of exchange relationships that an attempt to proceed along Walrasian lines would absorb all the energies and resources of contractors without perhaps ever achieving a 'solution'. Once more the paradox of equilibrium theory is exposed. If all information is costlessly available, the auctioneer will get it right first time. If the process of acquiring information is costly, endless pursuit of a general equilibrium is the ultimate example of the ideal becoming the enemy of the good.

6. THE EQUILIBRIUM METHOD

The purpose of our brief discussion of the salient features of general equilibrium theorising conducted above is not to develop a detailed critique or to question the intellectual achievement which it represents. It is important, however, to appreciate the nature of that achievement and the implications which it holds for the theory of the firm. General equilibrium theory represents an existence proof. Under tightly specified conditions in a world consisting of many individuals all with different tastes, skills and other endowments of resources, there will exist a set of relative prices of goods and factors compatible with universal market clearing. Equivalently there will exist a set of agreements between the individuals which no one will wish to change. The activities of all contractors will be perfectly reconciled. For any given set of preferences, resources and technological possibilities a 'solution' to the resource allocation problem exists in terms of specific outcomes.

Such a perfect coordination of all activity requires that agreements are concluded simultaneously and that transactions costs are zero. Knowledge of all technical possibilities both now and in the future must be assumed to be complete. The very passage of time itself can be admitted only in a very artificial sense. By extending the concept of consumers' preferences to embrace consumption in future time periods, and of production possibilities to include the 'transformation' via investment of goods today into goods tomorrow it is possible to envisage a set of equilibrium intertemporal prices. At some price ratio the right to consume apples in period 2 may be exchanged for the right to consume nuts in period 5. The final set of agreements will then embrace transactions extending over all future time periods. Time exists as a dimension on a graph. But outcomes over time are completely predetermined at the moment of general agreement. Time is incorporated into the analysis but only at the price of robbing the concept of all meaning. Formally 'apples today' and 'apples tomorrow' are simply two different commodities. Decisions concerning consumption and production levels are made 'now'.

Time implies uncertainty, and the uncertain future poses intractable problems for any theory of rational choice. For general equilibrium theorists a further extension of the Walrasian system to embrace transactions in 'state-contingent claims' is a possibility. Each transactor is assumed to possess a list of all possible future 'states of the world' along with some probability estimates attached to each state. Given initial resource endowments, the transactors exchange claims to resources contingent upon specified events. For example a claim to 1 1b of cocoa in period 3 contingent upon heavy rainfall in Ghana, might exchange in equilibrium for two claims to 1 1b of coffee in period 4 contingent upon no frost in Brazil.

Quite apart from the transactions costs problem mentioned earlier, this effort to achieve a determinate equilibrium in the face of uncertainty encounters even more fundamental difficulties. For the transactors are 'unboundedly rational'. All possible future states of the world are imaginable and nothing can occur which has not been imagined. Yet when the future is concerned there would appear to be no limits on the agenda of possible events, no boundaries on the contingencies which might be considered. Decision making in the face of such uncertainty cannot then be rational in the sense of making one best choice in the face of known opportunities. To quote Shackle (1972): 'it is plain that in order to achieve a theory of value applicable to the real human situation, reason must compromise with time' (p. 269).

7. INSTITUTIONS AND GROUPS

For the purposes of the theory of the firm the important point about the general equilibrium method is that by effectively excluding time and uncertainty from the analysis all transactions are costlessly and instantaneously reconciled. In this environment there are no institutional structures called firms. The efforts of all individuals are coordinated by a gigantic and complex web of contractual commitments simultaneously entered into. The economy is made up of a myriad of individual contractors, each one in an intricate and complex pattern or interrelationships with every other. As a description of economic life, however, this is clearly not very accurate. Institutions such as firms, clubs, political parties, trade unions and bureaucracies exist, and their existence, if it is not to be left unexplained or put down to chance, can be viewed as the outcome of the attempts by rational individuals to solve the resource allocation problems which confront them.

If firms help in the process of resource allocation they must represent a response to factors from which general equilibrium theory abstracts. The economy, to use the analogy of Simon (1969) and Loasby (1976), is not like a watch made up of thousands of parts placed separately in an appropriate position relative to all the others, but is more equivalent to a mechanism made up of several subassemblies the operating principles of which may be analysed separately even if their ultimate purposes may be fully understood only in the context of the complete item. A system of subassemblies places limits on the number of linkages which must be simultaneously considered and thereby reduces the costs of establishing them.

Firms are formed and survive as an institutional response to transactions costs. In a world of costless knowledge they have no rationale, but in a world in which opportunities are continually being discovered and in which the formation of agreements between individuals is a costly activity, firms may be seen as devices for reducing the costs of achieving coordinated effort. The ways in which transactions costs are reduced and the problems which arise as a result will be discussed in greater detail in future chapters. For present purposes it is sufficient to remember that 'firms' are characterised by a system of bilateral contracts. Each person comes to an agreement with 'the firm'. In the case of a small business a single proprietor might be the central contractual agent. In more complex cases the agreement will be between employees, managers, bondholders or landowners and a 'legal fiction' such as BP or US Steel. The firm is a 'nexus of contracts'.[8]

The nature of this set of contracts is of very great importance.

They are not highly specific contracts. They will not normally lay down extremely detailed provisions concerning when, where and how particular tasks are to be performed. When we join a firm as an employee we agree, within certain limits, to do whatever we are asked to do. We agree to be 'organised'. When we join as a manager we agree to organise resources, and have considerable discretion as to the way this may be done. Contracts, in other words, are *imperfectly specified*. This lack of specificity derives from the simple fact that the precise details of the actions required of the employees of a firm may be unknown at the time the contract is made. The decision-making process continues through time, and only time will reveal the decisions which may be made in the future concerning the best plan of action for the firm. If contracts had to be renegotiated with every small change of policy, the firm as a useful device for allocating resources would disappear.

Within the firm, information is collected concerning opportunities for productive collaboration, on the skills and attributes of employees, on new technical innovations, on the demands of consumers and so forth. This information must be transmitted to the relevant decision makers who must then choose and implement a plan of action. Resource allocation *within the firm* is not therefore the outcome of entirely decentralised decisions by individual people in response to their particular circumstances as in a market *process*. Nor is it the result of simultaneous agreement between all contractors as in a *state* of general equilibrium. Resources within firms are allocated by the conscious decisions of *planners*. The market *process* is replaced in the firm by a planning *process*. Firms are 'islands of conscious power in an ocean of unconscious co-operation', to use D. H. Robertson's vivid metaphor.[9]

It is important for readers to recognise that this initial characterisation of the firm will be amended in important respects in future chapters. As presented here, our definition depends upon a clear distinction being possible between a 'market process' and a 'planning process'. Later we shall question whether a clear dividing line can be drawn, and we will investigate in greater detail the spectrum of contractual relations which ranges from pure market types towards contracts involving more 'firm-like' characteristics.[10]

In timeless equilibrium, plan and market are indistinguishable, for they may both be envisaged in certain conditions as being consistent with the same final allocation of resources. Whether in the state of perfect knowledge the Walrasian auctioneer calls out the appropriate set of prices or tells people to consume and supply the appropriate quantities of goods and services could hardly matter less. But a market is not a final allocation, it is a way of proceeding. Similarly, planning as a mechanism of resource allocation implies a continuing method of coming to decisions rather than the achievement of any particular eternal outcomes.

The existence of firms suggests that, up to a point at least, a planning process may have advantages over the market. Groups of people may find it expedient to accept a system of imperfectly specified contracts with a single contractual agent who processes the information provided to him and allocates resources accordingly. It can be advantageous to be told what to do if the person making this decision is better informed about the opportunities available for cooperative effort than we are and can co-ordinate our activities with others in ways not achievable by alternative means. The potential benefits of the firm are associated with inevitable costs, however. For if contracts are not tightly specified it will often be costly to determine whether or not their provisions are being honoured. Incentives must be devised to induce employees to cooperate both in the provision of acccurate information to decision makers and in the efficient execution of the resulting decisions. Before investigating these problems in detail and analysing their effect on the internal structure of firms however, it is time to look more closely at the general nature of 'transactions costs' which play such a central part in the theory of the firm.

NOTES

1. For an elementary introduction to game theory *see* M. Bacharach (1976) *Economics and the Theory of Games*, Macmillan, London. The classic reference is J. Von Neumann and O. Morgenstern (1944).
2. Perceiving economic life as a discovery procedure and, by implication, the primary economic problem as an information problem, is especially associated with 'Austrian' thinkers; *see* Hayek (1978). The approach lends itself to the use of biological and particularly evolutionary analogies as new ideas are tried out and submitted to the test of survival in the market. A major contribution in this tradition is Alchian (1950).
3. Game theorists will recognise this table as representing the complete 'characteristic function' of our exchange game. For each possible

coalition the joint payoff is recorded; *see* Bacharach (1976, pp. 121–4).

4. This description of a bargaining process was used in the theoretical work of F. Y. Edgeworth, especially in his *Mathematical Psychics*. *See also* 'On the determinateness of economic equilibrium' in Edgeworth (1925) Vol. II. Thus: 'A "final settlement" is not reached until the market has hit upon a set of agreements which cannot be varied with advantage to all the re-contracting parties' (p. 314).
5. Gravelle and Rees (1981) present an intuitive discussion of the conditions under which this theorem will hold (pp. 266–70).
6. e.g. Gravelle and Rees (1981, pp. 263–5).
7. Walras (1965) *Elements of Pure Economics*. Translated by William Jaffé.
8. The 'nexus of contracts' idea goes back to Coase (1937). A more detailed discussion is undertaken in Chapter 2, and it forms the foundation for most of the rest of the analysis in this book.
9. D. H. Robertson and S. R. Dennison (1960, p. 73).
10. *See* especially Chapter 7 section 3.

2   Transactions costs

1. THE PROCESS OF EXCHANGE

All exchange transactions encounter problems of information and
enforcement. Consider for example the process of building houses.
Suppose that a person A wishes to build an extension to his home.
One possibility is that A will draw up his plans, submit them to the
relevant public authorities, dig his foundations, order the bricks,
mix the cement, build the walls, plaster the interior, put in the
doors and windows and undertake to install any electrical fitments
and plumbing. But elementary economic principles suggest this is
unlikely. Recognising the advantages to be gained from specialisation and exchange person A might instead decide to spend his time
in a suitably remunerative occupation and then to purchase the
services of specialist help. He could for example pay an architect
to draw his plans, another agent to obtain the necessary planning
consent, a bricklayer to build his walls and an electrician, a
carpenter, a plumber and so forth to fulfil their respective tasks.

By forming agreements with specialists person A will gain the
classic advantages from exchange. But he has also given himself
some problems.

(i) Like a cook consulting Hannah Glasse's *Art of Cookery* who
is there advised 'first catch your hare', A has to find the people who
are going to help him. As may be subtly suggested in this celebrated
mis-quote, in any process of co-ordination, obtaining the con-
stituent ingredients is not necessarily the easiest part.

(ii) Having located his bricklayer, architect or electrician, A has
to form some assessment of their professional competence. If the
bricklayer is more productive at laying bricks than is person A there
should be some advantage in using his services. But how does A
acquire such information? The existence of some other examples of

the bricklayer's handiwork which A can inspect, or the recommendation of other satisfied clients, are obvious possibilities, although many services and goods present greater difficulties. Person A may never be quite sure that he is not risking life and limb each time he switches on his electric kettle.

(iii) With each of his contacts, A will draw up a separate agreement. But this will not necessarily be as straightforward as it sounds. Person A knows what he wants to do in a very general sense. He wants to extend his house. The technical details of how this can be accomplished and the options available may, however, be quite beyond him. When he approaches his architect with a request to produce some plans he therefore confronts a significant problem. He cannot ask the architect to undertake a highly specific and carefully delineated task since at this level of detail A quite literally does not know what he wants. Instead he must ask the architect to act on his behalf. The architect is A's *agent* and is asked to make specific recommendations which are likely to satisfy the general requirements laid down by person A. Proceeding in this way enables A to gain the advantages of specialised advice, but as an intelligent and shrewd individual he is sure to be beset by a few nagging doubts.

If, for example, A does not like the architect's suggested plans and does not wish to proceed with the project, will he have to pay a fee to the architect? Clearly the architect is unlikely to agree to waive his fee simply because his client is dissatisfied. Such an arrangement would provide an enormous incentive to person A to dissemble. He would claim to see no merit in the plans whatever whilst secretly taking careful note of their contents. But the alternative arrangements by which the architect is paid a fee irrespective of the quality of his work is likewise fraught with difficulties, this time from the perspective of person A. Person A may wonder whether the architect has given his problem more than a moment's thought, or has perhaps delegated the case to some assistant of little talent and even less experience.

Similar considerations will play a part in person A's dealings with each of the other tradesmen involved in his project. The plumber, for example, cannot be told in detail how to proceed since only the broad objectives are defined by A. Technicalities such as the gauge and type of piping to be used, the potential heat output required of the boiler, the positioning of thermostats, the siting of the pumps, are all matters upon which A will accept the advice of the expert. The plumber will be asked to solve these detailed problems in ways which serve the interests of A. He should not install a boiler with the wrong characteristics simply because he stands to gain from an agreement with the suppliers, but his client will be in a weak position from which to detect such behaviour.

(iv) Overcoming the difficulties of formulating enforceable agreements with each individual is an important pre-requisite to the success of A's plans. Of equal significance, however, is the ability of A to *coordinate* the activities of each of his helpers. To build an extension to a house using specialist help involves many people cooperating together. Only in the simplest cases will the provisions of one person's contract be entirely independent of the provisions in another's. A decision, for example, to lay a concrete floor rather than a wooden suspended floor will influence the way in which the heating system is installed. Likewise the electrician and the plumber may have to work closely together at various stages. Thus A will find it difficult to finalise his agreement with any one person in the absence of agreements with all the others. Stolidly he contacts first one and then another, asking advice, modifying his original proposals and renegotiating terms until eventually he calculates that construction can begin. Inevitably there will be some residual uncertainty about his plans, some unforeseen difficulties which will arise and which will result in a continuing process of bargaining. Within rather vaguely defined limits his craftsmen accept the obligation to be flexible. Outside these limits they will claim that the job they are doing was not part of their original agreement and will wish to renegotiate terms.

As building starts, A becomes painfully aware that delays and problems in one area have implications for his plans in others. Bricklayers turn up but cannot build because the inspector has yet to see the foundations. A nevertheless pays them for their time. The nagging doubts which afflicted person A at the beginning now turn to serious concern. Indeed he begins to have nightmares. In his sleep he sees the extension to his house. Were those gaps in the roof really the latest thing in ventilation? And was it usual for walls to sway so far in the breeze? In the nearby hotel his architect and lawyer share a joke over a glass of whisky. It seems they are using his wallet to pay for their drinks. His gaze returns to his extension only to see the whole structure collapse in a cloud of dust. Across the rubble a shadowy figure advances towards him coughing and dusting his pin-stripe suit. The planner from the local authority serves him with a demolition order as a result of failure to comply with all necessary regulations. Person *A* wakes up sweating. He at least has discovered the primary message of this chapter. Whatever may be the potential advantages of specialisation and exchange, they certainly do not come free.

2. CONTRACTS AND INFORMATION

Our fictional story of person *A*'s building project was designed to highlight some of the difficulties everyone encounters at some time or other in the process of contracting. It is now necessary to look at the issues involved from a more analytical viewpoint. Perhaps the most important point about the hapless *A* is that his problems all derive from various forms of *information deficiency*. Were information costlessly available and all transactions costlessly enforceable most of his worries would be over. Consider now the various points at which *A* confronts the problem of his own ignorance.

(i) The first problem was that A did not know the location, skills or reliability of the tradesmen he required. Finding out this type of information requires time spent in search. More consideration will be given to the question of search in Chapter 3, but it should be evident from the discussion of Chapter 1 that to search exhaustively, that is to search until information is complete, would be to do nothing else. At some stage the costs of further search in terms of the perceived opportunities forgone will outweigh the benefits in terms of the expected new opportunities potentially discoverable. Further, certain types of ignorance are in their nature costly to dispel through search. Ignorance of the price of a very well-defined product can be mitigated by asking for quotes from an increasing number of sellers. But ignorance of product quality is more difficult. It may be worth paying more for the services of a more skilled person, but how is person *A* to tell a good and reliable craftsman from a poor one *ex ante*? Clearly, this problem ultimately derives from the difficulty of *precisely specifying* what services are required in a contract. If a contract between person *A* and a craftsman were clearly and unambiguously specified the 'reliability' or 'skill' of the craftsman would not be an issue. Either the provisions of the contract are fulfilled and the craftsman demonstrates sufficient skill or they are not fulfilled in which case the absence of sufficient skill results in a specified penalty. A skilled and reliable craftsman is valuable to person *A* because he may not have the technical knowledge required to specify precisely what is to be done. The absence of this knowledge, however, will make it difficult for *A* to discover the credentials of his potential workforce. All craftsmen, skilled or otherwise, will have an incentive to overstate their expertise in the process of negotiation, and the truly skilled will have difficulty in communicating their status to the doubting person *A*.

The problem which we have uncovered here is in fact of very widespread interest in economics. Essentially it relates to any transaction in which one of the parties is better informed than the other. Such transactions are said to be characterised by a structure of information which is *asymmetric*. Akerlof (1970) gives as an example of a market with asymmetric information, transactions in second-hand cars. It will often be very costly for a buyer of a second-hand car to determine accurately its true quality. He may or may not buy a 'lemon' (an American expression for a bad car) but *ex ante* there is not much he can do to avoid it. Ignorance on the part of buyers will imply therefore that both good and bad second-hand cars sell for the same price. *Sellers* of these cars, however, will have much better knowledge of their history and characteristics and therefore correspondingly better judgement about the probability of obtaining good or bad service in the future. The upshot will be that owners of good cars will tend to feel that the second-hand market value seriously understates their (better informed) valuation. The owners of 'lemons' on the other hand are more likely to sell. As the average quality of second-hand cars offered for sale falls the price that they fetch falls with it, and this accentuates the tendency for only the worst to be offered. It is at least possible to develop a model in which this *adverse selection* problem is so serious that no transactions will take place at all even though better-informed buyers would stand to gain.[1] Note the implied assumption, however, that contracts cannot be drawn up in such a way that failure of a car to meet the standards claimed for it would elicit penalties from the seller.

Perhaps the classic instance of adverse selection brought about by asymmetric information is in the realm of insurance. A provider of insurance against some undesired contingency (say ill health) may be less well informed about the probability of the occurrence of this event than the person seeking insurance. The terms quoted by an insurance company will be based upon certain basic pieces of information such as the age and medical history of the person buying the insurance, information which may be obtained at relatively low cost. This information may not be detailed enough, however, to distinguish with sufficient subtlety between relatively good and bad risks. Once more, people with good health prospects will regard the insurance terms offered as rather unfavourable while people with bad prospects will find the terms attractive. The people who are therefore most inclined to take out health insurance are those most likely to require health care. There is an 'adverse selection' problem based upon asymmetric information. *Ex ante* it may be very costly for an insurance company to distinguish between good and bad risks, just as, by assumption, buyers of cars in the last paragraph could not distinguish good and bad cars, and person *A* in our story found it difficult to distinguish between good and bad craftsmen.

In this context it is useful to note the importance of 'reputation' or 'goodwill' in markets with asymmetric information. A seller of second-hand cars who has established a reputation for providing good cars will be able to charge higher prices or establish markets where none existed before. Similarly person *A* found it expedient to use craftsmen with a good local reputation. The existence of 'goodwill' economises on transactions costs by reducing search and enables transactions to take place in higher-quality products and services than might otherwise be possible.

(ii) A second important problem facing *A* was that even after striking a bargain he did not know whether the other parties were fulfilling their obligations. The electrician seemed to have wired his house, but was it safe? Was the architect actually exerting himself on *A*'s behalf? Was the plumber using unnecessarily expensive equipment? Whereas under paragraph (i) above the problem was that *ex ante* a buyer may be ill informed about the qualities of a potential purchase (even though these may become perfectly clear *ex post*, as in the case of second-hand cars), the problem being considered now concerns the difficulty *ex post* of ascertaining whether the provisions of a contract have been fulfilled.

Conceptually we may distinguish a number of possible variations of this problem. Consider first the possibility that A is capable of drawing up a set of state-contingent contracts with his workmen. He agrees for example that *if* certain geological conditions are found to prevail the foundations will be strengthened or that extra drainage will be installed. He agrees that *if* weather conditions are unfavourable construction may be delayed and specified extra expenses incurred and so forth. This type of contract clearly requires that A and his workmen can agree on what 'state of the world' actually pertains. If for example it proved very costly for A to verify the correct position the workman would have an incentive to 'observe' any state of the world which he felt was most favourable to his own interests. Where it is expedient to discover problems the workman will duly discover them, and where it is inexpedient they will be ignored. When the plumber informs person A that he has 'hit problems' he is saying that 'I have observed a state of the world which permits me to take the following actions under the terms of our contract and which commits you to extra expenditure'. In many cases the problem will be sufficiently obvious to both parties. But in others person A may have to trust the workman. *Asymmetric information* therefore turns out to be at the root of A's difficulties once more.

A second variant of this transactional problem occurs when the probability of a given 'state of the world' occurring is influenced by one of the parties to a contract. Insurance contracts again supply the classic case. Suppose that person A in return for a specified payment now (an insurance premium) promises to pay to person B another specified sum in the event of person B being robbed. Our discussion so far has been limited to A's problem of deciding whether B is telling the truth when he claims to have been robbed or whether in reality the only person being robbed is person A. Even when the prevailing 'state of the world' is easily verified, however, there remains the possibility that the outcome was materially influenced by the activities of B. In other words the probability of being robbed is not entirely independent of B's behaviour. He is obviously more likely to be robbed if he spends long periods of time away from his house and habitually leaves the door open than if he installs a system of locks and alarms and never leaves his property unattended. This suggests the possibility that the insurance contract could specify conditions which commit person B to take certain precautions. Once more the problem of asymmetric information is confronted, however. If the contract states that *B* must always lock his door when leaving his house, how is *A* to know whether this provision was or was not complied with when *B* was robbed? Further, although it is easy enough to think of a few basic precautions against robbery, it would be extremely costly to investigate the detailed circumstances of person *B* in order to establish the actions required of him in every particular. Only *B* can have the kind of knowledge concerning specific circumstances which would be necessary to determine all the options available to discourage thieves. Once the insurance contract is agreed, however, *B* will clearly have a much smaller incentive to engage in thief-discouraging activities than before.

This general problem of verifying *ex post* whether the provisions of a contract have been fulfilled is called the problem of *moral hazard*. In the context of insurance markets Arrow (1962) summarises the issue as follows: 'The general principle is the difficulty of distinguishing between a state of nature and a decision by the insured. As a result, any insurance policy and in general any device for shifting risks can have the effect of dulling incentives' (p. 145). As we have already seen, however, these problems are not confined to insurance markets. Any contracts drawn up in conditions of asymmetric information may give rise to moral hazard. As Demsetz (1969) puts it: 'Moral hazard is a relevant cost of producing insurance; it is not different from the cost that arises from the tendency of men to shirk when their employer is not watching them.' (p. 167).

(iii) The third broad class of transactional problem facing person *A* which we may identify was the simple *magnitude* of the potential task of coordinating the activities of his workmen. This problem would exist even were information symmetrical, that is, available equally to *A* and the people he employs, and is therefore logically distinct from the issues discussed earlier in this section. Not only were the provisions of each person's contract inter-dependent but they would vary with all sorts of possible contingencies which might arise as work proceeded. The capacity of person *A* to imagine all possible future contingencies and then process the information required to allow for these different contingencies in the contracts of each person he hires is obviously limited. Person *A* faces, in other words, a problem which is now usually referred to as '*bounded rationality*'.

The idea of 'bounded rationality' is especially associated with the work of H. A. Simon (1957, 1969, 1979) and O. E. Williamson (1975). Both writers use the example of the game of chess to illustrate the issues involved. Given the rules which govern the movement of the pieces on a chess-board we might in principle consider constructing a list of all possible games. We might start by recording all possible opening moves and then for each one record all possible legal responses, and so on until we have built up an entire 'decision tree'. The problem of course, and the factor which prevents chess becoming a totally trivial pastime, is that the decision tree would be of such size and complexity that it beggars the imagination. Even the best chess players must make their decisions in the absence of a complete list of future contingencies which might possibly flow from them, and resort must be made to a limited set of considerations which experience has suggested are important.

If rationality is conceived as selecting the best possible course of action for achieving a specified objective, chess moves evidently do not qualify. Yet most people would baulk at describing chess decisions as irrational. Indeed chess is widely regarded as the board game requiring the powers of reason in the highest degree. Chess problems are susceptible to the application of reason, but the complexity of the game is such that decisions are effectively taken under conditions of uncertainty. This is why Williamson (1975, p. 23) argues that 'the distinction between deterministic complexity and uncertainty is inessential.... As long as either uncertainty or complexity is present in requisite degree, the bounded rationality problem arises...'.

It will be recalled that person *A* responded to his ignorance of all contingencies by formulating agreements embodying *some* flexibility (i.e. drawing up state-contingent contracts specifying appropriate responses to some of the more obvious possibilities) but outside these limits relying on a process of renegotiation as time advanced. In the following section, consideration is given to a number of different institutional responses to the problems we have been considering. Search costs, asymmetric information, moral hazard and bounded rationality are factors which exist and inevitably influence the ways in which people contract with one another. If gains from trade are potentially available it might be expected that institutions will be developed to facilitate their realisation, and this will involve mitigating the effects of some of the forces which stand in the way.

3. INSTITUTIONAL RESPONSES TO TRANSACTIONS COSTS

Information is costly to obtain. Finding out about the opportunities which are potentially available, about the quality of the goods and services on offer, and about the appropriate responses to various possible future contingencies, involves time and effort. The absence of information, as we have seen, can inhibit the process of exchange, but if the costs of acquiring the relevant information arc too great the failure of exchange to occur is both predictable and efficient. This was the essential bone of contention in the celebrated exchange between Arrow (1962) and Demsetz (1969) already referred to in the section above. To observe the failure of exchange to take place is not to prove inefficiency if information costs exist. To assert otherwise is, according to Demsetz, to commit the fallacy of the 'free lunch' (i.e. to assume that information is potentially available without cost). Alternatively, the fallacy involved might be described as the 'people could be different' fallacy (i.e. that somehow or other people could be induced *not* to exploit asymmetries in information and that the problem of moral hazard might go away).

As we have taken some pains to elaborate, however, the process of exchange inevitably entails overcoming these transactional difficulties. To assume away the problem of information is not very helpful if the object of study is the theory of the firm, but it would be equally unhelpful to assume that no attempts are made to mitigate the problem. If exchange is potentially advantageous we would expect the would-be transactors to devise mechanisms which enable it to proceed. Institutions will develop which economise on information costs and permit trades which would otherwise be impossible to take place.

(a) Money
The idea that institutions develop in response to transactions costs is familiar enough in certain areas. All students learn at an early stage the advantages associated with the use of money as a medium

of exchange relative to a system of barter. Elementary textbooks will usually contain examples of the difficulties faced by a fisherman vainly searching for a cobbler who wants a piece of haddock, to use D. H. Robertson's example. The problem of establishing a 'double coincidence of wants' is a slightly misleading way of looking at the issue of barter, however. A barter system, that is, a system involving the direct exchange of goods and services without the use of money, does not strictly require a 'double coincidence of wants' unless it is stipulated that all exchange transactions must be bilateral ones. A fisherman can obtain shoes from a cobbler under a system of barter even if the cobbler has no taste for fish, but to do so it will be necessary to involve other parties in a joint *multilateral* agreement. For example, a baker may agree to provide a certain quantity of bread to the cobbler. In exchange the fisherman provides the baker with fish and receives shoes from the cobbler. Finding the parties willing to take part in this 'triangular trade' and negotiating the terms of the contract, however, is clearly going to be more costly and require greater information than a simple bilateral deal. In principle it is possible to envisage more and more individuals taking part in these multilateral negotiations, but, as discussed in Chaper 1, obtaining a simultaneous agreement between many contractors is likely to be extremely difficult.

Money enables contractors to escape from the requirement of forming agreements *simultaneously*. A complex pattern of exchange relationships can instead be entered into through a *sequence* of bilateral arrangements. To return to our simple example, the shoemaker might accept fish in exchange for his shoes even when he dislikes fish if he knows of a baker who will be happy to exchange bread for fish. In this case the fish is being used in the form of a medium of exchange since its value to the shoemaker depends entirely on its ability to procure him something else. Clearly, if the agreements described here are not entered into simultaneously the cobbler will want to be confident of the willingness of the baker to accept fish, and it is apparent that this is not necessarily or usually going to be the case. A medium of exchange will be more acceptable to the shoemaker the more widely acceptable it is known to be to other people. Where confidence in the wide acceptability of a medium of exchange is strong it will not be necessary for the shoemaker to have knowledge of the demands of any particular baker. Any baker he knows will be happy to supply him with bread in exchange for money. This view of the origins of money is particularly associated with Carl Menger (see *Principles of Economics*, Chapter VIII):

As each economising individual becomes increasingly more aware of his economic interest, he is led by this interest, without any agreement, without legislative compulsion and even without regard to the public interest, to give his commodities in exchange for other, more saleable, commodities, even if he does not need them for any immediate consumption purpose (p. 260)

This passage from Menger raises the important question of what is meant by 'more saleable' commodities. Alchian (1977) provides a persuasive answer. Imagine a world in which four commodities exist; Alchian supposes that these are called oil, wheat, diamonds and 'C'. He notes that people cannot be expected to have expert knowledge of the characteristics of all the commodities in which they trade. Transactions costs, he assumes, will be highest when two 'novices' trade together, and will be lowest when the two traders are 'experts' in both commodities traded. We have already noted in our earlier discussion of asymmetric information that traders in certain products will have to establish a 'reputation' for trustworthiness if exchange is to take place. Let us suppose that by specialising in the trade of wheat in the sense that every exchange involves either its purchase or sale, a person becomes both an expert in assessing its quality and comes to command a high reputation. Such a reputation in a single commodity will be of little use, however, if the 'expert' wheat dealer is faced with the problem of assessing the qualities of oil or diamonds in the process of exchange. What is required if transactions costs are to be substantially reduced is a commodity in which *everyone is an 'expert'*. Such a commodity will be one the qualities of which are very easy to assay. This is the primary characteristic of 'money' and is implicit in Menger's use of term 'more saleable commodities' as a description of money. Commodities are 'more saleable' if large numbers of people find their qualities can be assessed at very low cost. The use of money as an exchange medium reduces transactions costs because, in conjunction with the existence of specialist traders in other commodities, it increases the knowledge possessed by each contractor involved in an exchange. The specialist wheat trader will be an 'expert' in both wheat *and* money, while his customer (either buyer or seller of wheat) will at least be an 'expert' in money. Of course this in no way alters the fact that most of the specialist traders' customers will be novices in wheat, and the implications of this have already been considered in the context of second-hand cars. But in the absence of money both parties to an exchange would usually be novices, while it is the use of money which permits the growth of specialised traders whose accumulated expertise and pursuit of goodwill are a response to the twin problems of asymmetric information and adverse selection.

Although a person accepting money in exchange for some good or service will feel confident that it can be used to procure other things, the precise terms of any future trades will not be known with certainty. Money is accepted in *the expectation* that it will permit the achievement of desired ends. It may even be the case that money is accepted with no *specific and determinate* ideas as to what is to be done with it. Instead the person may prefer to wait upon events, and spend time searching for suitable opportunities. By reducing transactions costs, in other words, money permits wider search, and a more extensive and complex system of exchange transactions can occur than would otherwise be possible. Pigou (1949, p. 25) likened money to 'a railway through the air, the loss of which would inflict on us the same sort of damage as we should suffer if the actual railways and roads, by which the different parts of the country are physically linked together were destroyed'. Money, that is, like the transport system, enables a wider range of transactions to take place.

But the existence of money implies more than simple widening of possibilities. It implies that these possibilities are discovered by a *process* which continues over time. People hold money speculatively in the hope that to commit themselves later will be advantageous compared with deciding on a course of action immediately. The cobbler for example *might* have bartered his shoes immediately for fish. In fact he preferred money because he expected to be able to use it later in ways yielding him greater satisfaction. The fact that in many everyday cases the time period involved might be quite short, and the cobbler may have intentions concerning the use of his money which are usually and routinely realised (he is very sure of the terms on which he can buy bread at the bakers) in no way changes the general principle.

Ignorance inevitably restricts exchange. Institutions which help to overcome the problems posed by ignorance are therefore expected to take root. To quote Loasby (1976): 'Money, like the firm, is a means of handling the consequences of the excessive cost or the sheer impossibility of abolishing ignorance...both imply a negation of the concept of general equilibrium in favour of the continuing management of emerging events' (p. 165).

(b) Political Institutions

The idea that a fundamental political institution such as 'the state' might be interpreted as a means of overcoming impediments to the process of exchange has a long history. Consider for example a celebrated passage from Hume:

Two neighbours may agree to drain a meadow, which they possess in common: because it is easy for them to know each other's mind; and each must perceive, that the immediate consequence of his failing in his part, is the abandoning of the whole project. But it is very difficult, and indeed impossible, that a thousand persons should agree in any such action; it being difficult for them to concert so complicated a design, and still more difficult for them to execute it; while each seeks a pretext to free himself of the trouble and expense, and would lay the whole burden on others. Political society easily remedies both these inconveniences....[2]

The focus of attention here is on the problem of 'public goods' (Samuelson, 1954, Musgrave, 1959). Some goods confer benefits not merely on a single consumer of the good but on a whole population of consumers simultaneously. Standard examples include defence, public health provisions, the services of lighthouses and so forth. Pure public goods are said to be 'non-rival' in consumption and 'non-excludable' (i.e. it is technically not possible, or at least enormously costly, to prevent any individual person from enjoying the benefits of a public good provided by others). The result of these two characteristics is that ordinary market processes 'fail' in the sense that a multilateral agreement which might potentially benefit all the parties to it will not emerge spontaneously. In Chapter 1 the costs of simultaneous multilateral contracting have already been discussed in the context of private goods. There it was argued that although simultaneous agreement would be impossibly costly to achieve, alternatives existed which would be preferable to completely independent activity for the parties concerned. Resources would be allocated not in a single all-embracing moment

of universal agreement but in a *process* involving bilateral exchanges and the use of money or the forming of institutions such
as 'firms' to manage events as time advanced. Public goods,
however, present us with a severe problem in that apparently the
only alternative to a widespread multilateral agreement is *no* agreement. Resolution of this dilemma requires the existence of the 'productive state' and the institution of collective processes in place of
market processes. Buchanan (1975) re-emphasises Hume's point if
in somewhat different style:

> Only through governmental-collective processes can individuals secure
> the net benefits of goods and services that are characterised by extreme
> jointness efficiencies and by extreme non-excludability, goods and services
> which would tend to be provided suboptimally or not at all in the absence
> of collective-governmental action (p. 97).

Public goods present obstacles to the formation of agreements of
a particularly intractable nature. But they are not in principle
different from those difficulties discussed in detail in section 2.2.
There it was seen that the failure of transactors to declare information honestly could conceivably totally inhibit the development
of certain insurance or other markets. Secondhand car salesmen
would always maintain their wares were more reliable than they
really were, and purchasers of insurance that the risks they faced
were less than they really were. People, in other words, cannot be
expected to declare honestly and voluntarily information which
adversely influences the terms upon which they will trade when
there are no cost-effective means of verifying the information.
Trade in public goods is no exception. Further, where the
simultaneous agreement of large numbers of individuals is involved
the problem of 'bounded rationality' cannot be overlooked. Thus
Hume's two 'inconveniences' which, he argues, political society
remedies, amount to the problems analysed earlier: 'bounded rationality' ('it being difficult for them to concert so complicated a
design') and an extreme form of information asymmetry leading to
opportunistic behaviour ('each seeks a pretext to free himself of the
trouble and expense').

(c) The Firm

A provisional rationalisation of the emergence of 'firms' was
suggested at the end of Chapter 1. From the standpoint of

economic theory the firm represented a 'nexus of contracts' so framed as to provide flexibility in the face of unpredictable events. Uncertainty, and the resulting difficulty of precisely specifying the terms of each person's contract, thus constituted the starting point for the theory of the firm. This approach has its origins in a celebrated paper by Coase (1937), and the discussion of transactional difficulties above (section 2), now permits a further appraisal.

For Coase: 'The main reason why it is profitable to establish a firm would seem to be that there is a cost of using the price mechanism' (p. 336). Coase is here referring to such matters as 'negotiating and concluding a separate contract for each exchange transaction' (p. 336). In the absence of a firm, each factor of production must contract with every other factor whose cooperation is required. Within the firm each factor negotiates a single contract. In an extreme case where 'n' individuals must all cooperate closely, a set of $n(n-1)/2$ bilateral contracts would be required to bind the parties together. For five individuals Figure 2.1 illustrates that ten agreements would be necessary. In a slightly different context, Williamson (1975, p. 46) refers to this as the 'all-channel network'. In the firm, on the other hand, one person would become the central contractual agent and a total of four contracts would be sufficient to link all the parties together.

It is important always to remember, however, that the advantages of the firm in terms of savings in contracting costs presuppose conditions of uncertainty. With costless knowledge there would be no advantages accruing to a reduced number of transactional bonds, since these bonds would be costless to establish. Uncertainty, on the other hand, implies not merely that the costs of

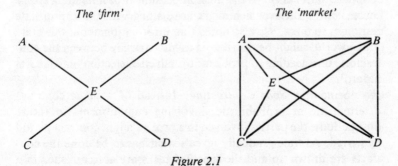

Figure 2.1

establishing contracts might reduce their numbers, but also that the *type of contract* established will be affected. As was seen at the end of Chapter 1, the firm involves the forging of rather loosely specified 'contracts of employment'. The employment relation involves the employee accepting the direction of his employer up to some limit. Thus in Coase's view of things the firm is characterised by the conscious organisation or direction of resources over time: 'When the direction of resources (within the limits of the contract) becomes dependent on the buyer in this way, that relationship which I term a "firm" may be obtained' (p. 337).

More recent contributions to this literature emphasise that the employment relation is one of several different possible 'transactions modes' (e.g. Williamson, 1975, pp. 64–72). In the fictional story of A's building project we have already considered some of these 'modes' and the problems which accompany them.

(i)   The Deterministic Contract   Under this sceme the contractors agree to perform specific services at certain points in time. The obvious problem is that, in the extreme, it completely lacks flexibility and presupposes that the contracting parties are able to determine exactly what they require at all relevant future points in time. It will be recalled that person A found it difficult to formulate a deterministic contract with his craftsmen because of the problem of predicting exactly what would be required of them at each stage.

(ii)   The State-Contingent Contract   In this type of contract, obligations are no longer deterministic and fixed. The requirements vary with the 'state of the world' which occurs. An example of such a contract was discussed in section 2. There it was argued that the specification of such a contract would be enormously time consuming and complex. Ultimately it would encounter the problem of 'bounded rationality' — the sheer impossibility of imagining all the future contingencies which might arise along with the appropriate responses to them. We also noted that information about the 'state of the world' might be distributed asymmetrically between the contractors, thus leading to problems of 'adverse selection' and 'moral hazard'.

(iii)   Sequential Spot Contracting   Instead of a *single* contract, deterministic or probabilistic, involving commitments in future time periods, the parties involved in a project might contract period by period. As time gradually reveals what has to be done the contracts are drawn up and the specified tasks are accomplished in a

sequence. This solution faces the objection emphasised by Coase that the number of contracts required to accomplish a given objective will be very large if they are continually renegotiated over time. The number of contracts, however, will not be the only problem. An equally important issue is the cost of establishing each one. In principle we might imagine the process of recontracting as a relatively simple operation. The buyer of labour services, for example, would ask a workman to do something at the established wage rate and acceptance of this 'request' would imply that the 'contract' had been duly renegotiated. According to this view, associated with Alchian and Demsetz (1972), the type of contract observed within a 'firm' is not a single long-term contract of employment involving 'direction' of resources by the buyer, as claimed by Coase. Instead there is an *implicit* process of continual renegotiation as in a system of sequential spot contracting.

(iv) The Employment Relation Where the process of recontracting operates as smoothly as suggested above there would be no advantage attached to a contract of employment. Indeed it would arguably be extremely difficult in practice to distinguish between the two methods of contracting. Whether an 'employee' is considered to 'renegotiate' his contract continually, or is seen as accepting contractually permissible 'instructions' may not in some circumstances be a matter of very great analytical importance. There will be occasions, however, when the renegotiation of contracts over time is likely to involve high bargaining costs, and when a relatively painless adjustment of activity to changed circumstances cannot be predicted. As Williamson emphasises, this is especially likely to be the case when the provider of a service gains specialised knowledge and experience over time. The employer will then find himself bargaining with a number of employees, each one of whom has certain 'idiosyncratic experience' which places them in a strong bargaining position relative to any outsider. These advantages which accrue to existing employees are termed by Williamson 'first-mover advantages' (i.e. the first person to undertake a particular task acquires experience which in future periods puts that person at an advantage relative to others).

A workforce which acquires specialised knowledge and skills over time is not, of course, undesirable in itself. The problem is simply the transactional one that continual renegotiation of contracts in these circumstances puts the employer in the sort of position faced by person A in our example of the building project. Each person with whom he is negotiating is in the possession of skills and information which he does not fully share. Striking a bargain is then inhibited by asymmetric information, and the incentive to act 'opportunistically', increases the cost of achieving agreement.

The essence of Williamson's contribution is his observation that 'the employment relation' does not offer a solution to the transactional difficulties posed by information asymmetries. Strictly the employment relation requires that it is possible to specify a list of 'acceptable' tasks from which the employer can choose. Any attempt at such exhaustive listing must, however, confront the information problem. The employer simply will not have sufficient knowledge to draw up a contract of this nature. If information is revealed over time, and if, further, this information accrues not to everyone but to particular individuals (it is 'impacted', to use Williamson's jargon), the crucial problem will be to set an environment in which people have an incentive to act cooperatively rather than opportunistically. Thus the employer is not a giver of instructions as in Coase's model, but a provider of incentives. The employee becomes not a passive receiver of orders but an active *agent* of the employer.

(v)   The Agency Relation   Under the agency relation one party (the agent) agrees to act in the interests of another party (the principal). The example of the architect and person A has already been discussed earlier in this chapter. Note that two important features are required to hold if the agency relation is to be interesting:

(a)   There must be a conflict of interest. The architect, by assumption, was interested in giving A's plans the minimum amount of attention he could get away with. Person A, of course, was interested in eliciting from his architect the greatest attention that was possible.

(b)   There must be an asymmetry in the information available to principal and agent. Person A may simply not know what actions are possible and how they may affect him. He may not be in a position even to tell what action if any, his agent has taken.

Clearly if there were no conflict of interest the existence of asymmetric information would not matter. The agent would always choose an action which accorded with the preferences of the principal. Similarly, if the information available to both principal and agent was the same, the conflict of interest would not matter since the principal would immediately detect any 'opportunistic' behaviour on the part of the agent. Where both asymmetric information and conflict of interest are present, the problem facing the principal will be to present the agent with a 'system of remuneration' sometimes called a 'fee structure' or 'incentive structure', which will produce the greatest payoff to himself.

In the case of the relationship between employer and employee, there are obvious parallels with the principal–agent problem. This was recognised by Coase who in a footnote in his 1937 paper wrote:

Of course, it is not possible to draw a hard and fast line which determines whether there is a firm or not. There may be more or less direction. It is similar to the legal question of whether there is the relationship of master and servant or principal and agent (p. 337).

The clear implication here is that only a contract of 'master and servant' which implies the *direction* of resources will be found in the Coasian firm. The relationship of principal and agent would not be compatible with the existence of a 'firm'. More recent theorists would not accept this judgement. As we have seen, Williamson's emphasis on the problems of bargaining in the face of asymmetrically distributed knowledge permits us to view the employee as an 'agent', and the firm as a response to the agency problem. The Coasian insight that the firm replaces a whole system of multilateral contracts with bilateral contracts betwen employer and employee is maintained. But the nature of the contract between employee and firm is no longer seen exclusively in terms of 'the employment relation' and the direction of resources. Whatever the strictly legal position, the economist can argue that perceiving the relationship between 'firm' and employee in terms of principal and agent may provide valuable insights into the way resources are allocated within the firm.

In Chapter 6 we will investigate how this type of approach has been expanded to explain some of the internal characteristics of firms. The existence of a hierarchical structure, with the possibility of promotion through the various grades from points of entry to compulsory retirement, can be explained in terms of the provision of a system of incentives which encourage cooperative behaviour, and which permit transactions to take place which would otherwise be inhibited by 'opportunistic' responses to informational asymmetries. The principal–agent paradigm will also permit us to discuss (Chapters 7 and 8) other important issues such as 'the division of ownership from control' (managers as agents of shareholders), the control of public enterprises (managers as agents of politicians), and a number of topics in the economics of bureaucracy. Before pursuing this analysis further, however, it is necessary to introduce another component which will play an important role in our general framework, the entrepreneur.

NOTES

1. Akerlof (1970), pp. 490–1) presents the following purely illustrative model. Suppose there are two types of transactor. Type 1 transactors have a stock of N cars with quality q uniformly distributed $0 < q < 2$. A type 1 person knows the quality of each car with certainty. The utility (U) of type 1 transactors is given by

$$U_1 = G + \sum_{i=1}^{n} q_i$$

where G = consumption of goods other than cars. Type 2 transactors have no cars to begin with and their utility is given by

$$U_2 = G + \sum_{i=1}^{n} q_i$$

The linear utility functions postulated may seem strange but the objective is merely to illustrate a possibility using as simple a framework as possible. Suppose that each transactor wishes to maximise expected utility. Further, let the price of other goods (G) be unity. Consider first the supply of cars. Suppose the market price of second-hand cars were p—how would type 1 transactors respond? Clearly those holding cars with quality $q_i < p$ will not sell them since to do so would reduce their utility. They would lose utility q_i from selling the car and gain utility p from buying other goods with the proceeds. Since $q_i > p$ there is a net loss. Those holding cars with quality $q_i < p$ will hasten to sell, however, since their utility index will rise. Given that the distribution of quality is uniform the proportion of cars offered for sale will be given by the shaded area in Figure 2.2. This shaded area will equal $p/2$ and the number of cars offered for sale with be $Np/2$.

   Given that the cars offered for sale are of uniformly distributed quality between o and p, the average quality of car offered ($\bar{q}$) will be $p/2$.

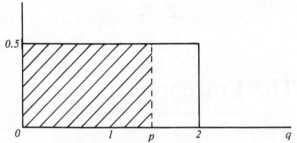

Figure 2.2: Probability distribution of quality (q);
$f(q) = 0.5, \ 0 \leqslant q \leqslant 2$

Now consider the demand side. Transactors of either type will only demand cars if the expected utility obtained per unit of expenditure on cars is greater than on other goods (i.e. greater than unity). The *expected* number of units of quality obtained per unit of expenditure on a car will be $\bar{q}/p$. For transactors of type 1, therefore, cars will be demanded only if $\bar{q}/p > 1$. Since $\bar{q} = p/2$ this condition can clearly never be fulfilled. For transactors of type 2, cars will be demanded if $k\bar{q} > 1$. Again since $\bar{q} = p/2$ we deduce that type 2 contractors will demand cars only if $k/2 > 1$, that is, if $k > 2$.

Thus if type 2 transactors have utility functions as specified with $0 < k < 2$, no cars will be demanded. This will be so even though examples can be constructed in which some type 1 transactors are prepared to supply cars of a quality and at a price that type 2 transactors would have been prepared to pay *if only they knew* the precise qualities of the cars on offer. Suppose for example k were 2. At a price of 1 a type 2 transactor would be prepared to buy any car with quality greater than $q_i = \frac{1}{2}$. And at a price of 1 there will be $N/4$ such cars offered for sale. The problem, of course, is that there will also be $N/4$ cars offered for sale with quality less than $\frac{1}{2}$ and our type 2 transactor by hypothesis cannot *ex ante* tell the difference between these two classes of car.

Kim (1985) presents a model in which traders are not designated as buyers or sellers but may choose whether to buy or sell. Traders are of differing types. They may also trade in the *new* car market. It is possible using this type of framework to derive results which contradict Akerlof's lemons principle. Traded used cars may be, on average, of higher quality than non-traded used cars.

2. D. Hume (1978) *Treatise of Human Nature*, P. H. Nidditch (ed). Oxford, Clarendon Press, p. 538. Originally published 1740.

3 The Entrepreneur

'The pivot on which everything turns.'
J. A. Schumpeter

In everyday parlance the word 'entrepreneur' has wide-ranging connotations. Certain individuals, both contemporary and historical, might by common assent be described as entrepreneurs. J. Pierpont Morgan, J. D. Rockefeller, A. Carnegie and the other personalities associated with the development of banking and finance, the railroad, oil and steel in nineteenth-century America (sometimes collectively referred to as the 'robber barons') would seem each to warrant the label 'entrepreneur'. Yet the pure scale of a person's activity, the opening up of whole continents, the development of entirely new industries, does not seem to be crucial. We might as easily apply the term to a local person often engaged in conventional, long-established trades, who nevertheless appears to possess those characteristics of energy, drive, inquisitiveness, acquisitiveness, shrewdness and perhaps even deviousness in the proportions required.

For energy and drive are in themselves insufficient to produce an entrepreneur. An entrepreneur must have the energy to act and the drive not to be discouraged by obstacles. But the blinkered determination of the fanatic is not an entrepreneurial quality. The entrepreneur requires not the momentum of the bulldozer to demolish all before him, but rather the agility and flexibility of the Landrover to circumvent the difficulties. Clearly such a strategy requires that the entrepreneur should look about, and the acquisitive and inquisitive aspects of the entrepreneurial character relate to this process. Both words derive from the Latin *'quaero'*, to seek, and the modern theory of the entrepreneur is concerned primarily with elaborating on this primary characteristic—the search for, or discovery of, new knowledge.

The entrepreneur uses the knowledge he has acquired to his own advantage by reallocating resources. This process of resource reallocation involves forming agreements with others, and it is here that the qualities of shrewdness and deviousness enter: shrewdness to judge the character and reliability of the people with whom agreements are formed, and deviousness to get the best of the bargains struck. As was noted in Chapter 2, in the process of bilateral bargaining it will be advantageous for each party to give the other a misleading impression of their true preferences. It is perhaps this component of the entrepreneurial character which gives the word entrepreneur its somewhat disparaging flavour, and helps to explain research findings which point to the success of poor immigrant people in entrepreneurial endeavours (see Hannah, 1983). Immigrants will look on established procedures with a new perspective, well aware that things may be done differently; the very act of migration suggests energy and ambition; while the costs of incurring the disapprobation of those inconvenienced by change will be lower for the outsider.[1]

The purpose of this chapter is not, however, to discuss the social origins of the entrepreneur or popular perceptions of the nature of entrepreneurship, but rather to outline the role of the entrepreneur in economic theory. A number of significant questions will arise. Are 'the firm' and 'the entrepreneur' necessarily always observed together or can we conceive of a firm without an entrepreneur? Are some people entrepreneurs and others not, or does the quality of entrepreneurship, as has been hinted above, inhere to a greater or lesser extent in all participants in the market? Is entrepreneurship a factor of production, a resource akin to land, capital or labour, receiving as its reward a factor payment; or is the return to the entrepreneur qualitatively different from the return to other factors? What exactly does the entrepreneur do?

CONTRASTING VIEWS OF THE ENTREPRENEUR

(a) The Classical Tradition
To summarise in a few lines the views of a range of writers spanning more than a century from the time of Adam Smith onwards is clearly a hazardous undertaking and one which is liable to result in

severe distortions to the work of some economists. As a generalisation, however, the classical tradition, at least in England, did not offer a very sophisticated account of the entrepreneur. Indeed this state of affairs has continued in the neoclassical analysis of the late nineteenth and twentieth centuries and for substantially similar reasons. Both traditions are concerned primarily with the analysis of the establishment of 'natural' or as we would now say 'equilibrium' prices. The emphasis on the final state rather than the process of getting there inevitably diverts attention from the distinctive contribution of the entrepreneur. Classical analysis recognised the role of superintendence and organisation in economic life, and in the conditions prevailing in the late eighteenth century the provider of capital and the organiser of production would usually be the same person. The result was a tendency to muddle together some sources of income and to reduce the significance of others. Thus the English classical writers, including Smith, Ricardo and Mill,[2] used the word 'profit' to describe the total return to the provider of capital even though this included elements which might more properly be termed 'wages of management', 'interest on capital', 'monopoly rents', 'windfalls' and so forth.

It is to the French classical tradition we must look for the origins of the idea that profit is a type of income quite distinct from that received by capital and that it goes to the entrepreneur. The early French contribution in this field is perhaps appropriately reflected in the fact that English economists have come to use the French word 'entrepreneur' rather than any English equivalent such as the term 'venturer'. J. B. Say[3] building on the ideas of Cantillon[4] insisted that profit was a quite separate category of income from interest, thus establishing the major distinction between English and French classical schools in this area. He did not, however, emphasise as did Cantillon the importance of risk but initially viewed profit as a wage accruing to the organiser of production. Within the French school, Knight in his review of theories of profit (p. 25) singles out Courcelle-Seneuil[5] as the contributor who most clearly argued that profit was a reward for the assumption of risk and was not in any sense a wage.

Mention should also be made of the German, and especially Von Thunen's contribution. Von Thunen[6] is most well known for his work on transport costs, land rents and the consequent spatial pattern of agricultural land use around a city. In the development of this analysis Von Thunen, who is said to have made extensive use of the financial records of his own estates, defines profit as a residual after the expenses of interest, insurance, and the wages of management have been met. By seeing profit as essentially a return for bearing *uninsurable risks*, Von Thunen was a close forerunner of Knight.

(b) F. Knight

Knight (1921) developed and elaborated the view that entrepreneurs receive a return for bearing uncertainty. His major criticism of theory up to that date was that even those who appreciated the importance of uncertainty were unclear about its nature and implications. One view, for example, was that profit arose from the fact of continuous change and development over time. Knight did not dispute that radical and less radical changes occurred continuously and that these *could* give rise to uncertainty and hence to profits. But he insisted that change *per se* was not the issue. If, for example, changes occurred whose consequences were entirely foreseeable no profits would be generated. Perfectly foreseen changes were compatible with a state of 'equilibrium' in which no profits would appear. This type of equilibrium is now often referred to as a 'Hayekian' equilibrium.[7] Change occurs, but because it is perfectly foreseen, no expectations are ever disappointed. A famous example is that of an approaching meteorite, the impact of which will occasion many changes but all of which may be calculated perfectly accurately (fire damage, loss of crops and buildings, etc.). The actual collision of the meteorite with the earth will then produce no profits since the prices of resources have long since adjusted to the certainty of the impact and nothing unforeseen has occurred. *Correct expectations*, however, are critical to this result. *No change* is compatible with profits and losses if change is confidently expected. If contrary to all known laws of physics the meteorite suddenly veers away from the earth and disappears into outer space, people will have to adjust to this unexpected continuation of the status quo, expectations will have been disappointed and profits and losses will appear.

According to Knight therefore it is not change but uncertainty and the possibility of incorrect expectations which give rise to profit. Further, the term uncertainty is used by Knight only to describe circumstances in which reliable probability values *cannot* be attached to possible future outcomes. Where future events can be assigned probabilities, Knight uses the term 'risk' to describe the situation, and argues that the existence of insurance markets will often enable people to avoid such risk.[8] True uncertainty cannot be avoided by paying an insurance premium. Important consequences follow from the recognition that much of economic life represents a response to the existence of uncertainty. As Knight puts it:

With Uncertainty present doing things, the actual execution of activity becomes in a real sense a secondary part of life; the primary problem or function is deciding what to do and how to do it (p. 268).

This 'primary function' is the entrepreneurial function. The job of deciding *how* various objectives are to be achieved and of predicting what objectives are worth achieving devolves on the entrepreneur, a specialist who is prepared to bear the costs of uncertainty.

The confident and venturesome assume the risk or insure the doubtful and timid by guaranteeing to the latter a specified income in return for an assignment of the actual result (pp. 269–70).

It is not clear from this that the confident and venturesome should *employ* the doubtful and timid, or that the entrepreneur should own and organise 'a firm', although Knight appears to have thought that this necessarily follows. This point will be taken up later on. For present purposes, however, the main result of Knight's analysis is that the entrepreneur's function is to make judgements about the uncertain future, and the reward associated with this function 'profit' is a return to uncertainty bearing.

It is our imperfect knowledge of the future...which is crucial for the understanding of our problem (p. 198).

This 'Knightian' view of the entrepreneur has a powerful intuitive appeal. Clearly the exercise of entrepreneurship *is* usually associated with uncertainty bearing and has something to do with imperfect knowledge. But there are equally powerful objections to it. As Schumpeter emphasised (1954, p. 556) if a person is to make a profit from uncertain turns of events, that person will do so as the owner of some marketable resource. Thus uncertainty is borne by resource owners who have to accept the consequences for the value on the market of their resources of unexpected change. If we are prepared to define resource owners as 'capitalists' (i.e. we suppress the distinctions between land, natural resources, buildings, physical and human capital) then uninsurable risks must be borne by capitalists. It may be objected that the entrepreneur may borrow from the capitalist at a fixed interest and that, if so, the entrepreneur not the capitalist bears the risk. But in this case, if the entrepreneur has no resources of his own, failure of his enterprise must mean default on the loan and the capitalist is an uncertainty bearer. Where the entrepreneur has other resources which permit him to repay his debt in the event of failure, clearly the entrepreneur bears the uncertainty but only in so far as he is also a capitalist.

If uninsurable risk is borne by resource owners, what becomes of the distinctive contribution of 'the entrepreneur'? Modern analysis of the entrepreneur reverts to and develops Say's insight that the organisation of production, the combining together of resource inputs, requires skills of a different order than those of routine labour. Knights' 'primary function' of 'deciding what to do and how to do it' is indeed an entrepreneurial activity, but it is conceptually a quite separate activity from bearing uninsurable risks, even though the latter may be associated with it. Recent theory therefore emphasises that the entrepreneur does not merely put up with the consequences of imperfect knowledge, but rather reaps the rewards of discovering and using new knowledge. The English tradition, in which industry appears to 'run itself' using inputs of capital and labour in an apparently routine and 'mindless' fashion, failed to recognise the importance of the coordinator, the person who decides how and what things shall be done as distinct from the person who merely ensures that they are done. In the next section a more careful elaboration of this view of the entrepreneur is attempted using the work of the most influential modern theorist in the subject, Israel Kirzner.

(c) I. Kirzner
In Chapter 1 we spent some time in the elementary task of showing how a community of four individuals (A, B, C and D) could gain through specialisation and exchange. Each person, we assumed,

faced different 'production possibilities'. If each remained independent and isolated, their consumption patterns would be those of Table 1.1. Total output would be 8 units of x and 8 units of y. Specialisation, it was found, enabled total output to rise to 10 units of x and 10 units of y. Agreements to specialise in the appropriate way and distribute the output as in Tables 1.4 and 1.5 represented various 'solutions' to the exchange game (the 'core'). We further saw that the establishment of appropriate prices for x and y would induce people to specialise and exchange their output on the market, and that the final position would be equivalent to a 'core' solution. At each stage it was emphasised that the theory as presented did not provide a persuasive account of the exchange *process*. 'Core' solutions could be *calculated* and equilibrium prices *deduced* once all the information necessary had been acquired. But there was only a limited discussion of *how* and to whom this information is made available.

In Edgeworth's bargaining approach the core solution emerges after a process of haggling involving all the contractors in the market. In Walras' 'tatonnement' the solution emerges from a trial and error sequence of price setting by the auctioneer. In both cases it is assumed that no final decisions concerning the allocation of resources are made until the bargaining or tatonnement processes are completed. As we have seen, this is paradoxical, for it effectively implies that the information problem has to be completely solved *before* the stage of actual resource allocation can begin, and yet this solution of the information problem apparently requires no resources itself and hence involves no opportunity costs. These two ideas that contractors in the market must all be fully informed before anything of consequence can happen, and that the achievement of this state of full information does not in itself imply that anything of consequence has already happened, should not be rejected simply on the grounds that they are 'unrealistic'. Within the framework of general equilibrium theory, and given the objectives and purposes of that theory, they may be perfectly defensible. Further, it is by considering the conditions imposed by the requirements of general equilibrium that role of the entrepreneur is perhaps most easily appreciated.[9]

For the entrepreneur is central to the *process* by which contractors come *to perceive* the opportunities presented by specialisation and exchange. Clearly, if everyone already knows the production possibility curves and preferences of each contractor, and if everyone is a rational, calculating, individual, one of the suggested solutions of Tables 1.4 and 1.5 will be adopted. But if each person is only partially informed, the acquisition of knowledge about potential gains from exchange becomes the pivotal economic problem. It is at this point that the 'Austrian' tradition in economic theory, here represented mainly by the work of Kirzner, emphasies the role of the entrepreneur. Essentially, an entrepreneur is any person who is 'alert' to hitherto unexploited possibilities for exchange. Spotting such possibilities enables the entrepreneur to benefit by acting as the 'middleman' who effects the change.

(i) The entrepreneur as a 'middleman' Consider once more the four individuals in Chapter 1. The production possibilities facing each were assumed to be:

A: $10 - 4x = Y$
B: $12 - 3x = Y$
C: $6 - 2x = Y$
D: $3 - x = 2Y$.

Suppose now that another individual (an entrepreneur E) turns up on the scene (there is yet another shipwreck). This individual is washed up with no resources to his name but, being alert to new opportunities, he rapidly observes that the four inhabitants he meets would be much better off if they specialised along the lines we have already discussed and thus coordinated their activities. It will be recalled that the 'no trade' consumption pattern was as shown in the left-hand side of Table 3.1. Imagine that E first contacts A and persuades A to provide him with 8 units of y in exchange for 2 units of x. A will just be prepared to do this since by specialising in y production (10 units) and accepting E's offer his final consumption level of 2 units of each commodity will be unchanged. E then approaches person B and suggests that the latter should provide 1 unit of x in exchange for 3 units of y (see Chapter 1 p. 14). Once more if person B specialises in x production (4 units) and accepts E's offer, his final consumption level of 3 units of each commodity would be unchanged. These are, of course, very 'hard bargains' and we might expect in general A and B to benefit from their acquaintance with E. For the moment, however, we will assume simply that E offers to purchase y at a price of $\frac{1}{4}x$ (i.e. sell

Table 3.1

| | No trade | | With entrepreneur | | |
	X	Y	X	Y	Gain
A	2.00	2.00	2.00	2.00	(0.00)
B	3.00	3.00	3.00	3.00	(0.00)
C	2.00	2.00	2.25	2.25	(+0.25)
D	1.00	1.00	2.25	2.25	(+1.25)
E	—	—	0.50	0.50	(+0.50)
Total	8.00	8.00	10.00	10.00	(+2.00)

x at price of $4y$) and sell y at a price of $\frac{1}{3}x$ (i.e. purchase x at a price of $3y$) and we have seen that this would leave A and B no better or worse off than before. Person C, on the other hand, will benefit noticeably from trade with E assuming he faces the same price ratio as B. By specialising in x (3 units), C can trade 0.75 units of x for 2.25 units of y. Similarly, person D can specialise in x (3 units) and through trade achieve the same position as C. The argument is precisely the same as was presented in Chapter 1 p. 15 and the entries on the right-hand side of Table 3.1 are a combination of the first two lines of Table 1.5.

The important difference is that, whereas in Chapter 1 we assumed in each line of Table 1.5 that every contractor faced the *same* price ratio set by an auctioneer, in Table 3.1 we have assumed that contractors B, C and D faced a different price ratio to contractor A, and that these price ratios were negotiated with an entrepreneur. The entrepreneur in this simple situation acts merely as an *intermediary*. By spotting that currently unexploited gains from trade existed, the entrepreneur was able to use that knowledge both to realise the gains and to appropriate a proportion of them for himself. Each person's individual benefit (in terms of units of x and y) from the reallocation of resources initiated by the entrepreneur is recorded in parenthesis in the last column of Table 3.1. Person D appears to have gained most of all, but this, of course, is the result of our simple assumption that E offered the same terms of trade to all sellers of x. If the entrepreneur could have kept B, C and D apart and negotiated individually with them, then a sufficiently 'hard-nosed' approach might have diverted a larger proportion of the gains from trade in E's direction. However, in the

particular arithmetical example presented, the entrepreneur gains
0.5 units of x and 0.5 of y. Of the 8 units of y supplied by person
A, 7.5 units are given to B, C and D; while of the 2.5 units of x
supplied by B, C and D, only 2 units are given to A.

Person E achieves a consumption level of $0.5x$ and $0.5y$. This
represents '*pure entrepreneurial profit*'. It has nothing to do with
interest payments on capital employed. Indeed it has nothing to do
with a return to any 'factor' as conventionally defined. It arises out
of entrepreneurial activity and the possession of a particular kind
of knowledge: the knowledge that opportunities exist which no one
has spotted before. The entrepreneur acts as a coordinator of
resources, and his profit is taken from the gains in efficiency which
accompany his activity. Note that the gains to persons C and D
recorded in Table 3.1 are *not* entrepreneurial profits even though
they also are part of the efficiency gain resulting from the reallocation of resources. Persons C and D did not spot the potential
benefits available from change; they merely responded to the entrepreneur's offer. Their gain is therefore a type of 'windfall', a portion of the increased output which eluded the grasp of the
entrepreneur.

An important problem was studiously ignored in the paragraphs
above, however. Clearly the entrepreneur does not negotiate with
all the people playing a part in his plans simultaneously. If he did,
he would be unable to offer person A different terms of trade from
the others, and the mechanism which enables some profit to be
realised would be ineffective. In effect, the entrepreneur's knowledge would be instantly available to the others and no entrepreneurial profit could therefore be derived from it. As Richardson
(1960 p. 57) puts it:

a general profit opportunity, which is both known to everyone and equally
capable of being exploited by everyone, is, in an important sense, a profit
opportunity for no one in particular.

But, on the other hand, if the entrepreneur, who it will be recalled
has no resources of his own, is to trade with A first, where is he to
find the units of x required to make an offer? One solution to this
problem might involve E persuading person A to supply the 8 units
of y in advance of E's delivery of the x. In this case, person A
would be acting as a capitalist supplying the entrepreneur with the
resources required to test his hunch in the market. We would then

expect that person *A* would require compensation both for the delay and for the perceived uncertainty associated with the ultimate delivery of *x*. *A* would have to take the risk that *E*'s confidence in his ability to deliver a given quantity of *x* by a certain date is misplaced and that his entrepreneurial plan fails. For Knight, as we have seen, this bearing of uncertainty would make person *A* an entrepreneur. But for Kirzner this is not *necessarily* the case. *E* is the person who thinks he has spotted new opportunities, and it is *E* who stands to gain pure entrepreneurial profits if this judgement proves correct. Kirzner (1979) is quite specific on this point:

Entrepreneurial profits...are not captured by owners, in their capacity as owners, at all. They are captured, instead, by men who exercise pure entrepreneurship, for which ownership is *never* a condition (p. 94).

Where time must elapse between purchase and sale:

It is still correct to insist that the entrepreneur requires no investment of any kind. If the surplus...is sufficient to enable the entrepreneur to offer an interest payment attractive enough to persuade someone to advance the necessary funds,...the entrepreneur has discovered a way of obtaining pure profit, without the need to invest anything at all (Kirzner, 1973, p. 49).

Of course, nothing guarantees that the penniless entrepreneur will succeed in persuading capitalists to advance their funds. But, as was emphasised in Chapter 2:

These costs of securing recognition of one's competence and trust-worthiness are truly social costs. They would exist under any system of economic organisation...(Kirzner, 1979, p. 101).

All that can be said is that an entrepreneur who is also a resource owner will find it easier to back his hunches and benefit from his knowledge since these transactions costs can be avoided.[10] The entrepreneur lends to himself.[11]

(ii) Entrepreneurship and Knowledge For Kirzner the entrepreneur is the person who perceives the opportunities and hence benefits from the possession of knowledge not apparently possessed by others. Thus entrepreneurship is central to the *process* by which information is disseminated throughout the economy. This emphasis on *process* is distinctive of the modern 'Austrian' school of

thought, and it was noted in Chapter 1 that the major Austrian criticism of neoclassical equilibrium theory is the implicit assumption of perfect knowledge which underlies it.

It would, however, be totally misleading simply to leave the impression that neoclassical theory has nothing of substance to say about the problem of information. Our discussion of the information requirements underlying general equilibrium theory still stands, but neoclassical economists have developed tools which enable them to handle some problems in the economics of information very effectively. Since the early 1960s the assumption of 'costless knowledge' has been dropped and replaced by the idea that knowledge is a valuable good which it is costly to acquire. This opens the way to the study of the behaviour of rational, maximising, calculating agents in the field of acquiring knowledge. A good example of such an approach is the analysis of 'search behaviour', a literature which emanates from Stigler's (1961) paper on the economics of information. Essentially the idea is simply that resources will be invested in search (i.e. acquiring information) up to the point at which the marginal expected benefits of the information thus obtained equal the marginal costs of obtaining it.

It is worth taking a brief look at the elements of this literature in order to draw out the contrast between the approach of the Austrians and that of 'standard' theory to the problem of information. Take the very simplest case discussed by Stigler (1961). Suppose that a person wishes to purchase a certain commodity. In the textbook world of perfect competition the price of this commodity is known with certainty by every transactor. But in reality, of course, the price quoted by some sellers will be higher than others, and consumers will usually benefit by 'shopping around'. Imagine now that the consumer knows something about the *probability* of being quoted a price within certain ranges upon any given enquiry. Indeed suppose that he knows that the distribution of quoted prices is rectangular and that the price quoted may vary between £0 and £1. Such a person might argue that if he simply plans to buy from the first person he contacts he will expect to pay a price of £0.5. But of course there is a 0.5 probability that he will pay a price *greater* than £0.5. If he obtains two price quotes and then accepts the minimum of these two prices, the person will reduce the expected price that he pays. The probability of paying more than £0.5 for the item (i.e. that both quotes were greater than

£0.5) would be reduced to 0.25, while the probability that at least *one* of the two quotes is less than £0.5 would be 0.75. Clearly, 'shopping around' favourably affects the probability distribution of the minimum price encountered. It can be shown in this case[12] that if n is the number of price quotes obtained, the distribution of the minimum price will be

$$\hat{f}_n(p^*) = n(1 - p^*)^{n-1}$$

where p^* is the minimum price encountered, and the mathematical expectation of the price paid will be

$$E_n(p^*) = \int_0^1 p^* n(1 - p^*)^{n-1} \, \mathrm{d}p^* = \frac{1}{n+1}.$$

If we now assume that the person intends to buy a quantity q of the commodity (which for simplicity we take as independent of the minimum price quoted) and that the extra cost of getting one more price quote is a constant c, it is a routine minimisation problem to calculate the number of searches which will minimise the expected total cost (expenditure plus search costs) of buying q units of the commodity. In order to do so it is necessary to treat n as a continuous variable even though it can, of course, only take integer values. Let $T = qp^* + nc$ where $T =$ total cost of acquiring q units of a commodity after n searches.

Then $E(T) = qE_n(p^*) + nc = q(n + 1)^{-1} + nc$.

The first-order condition for expected cost minimisation is

$$\frac{\partial E(T)}{\partial n} = -q(n + 1)^{-2} + c = 0.$$

Hence $n = \left(\dfrac{q}{c}\right)^{1/2} - 1$

Further $\partial^2 E(T)/\partial n^2 > 0$ as required by the second-order conditions for a minimum.

If, for example, the person is to purchase a single unit of the commodity (Stigler uses once more the example of a second-hand car!) and if $c = \frac{1}{9}$ then the first-order condition tells us that two price quotes will be optimal. Clearly the lower the cost of search c, the greater the optimal number of searches (if $c = 1/100, n = 9$).

And not surprisingly the more units of the commodity to be purchased, the greater the optimal search effort (with $q = 100$ and $c = 1/100$, $n = 99$).

Stigler's analysis therefore involves the searcher in calculating the best sample size of price offers to choose. Once the problem is solved, the searcher goes out into the market and contacts the requisite number of sellers. This *predetermined sample size* strategy, however, clearly has its disadvantages. If $q = 1$ and $c = \frac{1}{9}$ and the buyer approaches the first of the two sellers he is going to sample and finds that he is offered a price of £0.1, it is not at all clear that the person should bother to contact anyone else. Rather than a *predetermined* sample size strategy, therefore, it has been suggested that a *sequential* search strategy would be more sensible. At each stage the searcher asks himself whether, given the known frequency distribution of price offers and given the lowest price so far encountered, a further unit of search would be worthwhile.

Assuming that $q = 1$ and the frequency distribution is rectangular, as above, it is a simple matter to show [13] that further search at any stage will not be worth while (in terms of reducing expected costs) if

$$p^* < \sqrt{(2c)} .$$

If the most recent price offer is less than $\sqrt{(2c)}$ it is best to accept it and search no more. $\sqrt{(2c)}$ is called a 'reservation price'. The sequential search strategy therefore comes down to the calculation of the optimal reservation price. Search then continues until a price below this level is quoted. [14]

This brief excursion into neoclassical search theory is sufficient at least to uncover the essential rationale of the approach. Neoclassical theory is evidently quite capable of analysing some types of search. But, if this is so, what is it that distinguishes Kirzner's 'alert' entrepreneur who discovers new information from Stigler's searcher after new information? And is the distinction of any importance?

The idea of a rational investment programme in the acquisition of new knowledge, as suggested by neoclassical search theory, is in some respects rather odd. For it implies that it is possible to estimate the value of new knowledge in advance of its discovery. Yet presumably this will only be possible if, in some sense, we already know what we are looking for along with probability of finding it. It is rather as if we are searching for something of which we once had full knowledge but have inadvertently mislaid. Stigler's searcher decides how much time it is worth spending rummaging through dusty attics and untidy drawers looking for a sketch which (the family recalls) Aunt Enid thought might be by Lautrec. Kirzner's entrepreneur enters a house and glances lazily at the pictures which have been hanging in the same place for years. 'Isn't that a Lautrec on the wall?'.[15]

For Kirzner, entrepreneurial knowledge is not the sort of knowledge which is the yield to a rational investment policy in search. Entrepreneurial knowledge does not involve resource inputs but is 'costless'. It arises when someone notices an opportunity which may have been available all along—something which was staring everyone in the face but had somehow escaped their attention (Kirzner, 1979, pp. 129–31). 'Why didn't I think of that?' is the exasperated cry of most of us when confronted with some simple and effective piece of enterprise. Part of our exasperation derives from the appreciation that we may have possessed all the individual pieces of information required to perceive the same opportunity. The significance of the information somehow unfortunately escaped us, and we failed to 'put it together' to form a coherent and profitable picture. Such self-admonishment is quite out of place in the world of neoclassical search. For in that world there are no mistakes and regrets whether deriving from omission or commission. True, a decision having been made, a person may later acquire knowledge which reveals how much better some alternative decision might have been. But providing that *within the context of the knowledge available at the time* the decision was correct, and providing that investment in information had been carried to the optimal point, no real 'error' can be said to have occurred. The neoclassical world must always ultimately be a world of calculation in which 'observation' is taken for granted.

(d)   J. A. Schumpeter

(i)   Entrepreneurship and Equilibrium As we have seen, Kirzner's approach to the entrepreneur is that he is alert to hitherto unexploited gains from trade. At any one time, economic life consists of a complex pattern of exchange relationships. The entrepreneur acts as the catalyst which loosens some transactional bonds and

forges new ones. In our simple example (p. 51) the entrepreneur was the motive force impelling society towards some ultimate 'solution' represented by the figures in Tables 1.4 and 1.5. Once this position is achieved no further possible entrepreneurial profits are available. By definition, if the allocation of resources is a 'core' allocation, no reallocation can benefit any group of people, and hence all the 'alertness' in the world will be of no avail in the spotting of further efficiency gains. Thus, for Kirzner, entrepreneurship is associated with *disequilibrium*, and concerns the process by which the economy moves *towards* equilibrium.

The very notion of the entrepreneur as a trader and middleman suggests the gradual and incremental approach to equilibrium as differences in relative prices are spotted and arbitrage takes place. As Loasby (1982) emphasises, there is a similarity here with Marshall's[16] approach to economic change with its emphasis on numberless small modifications of established procedures tested out in the marketplace by 'the alert businessman'. It is the tradition of Mises and of Hayek who both emphasise the small scale and 'local' character of much entrepreneurship and the dependence of this entrepreneurship on 'knowledge of time and place'[17] or 'tacit knowledge' which 'by its nature cannot enter into statistics' (Hayek, 1945, p. 21).

There is, however, a more heroic conception of the entrepreneur than this. It is easy to see how Kirzner's approach might lead to the conclusion that virtually everyone acts entrepreneurially, at least to some degree. For Schumpeter (1943), on the other hand, the entrepreneur is an extraordinary person who brings about extraordinary events. In Schumpeter's view, the entrepreneur is a revolutionary, an innovator overturning tried and tested convention and producing novelty. Such boldness and confidence 'requires aptitudes that are present only in a small fraction of the population' (p. 132) and represents a 'distinct economic function'. This function of the entrepreneur 'is to reform or revolutionise the pattern of production by exploiting an invention or, more generally, an untried technological possibility for producing a new commodity or producing an old one in a new way, by opening up a new source of supply of materials or a new outlet for products, by reorganising an industry and so on' (p. 132).

In order not to give a misleading impression it should be added that Schumpeter is careful to say that railroad construction or the generation of electrical power were 'spectacular instances' and that his conception of entrepreneurship would include introducing a new kind of 'sausage or toothbrush'. The crucial characteristic is not scale as such but novelty *in a technological sense*. New products, new processes or new types of organisation are thrust upon the world, often in the face of violent opposition. The military analogy with generalship or the 'medieval warlords, great or small' (p. 133) is considered by Schumpeter most appropriate because of the importance of 'individual leadership acting by virtue of personal force and personal responsibility for success'.

Because of this emphasis on the *energy* of individual entrepreneurs and the introduction of new products and processes, Schumpeter sees entrepreneurship as a disruptive, destabilising force, responsible for cycles of prosperity and depression. He refers explicitly to 'the *disequilibrating* impact of the new products or methods' (my emphasis) (p. 132). This is clearly a rather different conception from that of Kirzner. Kirzner's entrepreneur is engaged in spotting ways of making the best of a given set of technical circumstances. Technology, the state of the arts, of skills and scientific knowledge, are a backdrop to, rather than the outcome of, entrepreneurial activities. The possibilities for the full use of available resources in given technical circumstances still have to be uncovered, but this is all the entrepreneur is seen as doing. The production possibility curves applying to each of the four contractors in our arithmetical example were drawn on the assumption that they represented the outer bound of all the possible points attainable in the prevailing state of *technological knowledge* available to each individual. These curves would alter with changes in scientific and technical information. Thus it is usual to contrast Kirzner's approach with Schumpeter's by arguing that Kirzner's entrepreneur will get us to point *A* in Figure 1.1, a point on the community production possibility frontier representing a given state of technical knowledge; while Schumpeter's entrepreneur is engaged in *shifting* the production possibility frontier by instituting innovations. It is in this sense that Kirzner's entrepreneur gets us to an equilibrium point *A*, while Schumpeter's entrepreneur disturbs this position of equilibrium by redefining the technical constraints.

This distinction between two types of entrepreneur, one an equilibrating the other a disequilibrating force, is not, however, as clear-cut as at first sight it might appear. For it would seem inconsistent with Kirzner's basic philosophy to assume that people are aware of all the purely technical possibilities available to them, and that their lack of knowledge concerns only the possibilities of benefiting through the process of exchange. Rather, consistency requires us to argue that each person will have limited *technical* knowledge, that over time whether by accident or design they will acquire additional technical knowledge, and that entrepreneurial perception will be as significant in appreciating the consequences of newly acquired technical knowledge as knowledge of price differentials or any other objective pieces of information. It is difficult to see why the person who, upon becoming acquainted with the properties of some artificial fibre, realises that, using this fibre, toothbrushes might be made more cheaply than with natural fibre, is acting as a Schumpeterian rather than Kirznerian entrepreneur. If ultimately it is the perception of opportunities which defines the entrepreneur, then Kirzner's framework must surely embrace the marketing of new sausages and toothbrushes.

To maintain the distinction between equilibrating and disequilibrating entrepreneurs therefore seems to require that we distinguish between the use of 'new' technical knowledge, and the new use of technical knowledge which has been known for some time—at least known to some people. Thus the person who first manufactures and uses an artificial fibre is Schumpeterian, whereas the people who gradually come to perceive the multifarious possible applications are Kirznerian. This distinction would certainly seem consistent with the 'flavour' of the two writers, but whether it is tenable is a question which for the present moment we will simply ignore.

(ii) The fate of the entrepreneur Given the differences in emphasis between Schumpeter and Kirzner it is somewhat surprising to find one strand of thought common to both. Entrepreneurial activity serves to render obsolete the entrepreneur. This is perhaps easier to understand in the case of Kirzner since we have already drawn attention to the fact that, as advantage is taken of the available opportunities, the approach of equilibrium reduces the scope for further entrepreneurial insights. Kirzner, it should be emphasised, does not explicitly predict the demise of the entrepreneur as does Schumpeter. Exogenous changes in tastes and technology can be relied upon to create continuous opportunities for entrepreneurship. But it does appear to be a characteristic of

Kirzner's system that it would run down in the absence of these outside forces.

In the case of Schumpeter, the idea of the entrepreneur as a *destabiliser* might suggest the conclusion that the commercial exploitation of new inventions could go on indefinitely and with it the distinctive role of the entrepreneur. Schumpeter, however, took a quite different view. The progress of capitalism, he asserted, would eventually reduce the importance of the entrepreneur. The entrepreneur was required initially to overcome resistance to change but now 'innovation itself is being reduced to routine. Technological progress is increasingly becoming the business of teams of trained specialists who turn out what is required and make it work in predictable ways' (p. 132)... 'Economic progress tends to become depersonalised and automatised' (p. 133). The giant industrial unit 'ousts the entrepreneur' and the specialist instigators of progress eventually receive 'wages such as are paid for current administrative work' (p. 134).

This conception is of course, quite alien to Kirzner since 'alertness' to new opportunities could hardly be 'depersonalised' as envisaged by Schumpeter. Clearly 'perception' as such is not considered by Schumpeter to give rise to any special problems. Progress derives from technological change, and this can apparently develop a momentum of its own. The entrepreneur is required to galvanise the economic system into motion after which, like some material object in Newtonian physics, all resisting forces having been removed, it continues indefinitely along its predicted path.[18]

Schumpeter's prediction of the obsolescence of the entrepreneur is one of the most celebrated aspects of his work. It has naturally attracted considerable critical attention which cannot be considered here in detail. However, the different interpretations that can be placed on similar observations is startling in the study of economics. Whereas large corporate entities in Schumpeter's view 'oust the entrepreneur', Kirzner sees them as magnets attracting entrepreneurial talent. The corporation is 'an ingenious, unplanned device that eases the access of entrepreneurial talent to sources of large-scale financing' (1979, p. 105). It reduces the transactions costs, considered earlier, involved in gaining access to capitalists' funds.[19] Schumpeter observes the large corporation and finds in it an environment unconducive to the survival of the entrepreneur.

Kirzner observes the same phenomenon and pronounces it a structure which has evolved to permit a more effective use of entrepreneurial alertness. Further, Schumpeter's view that, within the corporation, technical progress becomes automatic was greeted even at the time with scepticism if not disbelief from some quarters. One such critic (Jewkes, 1948), with barely concealed contempt for a view which so contradicted his experience of aircraft production and research during the Second World War in the UK wrote that:

Left to themselves, and having no particular reasons for taking risks, teams of technicians will almost invariably bog themselves down without direction or purpose. . . . Take away the motive force of innovation—the business man—and the cautious and conservative habits of the consumer and technician would roll back over us with deadening effect (p. 21).

(e) G. L. S. Shackle

Shackle is celebrated not so much for his specific views on the entrepreneur as for his writing on the nature of choice in general. A brief consideration of his work is relevant here, however, because it impinges directly on the issues under discussion. We have seen how, in Kirzner's conception of things, the entrepreneur *perceives* opportunities. Shackle would insist that the entrepreneur must *imagine* these opportunities. This is not to use the word 'imagine' in the popular sense to imply that the opportunities are illusions, but rather simply to assert that *any* choice involves the exercise of imagining a possible future state of affairs. We do not choose between 'facts' or 'certainties'. When we act, it is on the basis of the imagined consequences. Even in the simplest possible case of choosing between a loaf of bread and a pint of beer we must choose on the basis of how we imagine our feelings will be when we actually get round to eating the bread or drinking the beer. This is so even if this occurrence follows the act of choice by a mere fraction of a second. Once we have drunk the beer we *know* what it was like, but this information is not relevant to any act of choice. When we approach the bar for our second pint we will of course, remember the experience of drinking the first, but it is strictly not this recollection of past drinks which determines our choice, but the consequent expectation of the future drink. Thus, Shackle is the complete subjectivist. All neoclassical economists are subjectivists in the sense that they accept that my valuation of beer in terms of the amount of something else I am prepared to sacrifice to get another pint is simply an expression of my own subjective preferences. But Shackle goes further to argue that the so-called 'objects of choice' (the bread and the beer) are not objects at all, but subjective impressions about the future:

If my theme be accepted, there is nothing among which the individual can make a choice, except the creations of his own thought (1979, p. 26)

Such radical subjectivism has immediate implications for his view of the entrepreneur. Shackle, like Kirzner, is often placed within the group of writers called 'Austrian'. Yet the implications of Shackle's philosophy are so subversive that by comparison the main Austrian camp appears a haven of conservatism. Kirzner's entrepreneur gradually uncovers the opportunities presented by objectively given constraints. In the process he takes us to an equilibrium in which all opportunities are finally exploited. But if opportunities do not have an objective existence independent of their discoverer, if opportunities spring from each person's imagination, they cannot be recorded, even conceptually, in a finite list unless the human imagination itself is capable of exhaustion. Thus, for Shackle there can be no state of 'full coordination' no equilibrium representing the final resting place of the economy. Underlying Kirzner there is a form of historical determinism, a final destination. Underlying Shackle there is simply 'the anarchy of history' (1979, p. 31). His view is clearly anti-determinist, and rejects the whole concept of equilibrium.[20]

To refer once more to our arithmetical illustration of the four individuals, Kirzner's entrepreneur spots the possibilities presented by four different, but objectively existing, production possibility curves. But these constraints and the opportunities delimited by them are, for Shackle, simply what people at any given time *think* they are, and can never have the status of ultimate objective unchanging facts. Tomorrow person *A* may imagine new ways of using his resources for different or for similar purposes. Either way the established pattern is upset and new opportunities for entrepreneurship are created. As Loasby (1982) puts it: 'Kirzner's entrepreneurs are alert, Shackle's are creative' (p. 119). Shackle rejects conceptions of the economic process which 'rule a line under the sum of human knowledge, the total human inventive accomplishment' (Shackle, 1982, p. 225).

If comparisons are to be made, Shackle's entrepreneur has perhaps a greater affinity with that of Schumpeter than with that of Kirzner. The emphasis on innovation on the one hand (Schumpeter) and the creative imagination on the other (Shackle) are closely related.[21] Further, the ideas that entrepreneurial activity disrupts equilibrium on the one hand (Schumpeter) and denies the possibility of equilibrium on the other (Shackle), while clearly not formally compatible, nevertheless suggest a similar conception of its impact. But in other ways Schumpeter and Shackle are far apart. Neither Schumpeter's view that only a small proportion of people have the qualities to be entrepreneurs, nor his view that the entrepreneurial function is doomed to extinction, seem compatible with Shackle's philosophy. For Shackle's view is ultimately grounded on his response to the most fundamental question of what it really means 'to choose'. Everyone faces the necessity of choice, and in choosing they exercise the entrepreneurial faculty of imagination. Thus so long as there are human beings and choices to be made, so too will there be entrepreneurs. Shackle's approach to the entrepreneur therefore is not part of a theory of business enterprise as commonly understood, nor is it like Kirzner's framework an attempt to consider the *process* by which equilibrium is attained, rather it is an integral part of his whole approach to the theory of individual choice.

(f) M. Casson

To be told that entrepreneurship is an inevitable concomitant of the human condition, while important conceptually and philosophically, is light years away from the popular conception of the entrepreneur with which we started. In principle we may accept the case that all decisions are speculative. But we may also accept that some decisions are more speculative than others, and that some people are better at making these more speculative decisions than others. If the entrepreneur is ultimately to play a part within a theory of the firm there seems no escaping the idea that the entrepreneur possesses skills which are special, if not in kind then in degree. Thus Knight's entrepreneur is unusually willing to tolerate uncertainty, Kirzner's is especially alert, Schumpeter's is ruthlessly capable of smashing the opposition, and Shackle's is endowed with a particularly creative imagination.

Casson (1982) attempts to synthesise and extend these conceptions of the entrepreneur. His definition is as follows:

An entrepreneur is someone who specialises in taking judgemental decisions about the coordination of scarce resources (p. 23).

Central to this definition is the notion of a judgemental decision. This Casson defines as a decision 'where different individuals, sharing the same objectives and acting under similar circumstances, would make different decisions' (p. 24). They would make different decisions because they have 'different access to information, or different interpretation of it'. It follows from this definition that an entrepreneur will be a person whose judgement inevitably differs from the judgement of others. His reward then derives from backing his judgement and being proved right by subsequent events.

A single chapter does not allow the space carefully to develop every point of comparison between Casson's view of the entrepreneur and those which we have already encountered. Nevertheless a few observations may help to make clear the distinctive contribution of Casson and at the same time clarify some of the issues discussed in earlier sections.

(i)   Casson has one fundamental point of agreement with the 'Austrian' theorists. The entrepreneur's reward is a residual income not a contractual income, and it is derived from the process of exchange or 'market making activities'. For Casson the middleman is an entrepreneur just as for Kirzner. Entrepreneurs reallocate resources. To achieve such a resource reallocation they must trade in property rights (see Chapter 4) and if their attempts at coordination (i.e. resource reallocation) are successful they will derive a pure entrepreneurial profit. The person who judges that a firm could be reorganised profitably, purchases the firm, changes its operations (by recontracting with the inputs) and sells it for a gain is clearly an entrepreneur. The person who thinks that a group of people, at present working independently, would be more effective as a team, and who forms the team by employing each at a wage equivalent to their existing income, thereby appropriates the productivity gains achievable through team effort. Such a person is also clearly an entrepreneur.[22]

Even at this level there are, of course, differences of emphasis.

Thus, as we have seen, Casson insists that these 'market makers' or 'coordinators' are *specialists*, whereas Kirzner sees any alert person as a potential entrepreneur. Further Casson emphasises that entrepreneurs require command over resources if they are to back their judgements and that this is likely to imply personal wealth. He refers to people with entrepreneurial ability but no access to capital as 'unqualified' (p. 333). Kirzner would accept that lack of personal capital presents extra transactional difficulties (see above section c (i)) but would almost certainly argue that anyone with entrepreneurial talent could never be in an objective sense totally 'unqualified'. Entrepreneurial talent will find ways of securing control of resources, and 'alertness' to possible new ways of doing so is as much a part of entrepreneurial talent as alertness to possible new uses for the resources themselves.

(ii)   In other respects Casson and the Austrian theorists are far apart. For Schumpeter, Kirzner and Shackle, the 'pace of change' is determined by the activities of the entrepreneurs. Each had different ideas of the personal qualities which were important in instigating change, and they differed on the question of whether change thus instigated was disequilibrating or equilibrating. But each is clear that change and entrepreneurship go together like a horse and cart and that the entrepreneur is the horse. In Casson's scheme, however, there is a tendency to view 'the pace of change' as an accompaniment to entrepreneurial activity rather than as its result. This makes Casson's entrepreneur more akin to that of Knight—the person who, in an uncertain (changing) world, specialises in making difficult judgements and receives a profit for bearing uninsurable risk (Casson would say for exhibiting superior judgement). Indeed Casson himself writes that his work on the entrepreneur is in many parts 'simply a reformulation of ideas first presented by Knight' (p. 373).

Casson's entrepreneur requires Kirznerian perception perhaps to spot the information most pertinent to the judgemental decision at hand; he requires Shackle's imaginative faculty to ponder future possibilities; but these features are not greatly emphasised. The reason is straightforward and fundamental. Casson wants to discuss more than the *rationale* of the entrepreneur. He realises the importance of the entrepreneur to the process of resource coordination and wishes to consider further questions upon which an economic theory might cast some light. Ultimately Casson wishes to construct a *predictive theory of entrepreneurship*. Shackle's sublime epistemology is all very well but there are some important down-to-earth issues which it does not really help us to address. Why are some economic systems apparently more successful at resource reallocation than others? How are entrepreneurs 'allocated' to the task of making judgemental decisions? What institutional arrangements facilitate the exercise of entrepreneurship? What factors determine the 'supply' of entrepreneurial talent? The language in these questions, which clearly implies the notion of entrepreneurship as a 'resource' similar to other factors of production to be 'allocated', is clearly alien to the Austrian conception. But as Casson recognises early on (p. 9) 'the Austrian school...is committed to extreme subjectivism—a philosophical standpoint which makes a predictive theory of the entrepreneur impossible'. He accepts that no predictive theory of the behaviour of an individual entrepreneur is possible, but this does not rule out, he argues, a theory of the aggregate behaviour of a population of entrepreneurs. Fortified with this thought Casson braces the hostility of the entire Austrian camp and proceeds to consider entrepreneurship within a supply and demand framework.

Figure 3.1 reproduces Casson's diagrammatic apparatus. The curves, though labelled *DD'* and *SS'* should not be regarded as supply and demand curves as conventionally interpreted. Consider the *DD'* curve first. Along this curve is plotted the expected reward per entrepreneur as the number of active entrepreneurs increases. It is drawn *assuming a given pace of change* in the economy. Thus new opportunities are cropping up at a certain pace and it is the task of the entrepreneurs to spot them and take advantage of them. Notice how similar to Kirzner's is this conception. Whereas Kirzner sees the entrepreneur as gradually coming to perceive the opportunities latent *in given circumstances*, Casson sees the entrepreneur as spotting a certain proportion of the opportunities thrown up *as circumstances change*. It is as if Schumpeter's entrepreneurial horse has done its work and the cart is proceeding under its own momentum directed, not by teams of experts as Schumpeter expected, but by specialist Kirznerian entrepreneurs placed in this slightly different environment by Casson.

As the number of active entrepreneurs increases, the expected return to each declines. This is to imply the usual competitive postulate in a slightly unfamiliar guise. The more active entre-

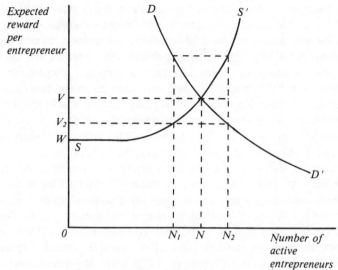

Figure 3.1

preneurs there are, the more likely it is that any given opportunity will have already been spotted by someone else, and the length of time elapsing before a newly spotted opportunity is emulated by others is reduced. Thus the curve *DD'* slopes downwards to the right and its position is dependent upon the pace of change. Curve *SS'* on the other hand is the supply curve of 'qualified' entrepreneurs (those with access to resources). It has a lower bound at the prevailing real wage on the reasonable grounds that no one will be an entrepreneur if the expected reward is below the wage rate. (This would, of course, not necessarily follow if entrepreneurs could be found who were risk lovers.) As the expected return to entrepreneurship rises above the wage rate, 'qualified' people desert employment to become specialist entrepreneurs. Further rises in the expected return induce yet others to become entrepreneurs who had before preferred leisure.

The position of the curve *SS'* depends on the stock of entrepreneurial talent existing in the population (i.e. the number of people who have the necessary judgemental qualities) and the proportion of these who are 'qualified' in Casson's sense of having command over resources. A person can become 'qualified' in three possible ways. He can have wealth of his own with which to pursue entrepreneurial ideas, he can have social contacts with wealth who know his character and appreciate his entrepreneurial potential, and he can gain command of resources from venture capitalists who do not know him but are specialists in screening for entre- preneurial flair, or from holding a senior position in a corporation.[23] Thus *SS'* will shift with changes in the distribution of wealth, changes in social mobility, and changes in institutional mechanisms for screening for entrepreneurial ability.

Intersection of the two curves *DD'* and *SS'* gives an 'equilibrium' solution and determines the number of active en- trepreneurs (N) and their expected rewards (V). These long-run 'equilibrium' expected rewards to entrepreneurship Casson inter- prets as a form of wage. In the short run the return to each entre- preneur is a return to superior (monopoly) knowledge. In the long run the expected return is 'simply compensation for time and effort, namely for the time and effort spent in identifying and making judgemental decisions' (p. 337). This long-run conception is not unlike that of J. B. Say which we encountered early on in this chapter. The number of active entrepreneurs (N), given the pace of change, will determine the proportion of new job opportunities that are exploited.

If this equilibrium or steady state is to be achieved it is necessary that potential entrepreneurs should know the total number of entrepreneurs operating at any given time, along with the underly- ing pace of change of the economy. This information will be re- quired if the expected return to entrepreneurship is to be assessed at each point and a decision made about the desirability of entry. It is worth noting that this mechanism will not necessarily lead smoothly to the equilibrium point. Suppose, for example, there were N_1 active entrepreneurs, all those entrepreneurs in the interval N_1N_2 would be attracted to enter. Casson supposes that the numbers gradually rise and the expected reward gradually falls until equilibrium is achieved. But since we have not assumed that each entrepreneur knows the opportunity costs faced by other entrepreneurs all we can really tell is that all entrepreneurs in the interval N_1N_2 will enter. Such a *mass* entry, however, will greatly depress the expected reward per entrepreneur (V_2). In this way a cycle could be generated not unlike the 'cobweb cycle' of principles of economics textbooks. It is also similar in conception to Schumpeter's view of cycles of entrepreneurial activity. Clearly the decision whether or not to become an entrepreneur is as 'judgemental' as the individual decisions the entrepreneur makes after he has entered. It would be ironical indeed to have to conclude that markets in general are coordinated by entrepreneurial activity, but that the market for entrepreneurs requires an auctioneer.

Casson's presentation of the market for entrepreneurs has many of the strengths which are associated with neoclassical ways of thinking. Drawing supply and demand curves can be a powerful aid to thought, which is presumably why they were invented and have proved so popular. Such diagrams immediately require us to specify what determines the shapes and positions of the curves, and in so doing we isolate what we think are the important influences on the market. Whether the concept of a steady-state equilibrium in the market for entrepreneurs is a theoretical advance, however, will have to be judged by future research effort. In principle the framework should permit comparative static properties to be deduced which are testable statistically. In practice it is not clear that some of the crucial variables in the model are amenable to statistical measurement, for example the social and institutional factors behind the supply curve. Further, economists of the Austrian school would argue that the attempt to introduce the equilibrium method into studies of entrepreneurship is fundamentally misconceived. For the DD' curve to mean anything it has to be assumed that all entrepreneurs know 'the pace of economic change' and can calculate the expected rewards from their entrepreneurial efforts. There seems to be no very clear explanation as to why such a construction is likely to exhibit much stability. In the context of a firm's market demand curve, Shackle (1982, p. 230) defends the geometrical figure as an aid to thought, but dismisses the possibility of knowing much about it in practice: 'It is a mere thread floating wildly in the gale'. There seems little possibility that he would take a different view of the demand for entrepreneurs.

THE ENTREPRENEUR AND THE FIRM

We have now considered in some detail the contribution of those economic theorists who have given the entrepreneur a place of importance in their thinking. There are clearly many different conceptions of the entrepreneur, but complex and subtle as are some of the arguments and distinctions that we have encountered, a few fundamental points seem particularly relevant for the theory of the firm. *Entrepreneurs are concerned with the process of coordination.* It is time and change which give rise to the possibility of entrepreneurial profit. This is so whether we emphasise alertness, imagination, skill in making judgemental decisions, willingness to bear uncertainty or energy to overcome resistance as the ultimate source of entrepreneurship. In Chapter 1 much space was devoted to the proposition that a world of perfect information required no firms and that the firm was an institutional response to uncertainty. Clearly, therefore, at this very fundamental level the entrepreneur and the firm are closely associated. Both are concerned with managing change.

It is important to remember that the entrepreneur is not a prisoner in the firm, and it is interesting that most of the theoretical work in the Austrian school concentrates, as we have seen, on intermediation in the market. But this is simply because these theorists are so interested in uncovering the ultimate source of entrepreneurial profit, and wish to emphasise their view that all economic life can be seen as a changing network of exchange relationships. Thus, as we saw in Chapter 2, the firm itself can be viewed as *a set of contracts* with a central authority, contracts so framed as to reduce the transactions costs associated with exchange in the market. The person who spots that possibilities for profitable collaboration exist, who puts together the necessary set of contracts between himself and the collaborating agents, and thus establishes a new enterprise or firm, is acting as an entrepreneur in the same way as the middleman in our earlier example. The difference between simple arbitrage and setting up a firm is one of the degree of complexity and the type of contract involved rather than any difference of economic principle. In both cases resources are reallocated, and if the reallocation makes it possible for everyone to benefit thereby the entrepreneur stands to gain a pure entrepreneurial profit. Entrepreneurship is central therefore to the establishment of new enterprises. As Knight recognised, 'A considerable and increasing number of individual promoters and corporations give their exclusive attention to the launching of new enterprises, withdrawing entirely as soon as the prospects of the business become fairly determinate' (p. 257).

Once the enterprise is established the scope for entrepreneurship does not cease. In principle the *continuation* of the same arrangements, the monitoring of the inputs and routine management are not entrepreneurial activities. But continuing change elsewhere is likely to involve a continuous process of adaptation by the firm, and no firm is likely to survive for long without the exercise of some entrepreneurial talent. It is in this context that Casson's approach has most to commend it. All firms require entrepreneurs, and a significant problem is how to make the most of available talent in the making of judgemental decisions. One of the most obvious problems faced by closely owned businesses is what happens when the sons or daughters of the founder lack their parent's business acumen. Indeed the growth of transferable shares and limited liability can be seen as a response to this very problem.[24]

The entrepreneur and the proprietor of a business enterprise are not synonymous. Clearly the single owner of the classical capitalist firm who supplies the capital and performs routine managerial tasks *may* also exercise entrepreneurial skills. But the owner is not necessarily an entrepreneur. Neither should we think in terms of a single entrepreneur associated with each firm. Especially in larger firms entrepreneurship, alertness to new opportunities, may exist throughout the organisation. The important thing is that entrepreneurs have the means of transferring their insights into personal gain. To consider the mechanisms by which this can be accomplished requires us to investigate in much more detail the nature of property rights and the way that different types of organisation reflect different structures of rights.

NOTES

1. Binks and Coyne (1983) briefly discuss the origins of entrepreneurs (pp. 15–16). In recent years the success of British–Asian entrepreneurs has been noted (Forester, 1978) while Bannock (1981) identifies 'the desperate, the non-conformist and the odd man out' as the instigator of new business enterprise.
2. A. Smith (1776) *The Wealth of Nations*.
   D. Ricardo (1817) *Principles of Political Economy and Taxation*.
   J. S. Mill (1848) *Principles of Political Economy with some of their Applications to Social Philosophy*.
3. Schumpeter (1954) writes of Say's work: 'His contribution is summed up in the pithy statement that the entrepreneur's function is to *combine* the factors of production into a producing organism. Such a statement may indeed mean much or little. He certainly failed to make full

use of it and presumably did not see all its analytic possibilities.'
(p. 555). Say's major work was the *Traite d'economie politique* (1803).

4. It is not clear that Say was consciously influenced by Cantillon.
   Richard Cantillon's 'Essai sur la nature de commerce en gènèral' was
   in circulation around 1730. He saw the farmer as an entrepreneur paying contractual sums to landlords and labourers and receiving an
   'uncertain' revenue from the sale of crops. This is a clear statement of
   the view of the entrepreneur as a recipient of 'residual' rather than
   'contractual' income.

5. Schumpeter takes a less exalted view of Courcelle-Seneuil's analytical
   contributions: 'His work illustrates our old truth that it is one thing
   to be a good economist and quite another to be a theorist'. (p. 498).
   Given his acknowledged 'practical turn of mind' however, it is appropriate, and perhaps even to be expected, that his view of profit and the
   entrepreneur was an advance on those of many more accomplished
   theorists. For, as Knight emphasises at many points, 'the absence of
   profit is the essential distinction between theoretical and actual
   economic society' (p. 51). In 'actual' economic society profits exist,
   and observers of such a society are therefore more likely to be interested in an explanation than are observers of 'theoretical' societies.

6. Von Thünen's major work *Der Isolierte Staat* was published in three
   volumes over a substantial period of time. The first volume was
   published in 1826: the third not until 1863.

7. For a discussion *see* Littlechild (1982), 'Equilibrium and the market
   process'.

8. Knight accepts that the 'moral factor' may make ordinary insurance
   inapplicable, but 'some other method of securing the same result will
   be developed and employed' (p. 47). The principal mechanism which
   Knight appears to have in mind is 'self-insurance' by taking on a
   variety of independent risks and increasing the scope of the operations
   of a single person or organisation (pp. 252–5). The growth of the corporate form of enterprise permits enormous size and scope and hence
   the pooling of risks, but is of course exposed to other moral hazards.
   These issues will be examined in detail in a later chapter.

9. Knight (1921) felt justified in devoting the whole of Part 2 of his book
   (over 140 pages) to a discussion of perfect competition, a state which
   involved 'the possession of accurate and certain knowledge of the
   whole economic situation by all the competitors' (p. 48). Similarly
   Schumpeter (1954) argued that all sound reasoning about the entrepreneur started from an appreciation of equilibrium theory, and the
   economist whose work he most admired was Walras: 'With perfect
   competition prevailing, firms would break-even in an equilibrium
   state—the proposition from which starts all clear thinking on profits'
   (p. 893)

10. Kirzner suggests at one point that capitalists *must* inevitably exercise
    the quality of entrepreneurship and quotes Mises to the effect that
    every human decision is speculative. This appears to the present writer
    to muddy the distinction between profit as a reward for 'perception'

and as a reward for uncertainty bearing. The capitalist *may* be an entrepreneur but it is difficult to see why he *must* be in Kirzner's sense. True, if a capitalist lends to an entrepreneur he may trivially have perceived what it is the entrepreneur is trying to accomplish. But there is a difference between perceiving a possible opportunity which is being, so to speak, presented on a plate by someone else, and independently perceiving the opportunity to begin with. Again, if the entrepreneur feels unwilling to divulge his plans to the capitalist for obvious reasons, the capitalist will lend only if he is convinced that the entrepreneur is a person of sound judgement. Being a good judge of character may therefore be a crucial part of becoming a successful capitalist, but it is not, in itself, the defining characteristic of an entrepreneur.

11. Borrowing from capitalists constitutes only one method by which an entrepreneur can obtain profit in the absence of resource ownership. We might have envisaged person E drawing up a contract with (say) person A by which E agreed to inform A about his entrepreneurial idea in exchange for a share in any resulting profit. This possible solution requires considerable trust between A and E, of course, but we have seen that the problem of establishing a reputation for integrity is common to virtually any contractual arrangement. Another possibility is that E negotiates with all the parties independently but arranges for all deliveries of goods to take place at the same time, thus eliminating the need to carry stock (the case of 'instantaneous arbitrage'). Again a substantial portion of Chapter 1 was devoted to the proposition that arranging for events to occur simultaneously is a costly activity.

12. If the distribution of quoted prices is rectangular we have

$$f(p) = 1. \quad 0 \leqslant p \leqslant 1 \ .$$

The probability that the price quoted is less than or equal to p^* on any one occasion will be

$$\int_0^{p^*} f(p) \ \mathrm{d}p = F(p^*) = p^*$$

where F is the cumulative distribution function. The probability that in n searches, all price quotes are *above* p^* will therefore be $(1 - p^*)^n$ and hence the probability that at least one quote will be less than or equal to p^* will be $1 - (1 - p^*)^n$. This therefore gives us an expression for the cumulative distribution function of p^* over n searches $(\hat{F}^n(p^*))$. Thus the $p \ \mathrm{d}f$ of p^* for n searches will be

$$\hat{f}_n(p^*) = \frac{\mathrm{d}}{\mathrm{d}p^*} \hat{F}_n(p^*) = n(1 - p^*)^{n-1}$$

Thus

$$E_n(p^*) = n \int_0^1 p^*(1 - p^*)^{n-1} \ \mathrm{d}p^* \ .$$

Integrating by parts we obtain

$$E_n(p^*) = \left[-p^*(1-p^*)^n - \frac{1}{(n+1)}(1-p^*)^{n+1} \right]_0^1 .$$

$$E_n(p^*) = \frac{1}{n+1} .$$

13. If the most recent price quote is accepted (p^*), this will be the 'cost' of the transaction. (Past search is a 'bygone.') If an extra unit of search is undertaken, what will be the expected cost of the transaction T?

$$T = c + p^*(1 - F(p^*)) + \int_0^{p^*} pf(p)\, \mathrm{d}p$$

c = search cost as before

$p^*(1 - F(p^*))$ = current lowest price times the probability that it continues to be the lowest price even after extra search.

Thus $\int_0^{p^*} pf(p)\, \mathrm{d}p + p^*(1 - F(p^*))$ = mathematical expectation of

lowest price available after one more search.

In the present case we simply subsitute $f(p) = 1$ and $F(p^*) = p^*$ into the above expression and obtain

$$T = c + p^* - \tfrac{1}{2}p^{*2} .$$

Clearly it is *not* worth searching any more if $T > p^*$, that is, if $c > \tfrac{1}{2}p^{*2}$. Thus we stop searching when $p^* < \sqrt(2c)$.

14. For a more detailed discussion of search models and an excellent introduction to the whole neoclassical framework for dealing with uncertainty see Hey (1979).

15. As a successful entrepreneur he will presumably express this possibility in tones sufficiently muted to be inaudible to any other occupant of the room.

16. Marshall did not expect all firms to adopt the same solutions to the problems they faced. People do not have the same information which will always lead to the same decisions: 'The tendency to variation is a chief cause of progress; and the abler are the undertakers in any trade the greater will this tendency be' (Marshall, 1925 p. 355). Different variations are then submitted to the test of the market. As Loasby (1982) puts it, 'Marshallian competition is a Hayekian discovery process' (p. 236) and his theory of economic progress is 'an incremental, experimental, evolutionary theory' (p. 239).

17. The concept of 'tacit knowledge' is of great importance to the understanding of the modern 'Austrian' writers. The term was coined by Polanyi (1958, 1967). 'We know more than we can tell' (1967 p. 4). In the neoclassical world, as was seen in section (ii), all knowledge is objective and hence discoverable by routine search and, potentially at

least, communicable to everyone. The prices quoted by sellers in the example of search considered earlier constitute objective pieces of information. Austrian theorists have argued that there is a category of knowledge which is of a different kind, information which cannot be communicated in simple statistical form to other people, information which can be acquired only through close association with particular circumstances, 'knowledge of people, of local conditions and of special circumstances' (Hayek, 1945 p. 20). Later in the same paper Hayek refers to 'knowledge of circumstances of the fleeting moment not known to others' (p. 20). In principle, the fundamental distinction is between knowledge of objective facts and knowledge of the opportunities which are present in any given situation (entrepreneurial knowledge in Kirzner's sense). The fact that circumstances are *fleeting* does not imply that the bits of information that make up these circumstances are not objective. Neither would the *complexity* of the information, as, for example, knowledge of character, necessarily imply lack of objectivity. But the ability to perceive the possibilities inherent in such fleeting or complex information is clearly to perceive information of a different order from the objective facts themselves. It is clear, however, that tacit knowledge will be particularly associated with the response to fleeting, complex, local conditions.

18. Schumpeter expresses the opinion that apart from special interests threatened by an innovation 'every other kind of resistance—the resistance, in particular, of consumers and producers to a new kind of thing because it is new—has well-nigh vanished already' (p. 133). Compare with Jewkes (1948, p. 21) quoted in the text.

19. The corporate form of enterprise will be considered in detail in a later chapter.

20. Littlechild (1979) considers this point in greater detail.

21. It should be said, however, that Schumpeter did not really see the entrepreneur as 'creating' new possibilities so much as *forcing through* those that existed.

22. *See* Chapter 4 for a fuller discussion of team production and the firm.

23. We have already met the idea of the corporation as a device to make use of otherwise 'unqualified' entrepreneurial talent in the section on Kirzner above.

24. Further discussion of this point is deferred until Chapter 4. *See also* Ekelund and Tollison (1980).

4   Property rights

In earlier chapters we have discussed at length the phenomenon of 'exchange'. But until now it has simply been assumed that exchange takes place in goods or services (or in the x and y of our arithmetical example) and that these goods and services are valued because of some physical or technical characteristics. Further progress in piecing together a coherent picture of the firm requires that we refine our concept of what it is that people trade with one another. Occasionally in microeconomics textbooks, the idea is encountered that utility or satisfaction derives not from 'goods' in themselves but from their 'characteristics'. Thus in Lancaster's (1966) framework we gain satisfaction not from toothpaste as such but from 'decay prevention' and 'mouth freshening' qualities which the toothpaste provides. Similarly in Becker's (1965) approach, households are ultimately concerned with 'commodities' which may be produced by using inputs of various market goods. Thus a visit to friends may be the desired end (the 'commodity') which requires us to use the 'goods' car service, petrol, shoe leather and so forth, along with a certain amount of time, if we are to achieve it.

These ideas suggest an even more general proposition. It is not goods in themselves which give satisfaction. *It is what people are entitled to do with these goods which really counts.* Of course, in the simple case involving an exchange of apples and nuts, so often explored in the economics textbook, the question of the ways in which we could use these physical entities to yield utility barely arises. Even here, however, we might observe that whereas the purchase of an apple entitles us to eat it, or cook it, we are not (say) entitled to propel it through our neighbour's window, or to drop the core carelessly on the public highway, or to ferment more than certain limited amounts of cider, and so forth. Thus, when people exchange apples and nuts the physical goods change hands. But that physical transaction is the visible manifestation of something more fundamental. The trade is more correctly seen as an *exchange of property rights* in the apples and the nuts.

In the case of more complex commodities the idea is more obvious. The market in the stock of housing, for example, involves the exchange of rights in the stock, and these property rights can be subdivided in such a way that several different people may have different rights in the same physical asset. Consider the legal 'owner' of a house. Such a person has the right to occupy the premises (*'usus'*), he may alternatively let the house to someone else and charge that person (the tenant) a rent (*'usus fructus'*), and within limits he may allow the house to deteriorate or he may improve it and change it in a beneficial way (*'abusus'*). But in all these things the owner is not entirely unconstrained. Ownership does not imply being able to do anything we like.

(i) If the owner occupies the premises himself there may be limitations on its use. He may be forbidden from keeping a caravan in his front garden or chickens in the back. He may be unable to paint his windows red. These activities may be forbidden because the original builder or developer of the house, wishing to create a favourable environment and thus to sell the houses for the highest possible price, judged that people will be prepared to pay more for houses free from the possible disamenities of neighbouring painters in tasteless red or lovers of noisy animals. By maintaining a right to prevent such activities, the developer is effectively instituting private 'zoning' arrangements which may be a less costly solution to these environmental problems than relying on negotiations between the occupants of neighbouring houses after they have all moved in. Whatever may be the economic rationale of the privately established 'chicken-free zone', for the moment the important point is that the bundle of rights purchased by the 'buyer' of a house is not all-encompassing.

(ii) If the owner lets his property he thereby transfers the rights of use to the tenant. The tenant now has a bundle of rights in the use of the house. The landlord can no longer enter the house when he likes, it is possible that he may be forbidden from charging more than a specified rent (if there is rent control), he may have to give a certain length of notice to the tenant. The tenant on the other hand has the right to live in the house and use the assets for a specified period of time. Under rent control the tenant may have 'security of tenure' so that he has the right to use the stock for as long as he pleases providing he pays the rent. This right of use might even be inherited by descendants of the tenant.

(iii) The right of an owner (or a tenant) to change the asset may be severely limited. As was mentioned in Chapter 2, building an extension to a house will normally require gaining the consent of the local authority planning department who thereby have considerable influence on the amount and type of development.

All these factors influence what a person can do with housing resources and hence the benefit that is derivable from them. The value to an individual of any resource thus depends on the property rights associated with it. As Demsetz (1967) puts it: 'Property rights are an instrument of society and derive their significance from the fact that they help a man form those expectations which he can reasonably hold in his dealings with others .... An owner of property rights possesses the consent of fellow men to allow him to act in particular ways' (p. 31).

TYPES OF PROPERTY RIGHTS

(1) Private Rights

When it is said that a person has *private* rights in any resource, it means that the *particular person concerned and no one else* has the authority to decide how the resource should be used. As we have seen, this does not imply that the person is unconstrained in his choice. The choice must be from a 'non-prohibited class of uses' (Alchian, 1965, p. 130). But the individual person with private property rights can prevent other people from using the resource in ways of which he does not approve. It is important to understand that this definition does not imply that *all* the property rights associated with a given resource are in the hands of a single person. Rights to use a resource may be *partitioned*, as in the case of landlord and tenant, between two or more individuals. But the rights held by the landlord and the rights held by the tenant in the housing stock are private rights. The landlord can prevent the tenant, or anyone else, physically changing the housing stock or subletting it to another person (unless of course the tenant has purchased the latter right from the landlord). The tenant can prevent the landlord from using the stock for his own private purposes. Thus the fact that different people have rights in the same physical asset does not necessarily imply that these rights are not private. So long as each person holds *different* rights, and that the exercise of one person of his rights in no way impinges upon the exercise of the other person of his rights, both people have *private* rights in the resource.

(ii) Communal Rights

There are instances in which a person's right to use a resource in a certain way is held in common with another person or group of people. My right to walk across common land is the same right as that held by everyone else with access to that land. I may use the resource for the purposes of walking, or gathering firewood, or grazing animals, or whatever, but so also can other people. Other important examples of communal rights might include the right to use a water course for the disposal of waste products, or the right to fish on a particular stretch of water or at sea, or the right to allow smoke or other waste gases to escape into the air. In each case a resource (a river, a lake, the sea or the air) may be used for the same purpose by many individuals. The analytical consequences of communal property will be discussed in a later section, but it will be obvious enough that the problems of 'congestion', 'over-fishing', and water and air 'pollution' are bound up with this question of property rights. Communal property rights, however, do not necessarily imply 'overuse' of resources if the group of people who hold these rights in common is restricted to an 'appropriate' size.[1] Thus a landowner with *private* rights to the fishing on a particular stretch of river may decide to restrict the use of the river to a selected group of other people. These people can buy a communal right to fish from the landlord, and any landlord wishing to maximise his income from selling these communal rights (licences) will wish to restrict their number.

(iii) Collective Rights

With communal rights each individual makes his or her decision as to when or how to exercise it. If I am going fishing, I do not have to consult the other people who may also have this right. In the case of a *collective* right or *shared* right, the decision about the use of a resource is taken as a group. For example a group of individuals may form a consortium which 'owns' a racehorse. This does not imply that any individual member of the consortium can enter the horse in whatever race he pleases, or that he can decide independently on how the horse should be treated. Rather it implies that *some collective decision* has to be taken about the training and sporting commitments of the horse. This will usually (though not necessarily) imply using some voting process to choose a particular person who will make the detailed decisions which most of the members of the consortium may be ill equipped to make. Once a person has been appointed to this position, the necessary private property rights which will enable him to execute decisions and prevent other non-qualified people from making decisions will inhere in that person. A *collective* right to determine the use of a resource and to share in the results is quite different therefore from a *private* right or indeed *communal* right. The managers of the resource will exercise the private rights which go with executive decision making.[2] These rights will remain for so long as the consortium believes they are being exercised sufficiently effectively on their behalf and it is therefore not worth the time and trouble involved in changing the manager.

Exchangeable Rights

All trade concerns the exchange of property rights. But not all property rights are tradable. Consider, for example, the tenant in a rent-controlled apartment. Such a tenant has the rights of use which we discussed earlier. These rights have no *market* value, however. The tenant cannot sell his rights to live in a particular house at a controlled rent to anyone else. This lack of tradability can have important consequences as the eclipse of the private rented sector in the UK helps to testify. Suppose, for example, the value of a house available for owner-occupation on the market was £50,000. Now imagine that the same house has a tenant paying a below-market rent set by a controlling agency. Clearly the value of the house with a sitting tenant will be less than £50,000 (perhaps £30,000) depending upon the level of the controlled rent, expectations concerning the future of rent control, or the likelihood that the tenant will move. The result is that the market value of the tenant's rights (zero) plus those of the landlord (£30,000) falls short of the value of the property unencumbered by the tenant (£50,000). It follows that both landlord and tenant will have a *mutual interest* in changing the allocation of property rights in the house. By creating a freehold there is a potential £20,000 of capital gain to be shared between them. Thus the tenant might offer the landlord (say) £40,000 for his rights in the house. This is £10,000 more than their value on the market. But by combining the landlord's and tenant's rights in this way, the tenant creates the freehold which as we saw was worth £50,000. Both landlord and tenant thus each make a gain of £10,000.

This example is an illustration of an important principle which will be encountered again in differing disguises. The nature of property rights in resources is expected to change when someone perceives that existing rights holders could all be better off by agreeing to such a change. Sometimes this will involve combining hitherto separately held rights in a single holder (as in the landlord–tenant example under rent control). Sometimes though, it might involve *disentangling* different rights at present held by a single person and then allocating them to different people. Financial markets provide examples of this process. A government bond which promises to pay £5 per year until repayment of the principal in the year 2010 can be held by a single person. But the right to £5 per year until 2010, and the right to the principal (say £100) in 2010, are quite distinct and could be sold separately on the market. If the market values of the two separate rights sum to more than the market value of the combined rights (the bond) it will pay some financial intermediary to buy bonds and split them down into their component parts.[3]

Just as private rights may be exchangeable or non-exchangeable, the same applies to collective and communal rights. Consider first the case of communal rights. The purchase of a licence to fish in a particular area results, as we saw, in a communal right (unless of course there is only a *single* licence). This right may or may not be tradable. If I break my arm after buying the licence I may be able to sell it to someone else, in which case possession of some document is presumably sufficient to procure admission. If on the other hand the licence applies to a single named individual, it is worthless to anyone else, and will have no exchangeable value. Membership of a club which allows people access to some communal property constitutes another example. Usually such communal rights are *not* marketable for the simple reason that when communal access to some resource is involved, the other members of the club will want a say in deciding the eligibility of new members. Willingness to pay the highest entry fee *may* not be the deciding criterion. Assessment of character and the probability that the new member will take due care of the communal property may be equally important. On the other hand the *incentive* to take care of communal property would appear to be stronger when rights of access are exchangeable than when they are not, since failure to do so will be reflected in a falling market value of club membership as facilities deteriorate.

Company shares represent the classic case of exchangeable collective rights. The member of the consortium which owned the racehorse in our earlier example would normally be able to sell his 'share' in the racehorse to another person. We will be investigating the property rights structure of different types of company in more detail shortly. Collective rights in assets taken into 'public ownership' such as nationalised undertakings and departments of state are clearly *not* exchangeable. This lack of transferability is the crucial distinction between collective rights in the assets of the state and collective rights in the private sector. As Alchian (1965) expresses it: 'The differences between public and private ownership arise from the inability of a public owner to sell his share of public ownership' (p. 138). Rights which cannot be traded are sometimes called 'inalienable rights'. Because they cannot be reassigned through the process of exchange the entrepreneurial function of intermediation which we discussed in Chapter 3 has no scope to operate in a world of inalienable rights. Some rights must be exchangeable if there is to be any coordination problem to solve.

(v) Exclusion

If rights are to be exchangeable on the market they must, of course, be denied to people who have not acquired them through gift or exchange. If people cannot effectively be excluded from fishing a stretch of river because the costs of policing the river bank are very high, the market price of a licence will be zero. No one will voluntarily pay for a right they can without penalty acquire for nothing.[4] Thus the ability to exclude others from using a resource is a necessary condition of exchangeability and hence of markets in property rights. If exclusion cannot be effected, the resource is perforce 'communal'; we all have a right to grab what we can get. *The converse does not hold*: communal property may or may not permit exclusion, as was seen in the section on communal rights.

THE DEVELOPMENT OF PROPERTY RIGHTS

Thus far, our attention has primarily been confined to describing property rights and presenting a simple taxonomy. Several questions now arise: Can we *explain* the development of different types of property rights? How will the nature of a person's rights influence behaviour? Do property rights matter? One possible response to these questions is that of Demsetz (1967, 1979). Demsetz concentrates on the issue of *economic efficiency*. We have already seen how the process of exchange gives rise to efficiency gains. If, as a result of resource reallocation, everyone is made better off (as in the example of Chapter 1) the new allocation of resources is said to be *'Pareto superior'* to the old allocation. It was from these 'efficiency gains' that the entrepreneur was seen to draw his 'pure entrepreneurial profit' in Chapter 3. In Chapter 2, on the other hand, the obstacles to the realisation of gains from exchange, 'transactions costs', were considered. Demsetz makes the point that transactions costs are not independent of the types of property rights in which trade is taking place. As a result some change in the structure of property rights in a resource may be required before potential efficiency gains can be appropriated.

Consider once more the case of the four islanders *A*, *B*, *C* and *D*. Let us suppose that somewhere on the island is a freshwater lake containing fish. Each person is equally skilled at catching fish and equally conveniently located with respect to access to the lake. The fish are a delicate species living in a finely balanced harmony with predators and prey. One person fishing the lake can take 10 fish per day, but two people fishing will find that only 15 fish per day are sustainable. A maximum yield per day of 18 fish can be achieved with three people, and any further fishing effort will actually reduce the sustainable yield of fish obtainable from the lake by depleting the stock of fish by more than can be compensated by the greater fishing effort. Table 4.1 records these illustrative figures for total social product of fish along with average and marginal social product schedules.

Table 4.1

Number of Fishermen	Total social product	Average social product	Marginal social product	Surplus
1	10	10	10	6
2	16	8	6	8
3	18	6	2	6
4	16	4	−2	0

From the firgures in Table 4.1 we see that each person fishing in the lake imposes on the others an *'external diseconomy'*. Suppose that *A* is fishing alone and taking home 10 fish per day. Person *B* now comes along and starts fishing. Both *A* and *B* each take home 8 fish per day. *B*'s fishing has *reduced A*'s catch by 2 fish per day. It would however be equally correct to say that *A*'s presence at the lake reduced *B*'s catch by 2 fish per day. The relationship is perfectly reciprocal. Each person imposes external diseconomies on the other. Real external diseconomies in production occur when one person's actions affect the production possibilities faced by others, and the four individuals around the island lake are clearly interdependent in this way. The fishing resouce is subject to *congestion* as reflected in the declining schedule of average social product (ASP) as the number of people fishing increases.

Assume now that all four islanders have a communal right to fish in the lake. No one is excluded from fishing, and hence the right to fish there has no market value. Each person will therefore fish as long as the product he takes home exceeds the value of the alternative uses of his time (the value of the fish exceeds its opportunity cost). Let this opportunity cost be the equivalent of 4 fish per day.[5] Since the private return to each person is the *average social product* (ASP) extra people will fish if ASP > 4 and this implies that all four people on the island will fish in the lake.

From the point of view of the group of islanders as a whole, of course, this outcome is not ideal. They could all be better off by restricting access to the lake. This is more easily seen by considering the 'surplus' which the community as a whole has derived from the resource. The 'surplus' is simply the total social product of fish minus the opportunity costs of catching it. For the case of three fishermen total product is 18 and total social cost is 12, thus resulting in a 'surplus' of 6. With four people fishing, this surplus has declined to zero. The presence of the lake has conferred *no* net benefit on the four individuals. Between them they have managed to sacrifice elsewhere things equivalent in value to the fish they have caught. If access to the lake were restricted to two people the social product would be unchanged at 16, while the other two people would be free to take leisure or to produce additional goods elsewhere, goods or leisure which we have assumed are valued as equivalent to 8 fish.

Restricting access to the lake implies changing the nature of the property rights which people hold. The lake can no longer be unrestricted common property. We might imagine many different ways in which this could come about.

(i) All four islanders might come to some mutual agreement whereby they renounce their communal rights in exchange for a collective right to a share in the produce of the lake. This 'fisheries consortium' will then have an incentive to ensure that only two people actually fish in the lake.

(ii) One of the islanders, perhaps the entrepreneur *E* of Chapter 3, might simply try to buy up the common rights of the others. Providing that the price of these rights is less than the surplus expected from the commercial exploitation of the lake, a profit will be achieved on the transactions. The bargaining and transactions costs involved in this strategy are likely to be considerable, however, because those who 'hold out' against the offers made by person *E* will in the end find themselves in a very strong bargaining position.[6] It is this problem which is often used to justify an element of coercion by the state when bargaining costs threaten the achievement of potential efficiency gains. The power of compulsory purchase, for example, has been defended as a method of reducing transactions costs in situations which would otherwise be subject to the problem of 'hold-out'.

(iii) A third possibility is that the only islander with a gun announces to the others that from henceforth they cannot fish in the lake without his consent. Common rights are confiscated by force and replaced by private rights.

Whatever the mechanism by which changes in property rights are effected, one result is the same. By restricting access to the resource, efficiency gains are achieved. The *distribution* of these gains will depend on the bargaining process between the islanders.

They may all accrue to the person with the gun, or to the entre-
peneur E, or they may be shared between members of the fisheries
consortium. A licence to fish in the lake set at a price equivalent to
4 fish would reduce the number of people fishing to two, and procure an income of 8 fish for the resource owner or owners.

Figure 4.1 illustrates the entire argument geometrically. The
average social product of fishing effort is depicted by curve ASP.
Since, by assumption all people are equally skilled at fishing, the
private return to extra fishing effort will equal the average social
return. This implies that people will continue to supply more fishing
effort as long as average social product exceeds marginal private
cost. Marginal private costs (equal to social costs) are assumed constant at c. Thus, with unrestricted entry into fishing we find a quantity of fishing effort F_1 provided. This is inefficient since the
marginal social product of fishing effort (MSP) is well below

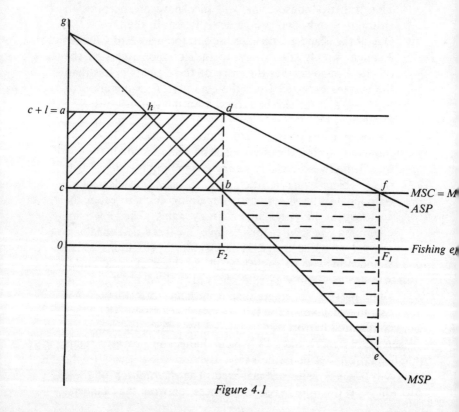

Figure 4.1

marginal social cost (MSC) at this level of effort. Efficiency requires a level of fishing effort F_2, where MSP = MSC. The vertical distance between ASP and MSP represents the external cost imposed on others by extra fishing effort. Similarly the vertical distance between ASP and MPC represents the private benefit accruing to extra fishing effort. Clearly if external costs exceed private benefit it will be possible for people to get together to bribe some of their number not to fish, since the bribers will gain from reduced congestion more than they have to pay in compensation to the people being bribed (see especially Coase, 1960).

The gain to restricting fishing effort in this way is given by area *bfe*. Once private rights to fishing have been established, a licence fee per unit of fishing effort (*l*) can be introduced, the private marginal costs of fishing will increase to $l + c = a$ and fishing effort will fall to F_2. Total revenue from the sale of licences will be area *acbd* and in these circumstances will precisely equal the efficiency gains achieved (area *bfe*).[7]

For Demsetz, therefore, property rights will change when people find that there are substantial efficiency gains (mutual benefits) to be derived from such a change. These benefits must be sufficient to compensate for the transactions costs involved in establishing and in policing the new structure of rights. If people cannot, except at prohibitively high cost, be prevented from fishing in the lake, no changes in the structure of rights will emerge. On the other hand 'prohibitive' here means 'relative to potential benefits', and the more congested the lake becomes the larger become the efficiency gains from mitigating the problem, and the more likely therefore that the policing costs are worth incurring.

Demsetz cites as an example of this process changes in the rights to use land among the Indians of Labrador. It appears that in the seventeenth century there was no restriction on hunting rights. The development of the fur trade, however, gave rise, according to this theory, to the division of territory among hunting bands. Clearly, without such rights each hunting party could impose severe external disbenefits on the others. When animals were hunted merely for food and clothing for the Indian population, the problem of external costs was insignificant. But with commercial development this was no longer the case and more restrictive property rights emerged. Demsetz then poses the question: why did a similar process not occur among the plains Indians of the south west? One answer is that the cost of defining and policing property rights on the plains would have been much higher than in the forests. Animals grazing on the plains wander over vast areas. Those in the forests are more restricted in their movements. Thus, simple delineation of a given policeable area is not sufficient to appropriate a right to tend and harvest a particular herd on the plains, and property rights remained common and open. The consequence of this structure of property rights for the buffalo herds is, of course, well known.

'TEAM PRODUCTION' AND THE CLASSICAL CAPITALIST FIRM

Just as the development of property rights in resources subject to congestion can be seen as an attempt to achieve efficiency gains, so the development of institutional structures such as firms can be viewed in the same light. In Chapter 2 the firm as a device to economise on transactions costs was considered in some detail. We did not emphasise at that stage, however, that the contractual relationships found within 'the firm' establish a structure of property rights in the use of resources. In a classic paper, Alchian and Demsetz (1972) elaborated on this theme and argued that the structure of property rights observed in the classical capitalist firm was a response to transactional problems, and in particular to the problem of 'team production'.

The essence of the firm for Alchian and Demsetz is that it permits people to work as a team. Team production occurs when an output is produced by the *simultaneous cooperation* of several team members. Production is not a sequence of identifiable stages by which a series of intermediate products are gradually transformed into the final output. Rather, the final output is the joint result of the combined efforts of all the inputs working *at the same time*. It follows that the individual contribution of each member of the team to the final output cannot be isolated and observed. All that can be observed in terms of output is the combined result of the entire team's efforts.

A further complication is that any one person's activity may affect the productivity of the other members of the team. In these circumstances there will exist an incentive for people to get together and agree to take account of external effects in their behaviour. In the last section we showed how people could gain by forming a 'fisheries consortium' if their fishing activities imposed external disbenefits on each other. Here the same argument can be used to show that a *collective* agreement to modify behaviour may be useful in the presence of external benefits. Person *A* agrees to work a little harder on the understanding that person *B* will do likewise. The benefits in terms of higher output of their *joint* decision to work harder will be sufficient to compensate them both, although any *individual* commitment to greater effort *in the absence of the other party* would not have conferred net private benefits on the person undertaking the extra work.

The situation is analogous to the public goods problem discussed in Chapter 2 (p. 35). No individual person may have an incentive to provide a public good, although a joint decision to produce one may confer benefits on everyone. It will be recalled that a joint decision was difficult to arrange because each person had an incentive to understate his or her true valuation of the public good in the hope that other people would pay to provide it. People, in other words, would tend 'to shirk' and fail voluntarily to pay their contributions. In the same way, a joint agreement to work harder in order to increase team output will be difficult to implement unless each person's behaviour can be monitored. Without monitoring, each person will 'shirk' and hope to 'free ride' on the effort of other people. Note that this problem would not arise if an identifiable output could be assigned costlessly to each person, for then a contract linking reward to performance would be possible. In the case of 'team production', however, there is a single output produced by the simultaneous cooperation of all members of the team, and the individual contribution of each member cannot be separately identified.

Problems of 'moral hazard' (see pp. 27–9) will therefore have to be overcome if the potential advantages of team production are to be achieved. The 'solution' suggested by Alchian and Demsetz is that the team requires a 'monitor' to observe the individual members and to check that their effort is satisfactory. Clearly, this solution requires that effort is observable and this will obviously not always be the case. Where the team is concerned with the coordination of fairly simple 'manual' operations, the observation of the inputs to ensure that they perform the tasks they contract to perform may not be very costly. In other cases, observation of *behaviour* may be a very imperfect guide to the effective input of the team member involved. Further, as we saw in Chapter 2, a monitor may not have the information to judge whether the actions taken by a particular person are or are not in the interests of the team as a whole. The problem is equivalent to person A's difficulty of contracting with his architect (p. 23).

Assuming for the time being that a monitor is capable of observing the effort of team members, the problem remains of providing the monitor with some incentive to bother. If the monitor is simply another member of the team whose job is to check that all other team members are fulfilling their contractual commitments, the monitor would have as much incentive to shirk as anyone else. It is for this reason, argue Alchian and Demsetz, that the monitor becomes a *residual claimant*. Each team member receives a contractual reward in the form of a wage, and the monitor receives whatever remains after these payments have been made. The more effectively the team operates, the bigger the residual will be, and hence the monitor will have a definite interest in promoting the efficiency of the team. All the benefits from improved coordination will accrue to the monitor instead of being shared amongst the team members.

If the status of residual claimant is to provide the monitor with an incentive rather than merely an interest, he must be able to discipline team members. It would be pointless monitoring the behaviour of team members if they could then ignore the monitor's criticisms. Thus the monitor becomes the common party to all contracts with the power to alter these contractual arrangements and to add and subtract from the team (to hire and fire). Note the difference here from Coase's view of the firm. Coase emphasised the costs of arranging detailed multilateral contracts as an explanation of the firm. Alchian and Demsetz emphasise the necessity of the monitor having control of contractual arrangements in the context of team production if shirking is to be reduced.

From the perspective of property rights theory therefore the traditional single proprietorship can be seen as a form of enterprise which concentrates property rights in the hands of a single person. The 'private' nature of these property rights gives the possessor the maximum incentive to consider the consequences of his actions for the market value of the rights. The more effectively the single contractual agent or proprietor monitors and organises the team, the greater is the residual claim and the more valuable will be his property rights on the market. Exchangeable, private rights to determine the use of team resources, to monitor operations, and to claim the residual, represent a response to the moral hazard problem posed by shirking in the context of team production.

Although Alchian and Demsetz in their original (1972) paper saw team production as the primary source of the moral hazard problem, it is evident from the arguments reviewed in Chapter 2 (pp. 25–31) that *even in the absence of team production* as we have conceived it, asymmetric information can lead to problems of moral hazard. Whenever it is difficult to assess the quality of an intermediate product, for example, the supplier may have an incentive to shirk and there will be an advantage to appointing a specialist monitor. In this way a purely market transaction becomes a transaction conducted within a firm. We will consider this process in more detail in a later chapter on the subject of vertical integration. For the present, it is merely necessary to note that the single proprietorship can be considered as a response to the 'shirking' problem and that this does not require us to assume conditions of team production but, as Williamson (1975, pp. 49–50) emphasises, may be an appropriate view wherever information difficulties lead to opportunistic behaviour.[8]

ALTERNATIVE STRUCTURES OF PROPERTY RIGHTS

In the last section we focused attention on the structure of property rights characteristic of the single proprietorship. Common observation tells us, however, that, numerous and economically important though such arrangements are (e.g. Storey, 1982; Bolton, 1971), the modern economy has developed institutions of far greater complexity. An explanation of these more complex institutions must ultimately reflect the idea that concentrating property rights in a single holder is not necessarily the most efficient structure. Sometimes the sharing of rights between people or the apportioning of different private rights between people may be efficient. Thus the full package of property rights held by a proprietor may instead be shared between two or more people in a 'partnership', or alternatively the right to claim the residual may be shared between one group of people and the right to monitor the inputs may be held by another as in a 'joint stock' company.

At first sight such a statement appears to contradict flatly all that was argued in the previous section concerning the necessity of overcoming the moral hazard problem posed by shirking and the resulting *concentration* of property rights. It is evident, however, that the complete avoidance of all moral hazard problems is neither feasible nor efficient. If this were not so it would be a simple matter to circumvent moral hazard by refraining from all contractual relations with other people and forgoing the benefits of division of labour and exchange. The maximum concern for fire prevention and theft prevention can be achieved no doubt by abolishing insurance markets, but few people would advocate such a move or claim that economic efficiency would be enhanced. It may be worth while tolerating reduced incentives if the benefits of a more efficient distribution of risk taking are sufficiently great. Conversely (and this is something we shall discuss in more detail in Chapter 5 on principal and agent) if a perfectly efficient distribution of risk taking involves severe problems of moral hazard it may be worth while sacrificing risk-sharing benefits in the interests of providing incentives. In other words we might expect observed contractual relations to reflect the available trade-off between risk-sharing benefits and effort incentives, a trade-off which will be affected in any given case by the costs of monitoring.

1. The Single Proprietor

Consider once more the single proprietor. A team endeavour requires a monitor if it is to operate effectively. The problem of providing incentives to the monitor is then encountered. This can be viewed as a classic 'agency' problem. If members of the team cannot tell whether the monitor is performing the promised services they have to devise some incentive structure based not on unobservable behaviour but on observable outcomes. The one thing that, by assumption, is observable by everyone is the final output of the entire team. Instead of a system in which this output is shared between all members of the team therefore, a form of organisation evolves in which team members receive a fixed wage (irrespective of overall team performance) and the monitor receives the residual. In Chapter 5 we shall investigate more carefully the circumstances in which we expect an agent to promise a principal a fixed sum in this way and thus to relieve the latter of all risk. However, it is not offensive to the intuition to learn that if the agent is risk neutral and the principal is risk averse the efficient contract between them will involve the agent bearing the entire risk.

It is very important to understand the nature of the 'thought experiment' conducted in the above paragraph. The single proprietor is clearly *not* an agent in a legal sense. As we saw in an earlier section the proprietor must be the *employer* not merely the agent of the team if he is to have the authority to influence team behaviour. However, in piecing together a *rationale* of the proprietorship, it is defensible and indeed enlightening as a first approximation to regard the structure of incentives embodied in this form of organisation as a solution to an agency problem. In a similar spirit we will later on consider how far and in what circumstances an employee might be considered an agent of the manager or the manager an agent of the shareholder.

Let us suppose now that the moral hazard problem is so severe that in the absence of a monitor-employer the team could not survive in any shape or form. On the other hand, assume that the returns to monitoring activities are substantial so that a proprietorship is viable. If the proprietor is risk neutral and the employees are risk averse the traditional structure with the proprietor receiving the residual and the employees a given wage will be efficient. Notice how akin to Knight's is this conception (Chapter 3 pp. 47–9) with the 'confident and venturesome' providing insurance for the 'doubtful and timid'. Alchian and Demsetz, however, explicitly reject the Knightian risk-sharing approach to the firm and prefer to concentrate instead on the advantages of team production. Yet any final organisational form, with its structure of property rights held by the members of the organisation, will presumably reflect all the forces which we have so far discussed:

(i) the potential advantages of further specialisation (division of labour) or team production;

(ii) the extent to which the exchange relationships involved in (i) give rise to problems of moral hazard;

(iii) the returns to monitoring;

(iv) the trade-off between risk-sharing benefits and incentives.

The single proprietorship is a 'solution' to the problem of organisational form under rather special circumstances:

(i) The potential advantages of specialisation or of team operations are limited to groups sufficiently small to be efficiently monitored by a single person;

(ii) moral hazard problems are severe but;

(iii) the returns to monitoring are such that at least over a certain range the extra output of the monitored team is more than sufficient to compensate the monitor for his effort;

(iv) (a) the returns to monitoring effort are *certain*; or
(b) monitoring effort favourably affects the probability distribution of the residual by increasing expected output net of monitoring and contractual costs *and* the monitor is risk neutral.

By setting out the conditions most favourable to the establishment of a single proprietorship in this way we begin to perceive the circumstances in which alternative organisational forms might be observed.

2. The Partnership

(a) Monitoring Costs We start by assuming that returns to monitoring effort are certain, as in (iv)a. In Figure 4.2 the curve labelled $MC_A = MC_B$ represents the marginal costs to monitors A and B of different levels of monitoring effort. It measures the extra monetary payment required to induce them to exert one more unit of effort. Curve MB_1 indicates the marginal returns to extra effort. We suppose that after a certain point (E_1) the marginal cost of monitoring effort rises and eventually becomes vertical as the limits of human endurance are reached. The returns to extra monitoring of the team decline throughout. A single proprietor (say person A) facing curve MB_1 would put in effort level E_1 where the extra returns from marginal effort are just equal to the compensation required. The final reward of the monitor will depend upon the level of effort required for the team to break even. Suppose for example, monitoring effort E_0 is required if contractual payments to other team members are to be met from the value of output. All further monitoring effort will produce a residual which can be claimed by the monitor. Since we have assumed that returns to monitoring effort are *certain* we would expect this residual will just be sufficient to compensate the monitor for the costs he incurs

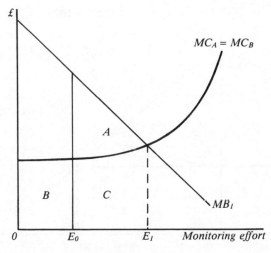

Figure 4.2

(including wages forgone as a team member).[9] Thus, the additional benefit to monitoring effort above E_0 (the value of the residual areas $A + C$) will be just equal to the costs incurred in being a monitor (areas $B + C$). Hence, under conditions of a certain return to monitoring effort area A = area B.

Now suppose that the returns to monitoring effort are given by MB_2 in Figure 4.3. Under these conditions a partnership of two people monitoring together will exert effort level $2E_1 = E_2$. The marginal cost of effort at this point is the same for each partner. But we might ask why a single proprietor should not monitor the team and exert effort level E_1'? The answer is that competition from the partnership form of organisation will undermine the single proprietorship. Once more assume that effort level E_0 is required for the team to break even. It follows as before, that where the returns to monitoring effort are certain, both partners will just be compensated for the costs of monitoring the team. Thus area $A'(abc)$ = area $B'(ofaE_0)$. But if area A' = area B', a single proprietor exerting effort E_1' would not be able to earn enough to compensate himself for the work involved. Clearly, the residual of the single proprietor will be $bdE_1'E_0$ which will fall short of total monitoring costs (the total area under MC_A up to E_1') since area

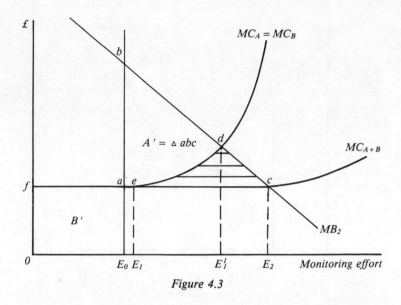

Figure 4.3

$aedb < B'$. The essential point is extremely obvious. If a partnership can monitor at the same marginal cost as a proprietorship or
lower up to E_1^1 and can further afford to monitor to a higher level
of intensity (E_2), the partnership form of enterprise will take over
from the proprietorship and the efficiency gains represented by area
edc will be the prize.

The assumption that the monitoring costs faced by each individual are uninfluenced by the forms of organisation is, of
course, crucial to this piece of analysis. A partnership involves an
agreement between two or more people to perform certain monitoring services in exchange for a specified *share* in the residual. Even
when the returns to monitoring effort are assumed to be certain,
therefore, contractual difficulties are likely to be encountered. If
the monitoring effort of each partner is perfectly and costlessly
observable by all the others, partnership arrangements will be a
predictable response to the increasing productivity of team effort
and hence will permit larger team sizes than would otherwise be
possible. But where the behaviour of each monitor is costly to
observe, Alchian and Demsetz's moral hazard problem reasserts
itself. The effort of one monitor (partner) confers benefits on the
others and the result will be an incentive to shirk. We therefore

deduce that partnerships are more likely to evolve where the process of monitoring is itself routine and susceptible to a degree of accountability than where the effort of each partner is almost impossible to observe or deduce. Where the returns to monitoring are certain, two partners should be able each to police the activity of the other since each will know their own effort and can deduce the effort of the other from the final team output.[10] As the number of partners increases, however, the incentive to shirk will rise since assigning individual responsibility for poor team performance may become impossible, and the effort of any individual partner will have a smaller and smaller effect on the value of his share.

Our discussion of the partnership thus far leads to the conclusion that sharing the right to the residual may hold out the possibility of potential efficiency gains by reducing the marginal cost of monitoring large teams. Against these potential gains we must set the extra problems of moral hazard which may arise when rights are shared in this way. If monitors begin to shirk, the efficiency gain (area *edc*) in Figure 4.3 may be dissipated and the single proprietorship will continue as the most effective organisational form. At any rate partnerships are likely to be fairly small and, given the trust which must exist between partners if they are to avoid the losses involved in opportunistic behaviour, it is expected that the use of close family connections and those amenable to peer group pressure will be frequent.

(b) *Risk Sharing* The assumption that returns to monitoring are *certain* is a convenient simplification when discussing the trade-off between monitoring costs and the hazards encountered when the residual is shared. But as was noted earlier the residual received by the monitor is unlikely to be deterministically related to monitoring effort. By accepting a residual reward, the monitor is exposed to risk. The fact that the residual may vary for reasons unrelated to monitoring effort has important implications.

(i) In the first place the suppliers of 'contractual' resources to the team effort will want assurances that, if the residual turns out to be negative, they will still receive the promised payment for services rendered. This implies that a monitor will require some personal wealth to act as 'collateral security'. We discussed at some length in Chapter 3 (pp. 54 and 67) the possibility that an entrepreneur with no wealth might presuade others to provide finance, but accepting that this *may* occur there are clear limits to the resource inputs which can be acquired in this way. Risk implies that the size of a single proprietorship will be limited by personal wealth and that partnerships will be necessary if firms are to grow beyond these limits.

It is worth emphasising that the above argument relies on the premise that the risk faced by the monitor is 'uninsurable'. Even if the residual could be represented by a probability distribution conditional upon effort and was thus 'risky' in Knight's strict sense, insurance markets would succumb to the moral hazard problem if the monitor's effort was not observable. If the monitor was certain of achieving a given residual through an insurance contract, the incentive to exert effort would be entirely lost, and with it the whole point of giving the monitor the residual claim.

(ii) Where the monitor is risk neutral, the concentration of risk is efficient as we have seen. Where, however, the monitor is risk averse along with other members of the team it makes no more sense to concentrate all the risk on such a person than to insist that someone confronting rapidly rising marginal costs of effort should do all the work. By taking a partner, the risks of the enterprise are shared, and where both partners are risk averse total risk-bearing costs will decline. Thus, just as we showed in section 2(a) that partnerships might permit lower monitoring costs, they may also permit lower risk-bearing costs. It is then the sum total of these two possible efficiency gains which must be set against the moral hazard problems arising from sharing a property right in the residual.

The history of the partnership form of enterprise illustrates the operation of these conflicting forces. Each partner, in addition to sharing in the residual, has rights to use and manage the resources of the team. The decisions of each can therefore bind the others, and the partners are responsible for all debts whether or not as individuals they were personally involved in incurring them. Indeed the English law of partnership developed the rule that each partner was liable 'to his last shilling and acre'. In the face of this stringent legal background of unlimited liability it is not surprising, as was noted earlier (p. 84) that the property rights of each partner are not freely tradable. If a partner withdraws or dies, the partnership is broken and has to be reconstituted. Thus it is very complicated and difficult for a partner to extricate his share of the resources from the business.

Because in the case of a partnership there is no *single* contractual agent but several agents capable of contracting on behalf of each other, the transactional difficulties involved in this type of enterprise are substantial. During the 1830s in the UK when dissatisfaction with the law of partnership was growing, one of the major issues concerned the difficulty faced by a third party in suing a partnership or vice versa, and the difficulty involved in one partner suing another. Grievances between partners were particularly troublesome given the difficulties of acquiring information and cases were reported 'which were upwards of thirty years in the Court of Chancery'.[11] The fact that the 1837 report on partnerships was particularly concerned 'with regard to the difficulties which exist in suing and being sued where partners are numerous' is indicative of the transactional problems encountered by large partnerships. These problems rapidly cancelled any risk-sharing or monitoring benefits available, and effectively placed a limit on the size to which a partnership could grow.[12]

3. The Joint-Stock Company

Large-scale enterprises involving the cooperation of thousands and even hundreds of thousands of individuals would clearly not have evolved had the property rights structures characteristic of the single proprietorship and the partnership been the only possibilities available. The potential gains available from the monitoring of large teams, the 'visible hand' as Chandler (1977) has termed it, required a new structure of rights to emerge, a structure which did not expose the managers of large-scale enterprise to a degree of risk which they were not prepared to shoulder, and which permitted capital to be supplied by many people who would play no part in day-to-day business decisions. This particular combination of characteristics was impossible to achieve under the strict law of partnership. Capital could be borrowed no doubt, at fixed interest from many people, but only at the cost of tolerating a very high 'gearing' or 'leverage' in the financial structure. Such high ratios of debt to proprietor's or partners' wealth would increase the risk of insolvency, a spectre made even more appalling by the provisions of unlimited liability which effectively meant personal ruin in the event of business failure on such a large scale. As we have seen, the alternative of growing through the addition of new partners was rendered unattractive because of the transactional difficulties involved and the enormous trust required in the integrity of other members of the partnership.

The joint-stock company developed as a response to these

difficulties. For our purposes there are three characteristics of great economic importance.

(a)   A joint-stock company has a legal existence quite distinct from the people who comprise the company at any given point in time. People may come and go but, unlike the partnership, the company continues in existence. Further, as a separate legal entity a joint stock company can sue and be sued. This greatly simplifies contractual relations with third parties and helps to overcome some of the difficulties alluded to in the previous section.

(b)   The shares of *public* companies are freely exchangeable. A market can therefore develop in these shared rights (the stock exchange) and it is a relatively costless exercise to buy or sell an interest in any particular company. Ekelund and Tollison (1980) argue that this ease of transferabilty was important in the early history of the development of the joint-stock form of enterprise. Lack of transferability would inhibit the most talented and qualified people gaining control of productive resources, which would instead remain in the same hands or in the same family for many years. Over the long run, the flexibility offered by joint-stock enterprises in reassigning property rights to more energetic people would give them an advantage over alternative institutional forms. [13]

(c)   The third important characteristic of joint-stock enterprises is that the liability of shareholders is limited. [14] With unlimited liability people will naturally be chary of business associations involving people they do not know personally. With limited liability the prospect of subscribing relatively small amounts to an enterprise will be more tolerable in the secure knowledge that the rest of a person's fortune is not inevitably at hazard in the same enterprise. Perhaps a more important implication of limited liability than the effect on the willingness of people to *supply finance* (as we have seen they could always lend at fixed interest to other types of enterprise) is the willingness of managers to raise finance. For the directors of a joint-stock company are themselves liable only to the extent of the shares they hold in the company and indeed there is no legal requirement that they should hold any. With risk spread widely in this way, rising costs of risk bearing do not constrain the size of operations as severely as they do in a partnership or proprietorship.

It is sometimes said that the coming of limited liability and the joint-stock enterprise lowered the 'cost' of finance. This is a somewhat misleading way of thinking, however. When people supply finance, whether by loan or by buying shares, they are aware of the institutional arrangements prevailing and are unlikely to ask for or expect a *lower* return when dealing with a limited liability company than with other forms of enterprise. They will 'pierce the veil of limited liability' and may adjust upwards their required return to allow for any perceived adverse effect on managerial incentives.[15] The advantage of limited liability is that even after these upward adjustments have been made, the possibilities opened up by large-scale operations may be more than adequate to compensate. Much depends here on terminology, however. A single proprietor with unlimited liability would be expected to undertake fewer projects than he would after turning his enterprise into a limited company. Even if the available projects were identical in the two cases, the additional risks faced by a proprietor will induce him to apply a higher discount rate, and fewer of the projects will yield expected returns which exceed the 'cost of capital'. Thus 'the cost of capital' to the enterprise, interpreted in this way, is very likely to be lower in the limited company. But this is just another way of saying that risk-bearing costs are lower *to the decision makers*.

Although Ekelund and Tollison emphasise the transferability of shares as a crucial force in the *origins* of the corporation in the sixteenth and seventeenth centuries therefore, by the mid nineteenth century the risk-sharing characteristics of the corporate form with limited liability appear to be a more decisive consideration. Hannah (1983, p. 23) reports that, in the UK, 80 per cent of joint-stock companies were private not public as late as 1914. Private companies are those which specifically restrict the right to transfer their shares while retaining the other characteristics of the joint-stock form including limited liability. It is instructive to consider the possible reason for this popularity of the *private* company in the UK into the twentieth century.

In terms of property rights the fundamental characteristic of the corporate form is that the 'right to claim the residual' is separated from the 'right to monitor the inputs'. This 'separation of ownership from control' has certain transactional advantages as we have seen, and it permits the development of a class of specialist managers, but it confronts the problem of managerial incentives which was so central to our earlier discussion of team production. The suspicion that joint-stock enterprises would result in inefficient if not corrupt management has a long history. Adam Smith, for example, wrote that 'negligence and profusion, therefore, must always prevail, more or less, in the management of the affairs of a joint stock company'.[16] Such 'negligence and profusion' will not prevent the emergence of the joint-stock form if potential efficiency gains exist which are sufficient to compensate, but it is clear that the problem of managerial incentives is central to this form of enterprise. The use of managers from a restricted family circle, each with a considerable shareholding and with limited ability to dispose of their holding, as in a *private* company, can obviously be viewed as a response to the incentives problem. Even successful *public* companies at the turn of the twentieth century in the UK used management from the families which founded and built the firms during the nineteenth century, firms such as J. and P. Coats, Imperial Tobacco, and Watney Combe Reid. As Hannah (1983) remarks, 'while this solved a fundamental problem of the corporate economy—that of maintaining managerial efficiency while divorcing ownership from control—it did so more by avoiding the issue than by devising new techniques of incentive and control' (p. 24). In the United States, on the other hand, the development of the corporate form occurred more rapidly than in the UK, and innovation in corporate structure was more advanced. Indeed Chandler (1976) attributes backwardness in the UK to the influence of family management and the failure to develop sufficiently quickly a class of professional managers. How far the former was the *cause* of the latter rather than a rational *response* to the latter, however, is a moot point.

A more formal analysis of the incentive problems associated with joint-stock enterprise is presented by Jensen and Meckling (1976). Their approach incorporates the use of debt instruments as well as equity in a sophisticated theory of 'ownership structure'. At this point we merely outline the simplest case, and consider the effect of outside equity holders on the market value of the firm. Suppose that the firm is of a given size, that it is financed entirely by equity and that *initially* all the equity is held by a single manager or 'peak coordinator'. In Figure 4.4 the market value of the firm is measured

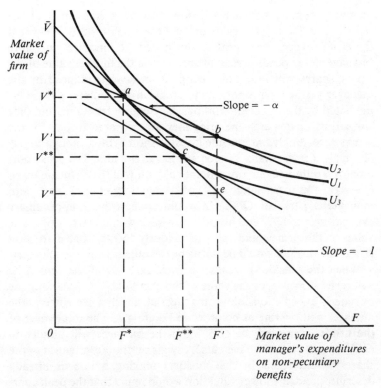

Figure 4.4: From Jensen and Meckling (1976), Fig. 1, p. 316

on the vertical axis and the market value of the stream of 'expenditures on non-pecuniary benefits' is measured along the horizontal axis. The slope of the constraint $\bar{V}F$ is -1, indicating that expenditures on non-pecuniary benefits are at the expense of pecuniary benefits. A single proprietor will operate at point 'a' where his indifference curve U_1 is tangential to the constraint $\bar{V}F$. The market value of the firm as a single proprietorship will be OV^* and the non-pecuniary benefits available will have a value of OF^*.

Now assume that the 'peak coordinator' can sell a fraction of his equity shares to outsiders. These shares, Jensen and Meckling assume, carry no voting rights. Suppose that the peak coordinator retains a proportion α of the shares and sells a proportion $1-\alpha$. Clearly the 'cost' to the coordinator of 'managerial' expenditures on non-pecuniary benefits will now only be a fraction α of the reduction in the market value of the firm which results. We would therefore expect the peak coordinator to indulge in more 'managerial' expenditures than before, and the market value of the equity shares will fall. This change in behaviour induced by the manager's smaller proportionate stake in the enterprise will be predicted by the outsiders who purchase equity from him and they will adjust downwards the price they are prepared to pay for the shares accordingly. An outside investor shortsighted enough to pay $(1 - \alpha)V^*$ for the shares offered would suffer a loss. The peak coordinator would not remain at point 'a' with wealth V^* (made up of $(1 - \alpha)V^*$ in cash and αV^* of remaining equity) and with managerial perks of OF^*. He would increase his non-pecuniary expenditures to OF' and his private wealth would fall to OV'. The value of the firm would fall precipitously to OV'' but a fraction $(1 - \alpha)$ of this fall would be borne by the outsider not the manager.

When the outsider purchases a fraction $1 - \alpha$ of the equity, he will revise downwards the value of the firm to OV^{**}. Assuming the outsider's expectations about managerial shirking are correct, the manager will operate at point 'c' in Figure 4.4. The total value of the firm's equity will be OV^{**} and the manager will indulge in OF^{**} of non-pecuniary benefits. Any higher initial valuation of the shares would result in the outsiders making a loss as already described, and any lower valuation would imply that the peak coordinator had sold for less than outsiders would have been prepared to pay. The distance OV^*-OV^{**} is termed by Jensen and Meckling the *gross agency cost* of the move to a fraction $1 - \alpha$ of outside equity. We should note that this fall in the value of the firm would not occur if an enforceable contract could be drawn up limiting the manager's non-pecuniary benefits to OF^*. Thus, even where monitoring is costly, some arrangement of this type might be in the interests of both parties.

If outside equity reduces the value of the firm and results in 'agency costs', why is it that all firms are not individually owned and managed? One answer might be that no single individual is wealthy enough to hold the entire equity. This does not explain however, why if this is so, capital could not be borrowed at fixed interest instead of raised by outside equity holders. The objection that proprietors would not like highly leveraged operations because of the risk of bankruptcy has less force in a world of limited liability than it did above (p. 101) when considering a situation of unlimited liability. Under limited liability the problem is not the risk aversion of the owner-manager but instead the incentives that a highly leverage structure will give to such a person to take very large risks. The costs of failure are borne by outside bondholders and the benefits of success go to the single equity holder. Clearly there are agency costs associated with the use of debt as well as outside equity.

Given the inescapable agency costs of outside finance Jensen and Meckling explain the existence of outside equity and debt holders primarily by reference to risk-spreading benefits. Selling equity claims to outsiders will reduce the value of the firm and hence the owner-manager's wealth, but if the benefits of a more widely diversified portfolio outweigh these agency costs the owner-manager will still prefer to reduce his holding. The optimal amount of outside financing will be reached when the marginal benefits from increased diversification equal the marginal agency costs incurred (Jensen and Meckling, pp. 349–51).

We have now completed our preliminary discussion of the forces moulding the broad types of business enterprise. Fairly definite distinctions have been drawn between the structures of property rights characteristic of proprietorships, partnerships, and joint-stock companies. In fact, of course, the possibilities of subtly different varieties of enterprise are wide ranging. Limited partnerships which provide for the existence of limited partners as a supplement to general partners with unlimited liability are possible, though rare. Further, the company form permits different varieties of shares to be issued including 'preference' shares carrying the right to a fixed return which must be honoured before payments can be made to ordinary shareholders; and 'preferred ordinary' shares which entitle the holder to a fixed return plus some claim on distributed profits smaller than that of the ordinary shareholder.[17] Later in this book we shall also discuss other types of enterprise, especially the nationalised enterprise and the labour managed enterprise in which the residual is shared among the labour force. The initial task of Part II however, is to consider in more detail the principles underlying the internal structure of firms, and the evolution of those 'new techniques of incentive and control' which have encouraged the development of the modern large corporate enterprise.

NOTES

1. The meaning of the words 'overuse' and 'appropriate' will be considered in a later section.
2. 'Public' property is often extremely 'private', as has frequently been noted. Custodians of assets which are collectively owned have little incentive to grant access to outsiders or even members of the owning consortium.
3. In a world of perfect certainty and no taxation, of course, the bond should sell for precisely the same sum as the right to interest plus the right to repayment of the principal. Where interest income and capital gains are taxed at different rates and the relative advantage of taking income in one form rather than another varies between people, this conclusion no longer holds.
4. This statement may appear rather strong to some people. It should be interpreted more as a basic assumption upon which much of the future analysis will depend rather than a complete denial of a 'social conscience' in individual people. Clearly people *do* leave money by an unattended pile of newspapers if the vendor is momentarily not there. But it would be difficult to maintain that social institutions have developed on the assumption that they will always do so. The contrary assumption that they will *never* do so is likely to get us further.
5. 'Leisure' might be valued by each person at four fish per day. Alternatively we have to imagine that a market in fish exists, perhaps involving other groups on the island and possibly on nearby islands. The product of a day's labour at x or y production might then exchange for four fish on this market.
6. The problem is identical to that of site assembly in the context of urban land development. A developer finds himself playing a game of 'chicken' (*see* note 10) with the last remaining holder of a parcel of land which is required if the project is to go ahead. The existing owner of this parcel of land effectively has a 'veto' on the development, and can hold out for a price which will appropriate for himself as much of the developer's profit as possible (*see* Davis and Whinston, 1961). In principle, of course, it would be foolish of an owner to so overplay his hand that the project did not go ahead and any potential efficiency gain should therefore be achieved. In practice, however, the possibility of being thwarted by a single person may act as a distinct disincentive to development.
7. $\Delta gcb \equiv \Delta bfe$.
   Also $\Delta gah \equiv \Delta hdb$
   Thus area $ahbc$ + area hdb = area bfe
8. The definition of the term 'team production' given by Alchian and Demsetz does not accord perfectly with the interpretation of this chapter. In their original presentation, Alchian and Demsetz cite the case of two people jointly lifting heavy cargo into trucks. They point out that 'it is impossible to determine each person's marginal produc-

tivity' (p. 779) More formally, 'Team production of z involves at least two inputs, X_i and X_j, with $\partial^2 z/(\partial X_i\,\partial X_j) \neq 0'$ (p. 779).

There seems to be a clear implication here that 'technological non-separabilities' are central to the concept of team production and lead to the difficulty of identifying the output attributable to each cooperating agent. If $\partial^2 z/(\partial X_i\,\partial X_j) = 0$ so that the marginal productivity of each input is *independent* of the activity of other inputs (the production function is *separable*) then 'this is not team production'. At the level of pure principle, however, it is difficult to see why a separable production function is sufficient to rule out team production in the sense of the impossibility of *observing* individual marginal products. Observability and separability are surely not synonymous, although Alchian and Demsetz appear to treat them as if they were.

Contrast the case of two people lifting a block of concrete with two people stirring a vat of paint or mixing cement. In the latter case, when the cement is thoroughly mixed, it would be impossible to separate out the contribution of each mixer by observing the output. On the other hand, it is by no means clear in this case that the mixing effort of one person necessarily influences the productivity of the mixing effort of the other. One thousand 'mixing motions' will achieve the result irrespective of who is doing the 'mixing' so that we might argue that the marginal product of mixing effort is independent of the activity of others in the team of mixers. The 'production function' is formally 'separable' but the contribution of each input cannot be physically observed. If lack of observability is the crucial problem (as we have argued in the text) it does not follow that separability will ensure observability.

Conversely, it is not clear that non-separability rules out observability. Imagine a production line in which a piece of metal is initially flattened, formed into some shape, polished and then packed. It might reasonably be conjectured that the better the metal is prepared the easier it is to form it into a correct shape, the better the shape the easier to polish, and the better it is polished the easier the product slips into its final container. The productivity of each input is not independent of the productivity of the others. Yet it is quite possible to observe the output at each stage and therefore to gauge each input's productivity. The production function is non-separable, but the contribution of each input *is* observable (even if not independent of the contribution of other team members).

It is for these reasons that the term 'team production' has been associated in the text with the *non-observability* of marginal product problem rather than non-separabilities. The problem of non-observability is obviously most severe in the case of the simultaneous cooperation of individuals in pursuit of a single common goal. It is this simultaneous use of inputs which characterises team endeavour. In such a team environment non-separabilities are very likely to exist, but they are not a sufficient condition for the existence of team production and if we were being pedantic we would also have to claim they are not absolutely *necessary*.

Williamson (1975) criticises the idea that non-separabilities underlie the supplanting of market transactions by monitoring and the employment relation. The basic problem, he insists, is the problem of 'information impactedness' (i.e. asymmetry) leading to opportunistic behaviour (shirking). 'Regarded in transactional terms, technological nonseparability represents a case where information impactedness is particularly severe; but I emphasize that this is merely a matter of degree' (p. 61). There are other sources of information impactedness of a less extreme form. Note here that Williamson accepts that non-separability and non-observability go together, a point of view which we have challenged above. On the other hand, Williamson argues forcefully that 'nonseparabilities are much less widespread than is commonly believed' (p. 49). In support of this contention he urges that 'most tasks appear to be separable in a buffer inventory sense' (p. 61), that is it is usually possible to see production as a succession of stages with the possibility of an inventory of the intermediate product at each stage. This is precisely the point which was discussed earlier in this note in the context of the production line process and the metal product. However, Williamson does not make it crystal clear that 'technological nonseparability' in Alchian and Demsetz's sense and 'nonseparability in a buffer inventory sense' are two quite distinct concepts. Alchian and Demsetz use a timeless neoclassical production function to illustrate their idea of separability: Williamson is concerned with separability in an inter-temporal context. The former relates to a formal mathematical type of separability, while the latter relates to separation in time. Functional separability in a mathematical sense may or may not imply separability in an inter-temporal sense.

9. We are here assuming 'free entry' into monitoring.
10. In the two-partner case the situation can be envisaged as a game of 'chicken'. Each partner has two strategies: 'monitor' and 'shirk'.

		Partner B	
		Monitor	Shirk
	Monitor	a	c
Partner A			
	Shirk	b	d

The entries in the matrix represent A's payoffs. In the 'chicken' game $b > a$, $a > c$, $b > d$ and $c > d$. If B monitors it is better for A to shirk; whatever A does he is better off if B monitors; but if B shirks it is better for A to monitor. This game will lead to 'bluffing'. Each partner will have an incentive to convince the other of his idleness in the hope that the other will be frightened into working. The 'chicken' game is representative of many situations which arise in the field of litigation (*see* Goetz, 1984). In the situation analysed in the text, however, it is necessary to remember that the game is repeated for as long as the partnership lasts. This 'discipline of continuous dealings' is likely to limit the advantage that will accrue to a partner from adopting a stance of exaggerated non-cooperation.

As the number of partners increases, however, the nature of the 'game' changes. In particular, eventually $d > c$. If the others shirk it is better for A to shirk also. This turns the game into a 'prisoner's dilemma'. Since $b > a$ and $d > c$, all parties will be induced to shirk. Shirking is a 'dominant strategy' since A is better off shirking whatever his partners do. Clearly a partnership will find it difficult to operate under these conditions. We may surmise that 'unlimited liability' would delay their establishment. Again we must bear in mind that the 'game' is repeated and we might expect partners to cooperate until the others cheat. In any game repeated a *finite* number of times, however, it can be shown that the dominant strategy is still to shirk. Infinite horizon games can produce cooperation as an equilibrium outcome. The case of the finite horizon prisoner's dilemma 'supergame' has been widely discussed. The 'non-cooperative' result is felt by many to be counter-intuitive and much effort has been devoted to achieving a more 'plausible' solution to this case (*See* Luce and Raiffa 1957 pp. 97–102 and Radner 1981).

11. *See* H. A. Shannon (1931, pp. 270–74). The quote as reported by Shannon is from Lord Ashburton's evidence to the *Report on Partnership* (1837).
12. There is in the UK a statutory limit to the number of partners. In general there should be no more than twenty.
13. 'The Cartel owner-managers had wealth maximising incentives to seek the development of a legal form of organisation under which they could more easily trade their property rights in these firms' (Ekelund and Tollison, 1980, p. 717).
14. General Limited Liability in the UK came with the Joint Stock Companies Act 1856.
15. *See* R. Meiners *et al.* (1979) and C. M. Jensen and W. H. Meckling (1976).
16. *Wealth of Nations* Vol. 2, p. 233.
17. Such shares will usually not carry the same voting rights as ordinary shares.

Part II
Internal Structure

Many hands make light work: too many cooks spoil the broth. How reconcile the implications of these two aphorisms, each in its way so sensible? The answer is that in modern industry they are not reconciled: and their mutual conflict is the source of the perpetual shifting of the sands of industrial structure

D. H. Robertson and S. R. Dennison

5 Principal and Agent

Cremated...10% of his ashes to be thrown in his agent's face.

Ted Ray

1. INTRODUCTION

Throughout Part I, attention was focused on the difficulties inherent in formulating agreements which permit specialisation and exchange to occur, when information is not 'public' that is, costlessly and equally available to everyone. Specialisation permits people to concentrate on those tasks in which they have a comparative advantage (Chapter 1), and it also has more dynamic effects. As Adam Smith[1] noted, specialisation results in the acquisition of enhanced levels of skill in particular operations as experience accumulates, it may permit the introduction of specialised machinery as various activities are broken down into basic components, and it may reduce the time which would otherwise be spent transferring attention from one job to the next.[2] If 'many hands make light work' however, they may also give rise to new problems. A person who 'saunters a little' between tasks will at least face the costs of his own sauntering if he is responsible for all stages in the production process. Much of Chapter 4 was devoted to the analysis of situations in which specialisation results in Adam Smith's 'sauntering' turning into Alchian and Demsetz's 'shirking' as people attempt to transfer the costs of their wavering attention onto others. Clearly, Smith in his example of pin making, was considering a case of division of labour which, we may infer, he did not expect would encounter substantial coordination and policing costs. But, in general, costs of coordination and policing are not negligible (Chapter 2) and the firm itself can be seen as a response to them. These costs underlie the saying that 'too many cooks spoil the broth', as well as the often heard remark 'if you want a job done properly you must do it yourself'.

The tension between the advantages of 'specialisation' and the costs of policing and monitoring (the advantages of 'integration') is a leitmotif which returns constantly in the theory of the firm. Robertson and Dennison, in the quote which precedes Part II, see the primary effects of the conflict of these two principles in the changing patterns of 'industrial structure'. But the same forces mould the internal structure of firms as delineate their boundaries, and, as will be seen later in this chapter, modern theory is even beginning to question whether clear economic distinctions can be drawn between transactions conducted within firms and transactions conducted between them. Already in Chapter 4 we have seen how different types of firm represent compromise solutions to the conflicting requirements of specialisation and incentives. In the classical proprietorship the tasks of capitalist, monitor and risk bearer are 'integrated' and the problem of managerial incentives thereby mitigated. The partnership and, even more, the joint-stock company permit the 'disintegration' of these functions and hence the potential advantages which may accrue from exchange—a specialised management and widely spread risks—but the problem of policing and incentives is more pronounced.

In this chapter our objective is to consider the contractual problem faced by principal and agent in greater analytical detail. This will help to clarify the nature of the trade-off between risk-sharing benefits and effort incentives, and will provide a useful framework for rationalising various contractual arrangements which are observed in practice. At the outset it is necessary to remember that the economist uses the word 'agent' in a much looser sense than does the lawyer. For the lawyer, an agent is 'a person invested with a legal power to alter the principal's legal relations with third parties'.[3] Thus two partners are one another's agents in a strict legal sense, since each can bind the other in contractual arrangements with third parties. The economist, however, is, for once, more in line with common usage in seeing the agent as a person who is employed to undertake some activity on behalf of someone else (the principal). This will cover cases of agency in the strict sense, but will also include other cases in which the same or similar incentive problems arise, although the legal term 'agent' would not be accurate.

2. OBSERVABILITY AND THE SHARECROPPER

As we have seen (Chapter 2, p. 40) a principal–agent relation exists when one party (the agent) agrees to act on behalf of another party (the principal). The problem then exists of devising a 'contract' which provides incentives for the agent to work in ways which benefit the principal. Let Π be the final *outcome* of the agent's activities, and let e represent his level of *effort*. Sharecropping represents the most commonly used illustrative case for discussing incentive contracts, with the landlord as the 'principal' and the sharecropper as his 'agent' (in the loose rather than the legal sense of these terms). In this case Π might represent the volume of the crop finally harvested (say bushels of wheat), while e would represent the input of the sharecropper's time and skill. Now suppose that the final outcome is deterministically related to the sharecropper's effort

$$\Pi = \Pi(e) \tag{5.1}$$

Assuming that both sharecropper and landlord can observe the final outcome and that this outcome is conceptually simple enough to appear in a contract, it is clear that there is no reason for the landlord to monitor effort. The contract merely has to stipulate the outcome desired (say $\overline{\Pi}$), and the payment to be made when it is achieved. Under these circumstances, perfect knowledge of the outcome gives us perfect information about the effort expended, and the result is a contract which is not a 'sharecropping' arrangement at all but simply a paid worker contract. The worker receives a specified reward upon completing the job he was hired to do. There is no incentive problem.

A case more germane to the problem of incentives occurs when the outcome depends not only on the labourer's effort but also upon other chance factors. In the agricultural example, the harvest may depend upon climatic conditions as well as work effort. Thus we might write

$$\Pi = \Pi^*(e, \theta) \tag{5.2}$$

where θ represents the 'state of the world'. For example θ might measure 'inches of rainfall' or 'hours of sunshine' or 'average temperature in July' and so forth. Any contract will now involve the sharing of risk in addition to the provision of incentives. Consider, once more, the paid worker contract which depends only on the achievement of a target outcome $\overline{\Pi}$. The labourer is unlikely to accept such an arrangement since it exposes him to considerable risk. The most careful husbandry could be powerless against adverse weather conditions and the labourer, if he is risk averse, will prefer that some account is taken either of his effort level, or of the state of the world prevailing. Clearly, however, the prospect of including e or θ in a contract depends upon whether or not they are 'observable'. Suppose, first of all, that θ can easily be verified by both parties. It follows, once more, that observation of the labourer's effort is unnecessary to provide incentives, and that a preferred distribution of risk can be achieved without confronting the shirking problem.

From (5.2) both landlord and labourer will be able to work out the result (Π) of a given amount of effort $\bar{e}$ in different states of the world (θ). The labourer's reward (A) can therefore be made to depend upon both outcome and state of the world: $A = A(\Pi, \theta)$. If the landlord receives an amount (P) which depends only on the state of the world $P(\theta)$, the labourer's return would be given by

$$A = \Pi - P(\theta). \tag{5.3}$$

In other words, the labourer would pay to the landlord an amount $P(\theta)$ which depended on the weather, and would keep the rest of the harvest for himself. The results of additional effort always accrue to the labourer, so that no incentive problem arises, while the characteristics of $P(\theta)$ enable risks to be shared between landlord and labourer in any way desired. Such arrangements typify the 'sharecropping' contract. If, for example, $P(\theta)$ were a constant $\overline{P}$, so that the labourer paid the *same* amount to the landlord in every state of the world, the labourer would effectively be bearing the entire risk and insuring the landlord against the vagaries of the weather. On the other hand, the landlord's share $P(\theta)$ could be so arranged that the remainder left for the labourer is always the same, providing the labourer puts in the standard effort $\bar{e}$. In this case it would be the landlord who would bear the risk and the labourer who would receive a definite predetermined return providing the standard effort $\bar{e}$ was forthcoming. If both landlord and labourer were risk averse, we would not expect either to bear the entire risk. Instead $P(\theta)$ would be defined so as to share risk efficiently between them. In the next section we will discuss in more detail what it means to share risk 'efficiently'.

Specifying a mutually agreeable contract becomes more complicated when we assume that the state of the world θ is not observable by the landlord (or principal). If effort e is unobservable also, then clearly any contract must of necessity depend upon the outcome Π alone. It is this case which we will discuss in detail in section 4. Even at this stage the essential character of the problem can be appreciated, however. The unobservability of the state variable θ and effort e means that it will in general be impossible to achieve an ideal distribution of risk between the parties without sacrificing effort incentives. Conversely the 'best' contract achievable will usually involve the sacrifice of risk-sharing benefits in the interests of providing incentives.

Consider the case in which the landlord or principal is risk neutral, and the labourer or agent is risk averse. Intuitively we have already asserted that the risk-neutral partner should ideally bear the entire risk (a proposition which we will justify in more detail in the next section). Where the state of the world θ is *observable* it has already been shown how this distribution of risk could be arranged whilst still eliciting the standard effort $\bar{e}$ from the labourer. The labourer would receive the same reward whatever the state of the world, but *only if he exerted the standard effort*. Where the contract must depend on the outcome alone, however, assuring the labourer of a given reward is to leave him with no incentive to do anything. If the principal can never form the faintest conception of how hard the agent worked, and can never become acquainted with the difficulties he encountered, these factors cannot enter the contract. But in such a case, a promise to pay a fixed determinate sum to the agent would be to make his remuneration completely independent of effort. The labourer would receive the same number of bushels of wheat from the landlord even if his only acquaintance with the fields to be cultivated occurred as he passed through them during his daily journeys to and from the village pub. Clearly, the provision of effort incentives requires that the labourer receives a bigger payment if the harvest is big than if the harvest is small. But because the harvest depends on the chance factors θ, this implies that the labourer must shoulder some risk even though his landlord is risk neutral and would, in conditions of 'observability', provide him with complete insurance.

The above paragraph suggests that information about the labourer's effort would be valuable in enabling both parties to a contract to achieve preferred positions. If we continue to assume that θ is unobservable by the principal, some observation of the agent's effort e might clearly benefit both parties. By checking that the labourer sowed the correct type of seed, applied the appropriate fertiliser and so forth it would be possible to move towards the ideal distribution of risk without diminishing effort incentives. In the extreme case of perfectly observable effort the (risk-averse) labourer would receive a payment dependent entirely on effort and would thus face no risk, while the (risk-neutral) landlord would receive the residual harvest. Monitoring will not usually be so reliable, however, and a further interesting question is whether information about effort containing errors which are subject to a known statistical distribution could be incorporated in a contract to the advantage of both parties. The landlord might check at random whether the labourer is actually working in the field. An unlucky labourer could find that the spot check occurred during the only five minutes he was away, and a lucky one that it occurred during the only five minutes he was there. But a series of such checks will provide information which, although not perfectly accurate, nevertheless contains potentially usable information about effort. Indeed it can be shown,[4] that, irrespective of the 'noise' associated with the information, there will always be an advantage to incorporating an informative signal into a contract if the agent is risk averse (assuming that the signal is costlessly received and that costs of writing the contract can be ignored). A more detailed illustration of what it means for a noisy signal to be 'informative' will be given in section 4.

In the case of a risk-neutral labourer or agent, information about effort or state of the world will be valueless. Even in conditions of complete non-observability of effort and state, all available risk-sharing benefits can be achieved without sacrificing incentives. As we noted above, a risk-neutral labourer will shoulder the entire risk and pay a fixed fee to the landlord. Because the fee is the same whatever the state of the world that occurs, it is clearly not necessary to observe the state. Neither will observation of the agent's effort confer any benefits since the agent will personally face the consequences of any 'sauntering' and cannot unload the costs onto the landlord. In effect, the agent simply pays a fixed fee for the use of the resources owned by the landlord for a specified period of time. This will obviously avoid any dangers associated with shirking, while the risk-neutrality assumption ensures that this arrangement is compatible with the efficient distribution of risk. The next two sections illustrate some of the above results using a set of simple diagrams.

3. RISK SHARING

Consider a case in which two people (person A and person P) wish to share the risk implied by a fluctuating harvest. Suppose that the harvest or outcome can take only two values Π_1 and Π_2 with $\Pi_1 > \Pi_2$. For the present we ignore the influence of effort on the harvest and simply asume that Π_1 and Π_2 occur with probabilities p_1 and $p_2 = (1 - p_1)$ respectively. Each person we assume will be entitled to a given portion of the harvest depending on whether the harvest is good or bad.

Thus, $\Pi_{1A} + \Pi_{1P} = \Pi_1$

and $\Pi_{2A} + \Pi_{2P} = \Pi_2$

where Π_{1A} is person A's entitlement when the harvest is good, Π_{2P} is person P's entitlement when the harvest is bad, and so forth. Presented with various different combinations of Π_{1A} and Π_{2A} it is assumed, as in elementary consumer theory, that person A is capable of ranking them in a weak ordering. The outcome of this ranking process can then be illustrated on a two-dimensional diagram using indifference curves. If person A's preferences accord with certain axioms—the von Neumann–Morgenstern axioms[5]— it can be shown that a utility function for person A can be constructed $U_A(\Pi_A)$ such that his preferences over risky prospects are consistent with the *expected utility* attached to the prospects. Indifference curves can then be thought of as lines of constant expected utility.[6]

The shape of A's indifference curves will depend upon his attitude to risk. In Figure 5.1 each point (Π_{1A}, Π_{2A}) represents a prospect. At point a for example, person A has a claim or entitlement to Π_{1A}' if the harvest is good and Π_{2A}' if the harvest is bad. Since as drawn $\Pi_{1A}' = \Pi_{2A}'$ this implies that, at such a point, person A would be *certain* of the outcome and would be bearing no risk. *Given* the probability of a good harvest p_1, it is clear that any portfolio of claims represented by a point in the shaded set to the north-

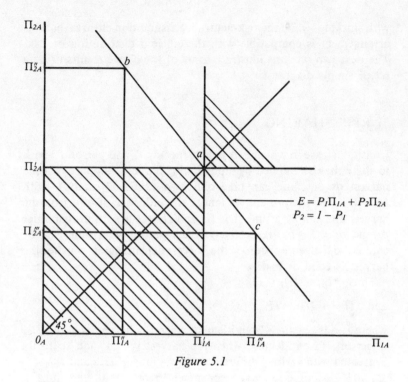

Figure 5.1

east of *a* will be preferred, and any portfolio represented by a point in the shaded set to the south-west of *a* will be less preferred, than the portfolio at *a*. Thus, just as in conventional consumer theory, indifference curves are expected to slope downwards from left to right. The curvature properties of the indifference curves are more complex, however.

Consider the straight line $P_1 \Pi_{1A} + P_2 \Pi_{2A} = E$ drawn through point *a*. By definition, all prospects along this line produce the same mathematical expectation of the outcome (E) as at point *a*. The slope of the line will be $-(P_1/P_2)$. Now consider a point such as *b* on this line. Will person *A* prefer *b* to *a* or vice versa? To answer this question we note that a move from *a* to *b* implies a move from a riskless environment to a risky one. Person *A* would risk losing ($\Pi_{1A}' - \Pi_{1A}''$) in the event of the harvest being good, but would stand the chance of gaining ($\Pi_{2A}'' - \Pi_{2A}'$) in the event of the harvest being bad. Since, the *expected* outcome for person *A* is constant all along the straight line, however, we know that the gamble involved in moving from *a* to *b* is a 'fair' gamble. A 'fair' gamble is one with an expected value of zero. Person *A* would expect, in a mathematical sense, neither to gain nor to lose because $P_2 (\Pi_{2A}'' - \Pi_{2A}') - P_1 (\Pi_{1A}' - \Pi_{1A}'') = 0$.

Whether person *A* would prefer point *a* or point *b* therefore reduces to the question of whether or not person *A* is prepared to take a 'fair' gamble. Any person who always rejects a 'fair' bet will prefer *a* to *b*. Such a person is 'risk averse'. A risk-averse person will move to lower and lower levels of satisfaction (expected utility) as he moves away from point *a* in either direction along the line of constant expected outcome. Thus the indifference curves of a risk-averse person will have the conventional convex shape familiar from elementary consumer theory. Figure 5.2 illustrates the preference map of a typical risk-averse person. An important characteristic of this preference map is that the slope of the indifference curves along the 45° line from the origin (e.g. at point *a*) will be equal to the slope of the constant expected outcome line $-(P_1/P_2)$. In other words, along the certainty line where $\Pi_{1A} = \Pi_{2A}$, each person will be prepared to exchange claims contingent upon a bad harvest for claims contingent on a good harvest in the ratio (P_1/P_2). This applies only to 'points such as *a*' and is therefore a proposition about limits. Although the person is risk

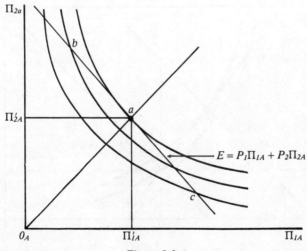

Figure 5.2

averse, he will *approach* indifference between point *a* and a fair gamble as the 'stakes' become vanishingly small. Some use will be made of this property of indifference curves in future sections.

Returning to Figure 5.1, a person who is indifferent between point *a* and any 'fair' gamble represented by another point on the constant expected outcome line (such as point *b* or point *c*) is termed 'risk neutral'. Variability of the outcome is of no consequence for such a person. The only matter of interest is the expected value of the outcome, and all combinations of claims which yield the same mathematically expected outcome are equally preferred. Thus the indifference curves of a risk-neutral person will be straight lines with slope $-(P_1/P_2)$ corresponding to lines of constant expected outcome. Maximising expected utility for this person will be the same as maximising the expected outcome. For completeness we should add that a person who *enjoys* taking fair bets will prefer point *b* to point *a*, and hence a 'risk-preferring' person will have concave indifference curves. The case is not illustrated and no future use will be made of it.

We are now in a position to discuss the risk-sharing problem. Figure 5.3 is a 'box diagram' with A's origin at the bottom left-hand corner and P's origin at the top right-hand corner. The

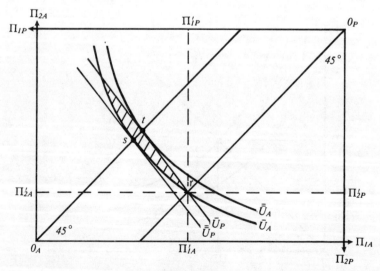

Figure 5.3

horizontal dimension of the box represents the total harvest if yields are good (Π_1) and the vertical dimension represents the total harvest if the yields are bad (Π_2). Any point within the box represents a division of the total harvest between the two people in both good times and bad. Thus, point r, for example, illustrates a case in which person A has entitlements given by distance $O_A \Pi_{1A}'$ if the harvest is good and $O_A \Pi_{2A}'$ if the harvest is bad; while person P has entitlements given by distance $O_p \Pi'_{1p}$ if the harvest is good and $O_p \Pi_{2p}'$ if the harvest is bad. Person A's claims *plus* person P's claims sum to the total harvest.

The question now arises: does point r represent an 'efficient' allocation of claims between persons A and P? The answer will depend upon the preferences of the people concerned and therefore Figure 5.3 illustrates one particular case. As drawn, person A is risk averse and his convex indifference curves are drawn with respect to an origin at O_A; while person P is assumed to be risk neutral and his straight line indifference curves are drawn with respect to an origin at O_p. At point r person A has utility index $\bar{U}_A$ and person P has utility index $\bar{U}_p$. It is clear, however, that by exchanging claims with one another both could be made better off; there are gains from trade to be had. Any allocation of claims represented by a point in the shaded set in Figure 5.3 will benefit at least one of the parties without harming the other, that is, they represent '*Pareto* improvements' on point r. 'Efficiency' is characterised by the absence of gains from trade, as was seen in Part I of this book. Points of tangency between A's indifference curves and P's indifference curves will be efficient points. An allocation represented by a point such as s, for example, is 'efficient'. Any move away from s must harm one or both of the parties, and therefore agreement to a move will be impossible to achieve.

As drawn in Figure 5.3 the locus of points of tangency between the indifference curves of the two parties lies along the 45° line out of A's origin. It will be recalled that P's indifference curves have a slope of $-(P_1/P_2)$ along their entire length whilst A's curves have a slope of $-(P_1/P_2)$ along A's certainty line. Thus tangency must occur along A's 45° line. The line between s and t represents the set of efficient allocations which are *Pareto* improvements on point r. By moving from point r to point t, for example, person P will be supplying person A with fair insurance. Fair insurance will benefit risk-averse A whose utility index increases to $\bar{\bar{U}}_A$. The risk taken by person P will be increased, but, for him, point t represents a fair gamble relative to point r and, being risk neutral, person P's utility index will be the same at t as at r. A move from r to s, on the other hand, will confer all the gains from trade on person P. Person P shoulders the entire risk still, but now on somewhat 'unfair' terms (in an actuarial sense) relative to point r. P's expected return and hence expected utility has increased, while A's expected return has decreased. The fall in the expected return to A does not result in a fall in expected *utility* because the greater certainty of the return at s compared with r is sufficient to compensate.

Figure 5.3 illustrates our earlier contention that efficient sharing of risk will involve a risk-neutral party providing complete insurance to the risk-averse party. Thus, in section 2, we saw that, where the state of the world θ was observable and the effort incentive problem could therefore be overcome, a risk-neutral landlord (employer) would take the entire risk and a risk-averse labourer (worker) would receive the same amount irrespective of whether the harvest turned out to be good or bad. Conversely, a risk-neutral labourer would pay a fixed fee to a risk-averse landlord and keep the residual harvest. Where both persons are risk averse, efficient allocations of claims will be between the two 45° lines in Figure 5.3 and both parties will bear some of the risk.

4. EFFORT INCENTIVES

The principal–agent problem proper can now be considered by assuming that the probability of a good harvest is not given and unalterable, but can be influenced by the activity of the agent, person A. To keep matters as simple as it is possible to make them, let us assume that by exerting effort e, the agent is capable of changing the probability of a good harvest from P_l to P_l^e where $P_l^e > P_l$. The agent has a simple choice between two levels of effort, zero or e. His effort, however, is assumed to be totally unobservable by the principal P. The final outcome or harvest can be observed by both parties, but this is all. Let the agent be risk averse and the principal be risk neutral.

Consider now the effect of effort on the agent's indifference map. Because effort increases the probability of a good harvest to P_l^e, the slope of all the agent's indifference curves along A's certainty line will steepen to $-(P_I^e/1 - P_I^e)$. At any particular point on this certainty line, however, the utility index will be lower, because effort we assume is unpleasant and reduces A's level of utility. In Figure 5.4 the indifference curve of the agent through θ is drawn assuming no effort is exerted. The slope at θ is $-(P_I/1 - P_I)$ and the utility index is $\bar{U}$. The curve through α is drawn on the assumption that effort e is exerted. Its slope at α is $-(P_I^e/1 - P_I^e)$ and the utility index is also $\bar{U}$. To show that it applies to situations where effort is being exerted the curve is labelled $\bar{U}_A^e$. Distance $\theta\alpha$ is a measure of the 'cost' to A of effort e.

These two curves $\bar{U}_A^e$ and $\bar{U}_A$ intersect at point r. A portfolio of claims represented by point r would just leave the agent indifferent between exerting effort e and not exerting any effort. At any point to the right of r and between $\bar{U}_A$ and $\bar{U}_A^e$ the agent would strictly prefer effort to no effort. At point s, for example, the agent will achieve a higher utility index by operating on his 'with effort' set of indifference curves than his 'without effort' set. By providing the agent with a portfolio of claims at s we can induce the effort e. No monitoring is possible and none is required. The agent's own self-interest will be sufficient to produce the effort. We have loaded his claims sufficiently heavily in favour of the good harvest that he has

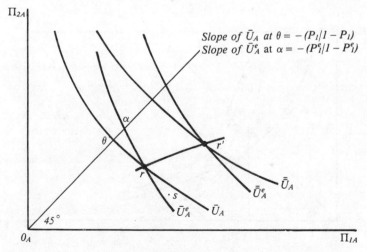

Figure 5.4

an interest in increasing the probability of this favoured event occurring, an interest powerful enough at s to overcome the disutility associated with effort.

By an identical process of reasoning we can deduce that at point r' in Figure 5.4, the agent is also indifferent between effort and no effort. At this point the agent's utility index is $\bar{\bar{U}} > \bar{U}$ whether or not effort is forthcoming. Joining up the points of intersection between 'with effort' and 'without effort' indifference curves applying to the same utility index, a locus such as rr' is traced out. Points to the right of rr' will induce effort e. Points to the left will not.

If it is possible to induce effort e from the agent, we still do not know whether both parties would *agree* to such a contract, or whether the principal would be as well off leaving the agent to relax in security at a point along his certainty line. It is this question which Figure 5.5 attempts to answer. At a point such as θ, risk would be efficiently shared between persons A and P as was shown in section 3. For effort to be forthcoming from the agent, however, a contract to the right of rr' must be agreed. Such a contract, by increasing the probability of a good harvest to P_I^e, will affect P's indifference curves and not merely person A's. P's indifference curves will now have a slope of $-(P_I^e/1-P_I^e)$ along their entire length. The new P indifference curve yielding the same utility index

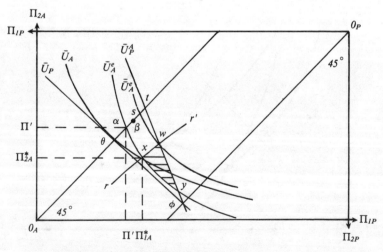

Figure 5.5

as at θ, but applying to a situation in which the agent is exerting effort, is labelled $\bar{U}_P^A$. Note that it cuts P's original indifference curve $\bar{U}_P$ at ϕ along P's certainty line. Clearly a given point on P's certainty line will yield the same utility index irrespective of the probability of a good harvest since, along that line, P is completely insulated from the effects of variations in the harvest.

Inspection of Figure 5.5 reveals that there exists a set of contracts (the shaded set *wxy*) which consists of *Pareto* improvements on the contract at θ. Points in the set *wxy* are between the curves $\bar{U}_A^e$ and $\bar{U}_P^A$, thus ensuring that the utility index of both principal and agent will be at least as great as at θ, and to the right of rr', thus ensuring that it is the 'with effort' indifference curves that will be relevant and that effort e will be forthcoming from the agent. Of this set of *Pareto* improvements on θ, *Pareto efficient contracts* will lie along the boundary between x and w. A move from point w, for example, to any other point in the shaded set will harm person A. A move from point x would harm person P. Conversely, from any point within the shaded set, it will be possible to find a point on the boundary which is preferred by both A and P.

It is important to notice that along the boundary xw risk is not shared efficiently between principal and agent. The indifference curves of principal and agent *intersect* (e.g. at point w) indicating that ideally there are risk-sharing benefits to be achieved by a move to A's certainty line between s and t. These benefits are unachievable, however, because of the observability problem. Figure 5.5 therefore illustrates clearly the distinction drawn in principal–agent theory between 'first-best' solutions (achievable only in an ideal world of perfect observability) which lie along A's certainty line and involve the efficient sharing of risk, and '*Pareto* efficient contracts' which lie along xw and are the best that can be achieved in the context of unobservable effort and state. Along xw risk-sharing benefits are sacrificed in the interests of providing incentives. The sacrifice will be worthwhile providing that the agent's effort is not too costly to him for any given effect on the probability of a good harvest, or conversely that for any given level of the disutility of effort the effect on the probability of a good harvest is sufficiently pronounced. It is possible to envisage a case in which the distance $\theta\alpha$ in Figure 5.5 is so large and $(P_I^e - P_I)$ is so small that the set of *Pareto* improvements on θ is empty.

Although a risk-averse agent may be made to bear some risk in

the efficient contract, it is worth noting that we will never observe
him bearing the entire risk. For a risk-averse agent to bear the entire risk we would have to imagine an efficient contract existing
somewhere along *P*'s certainty line. In terms of Figure 5.5, the
locus *xw* would have to cross *P*'s certainty line at some point. Risk
aversion and the resulting convexity of *A*'s indifference curves ensure, however, that the point *x* must always lie to the right of $\bar{U}_p$.
But points to the right of $\bar{U}_p$ along *P*'s certainty line will leave
person *P* with a lower utility index than at θ. Thus there can never
be an efficient contract on *P*'s certainty line which is *Pareto* preferred to θ when *A* is risk averse.

Where the agent is risk neutral, however, and the principal is risk
averse it is no longer necessary to sacrifice risk-sharing benefits to
achieve incentives. Incentives and risk sharing are compatible, as
can be seen from Figure 5.6, and the agent will optimally bear the
entire risk. The structure of the figure is the same as that of Figure
5.5. Once more contracts to the right of *rr'* provide an incentive
to *A* to exert effort level *e*. The set of contracts *Pareto* preferred
to θ is given by the shaded area. In this case, however, the boundary
xw no longer represents the set of *Pareto* efficient contracts. At *w*,
for example, the agent could be made better off without harming
the principal by a move to point ϕ, thereby achieving a more
efficient distribution of risk. Points along *P*'s certainty line share

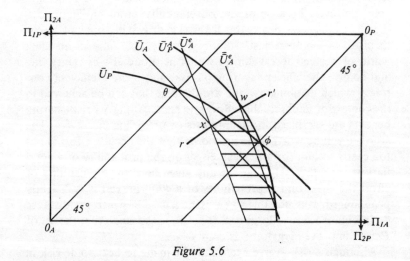

Figure 5.6

risk efficiently *and* induce effort *e* from the agent. '*Pareto* efficient contracts' are 'first best' even under conditions of unobservability. Information on the agent's effort or on the state of the world has no value to the principal. At ϕ the agent pays a fixed fee to the principal and is entitled to keep whatever remains of the harvest.

5. INFORMATION

A risk-averse agent and a risk-neutral principal (Figure 5.5) will have to sacrifice risk-sharing benefits if effort is to be induced under conditions of 'unobservability'. The ability to observe the agent's effort is therefore valuable because it enables risk-sharing benefits to be captured. Information about the agent's effort may be subject to error, however, and it is not immediately obvious whether principal and agent would both agree to use this kind of information in their contractual arrangements. As reported in section 2, abstracting from the costs of writing and enforcing an increasingly complex contract, an informative signal, no matter how noisy, can be used to increase the utility of both parties. In this section we illustrate this proposition using the simple example of principal and agent discussed in section 4.

Suppose to begin with that no information about the agent's effort is used in the contract. Efficient contracts will then lie along the locus rr' in Figure 5.5. Consider the efficient contract at x. As argued at length earlier, the agent at x will just be indifferent between effort and no effort. By exerting effort the agent faces one gamble and by not exerting effort he faces another (different) gamble. He is just indifferent between these two gambles. Specifically, if the agent remains idle he faces the following gamble:

$$G = (P_1, \Pi_{1A}^*; 1 - P_1, \Pi_{2A}^*).$$

Effort, on the other hand, produces a different gamble:

$$G^e = (P_1^e, \Pi_{1A}^{*e}; 1 - P_1^e, \Pi_{2A}^{*e}).$$

where in this case Π_{1A}^{*e} represents the outcome 'Π_{1A}^* bushels having exerted effort level e'. From our diagram we know that for person A, GIG^e, where I represents indifference.

Now let the principal (landlord) monitor the agent (labourer) through a series of spot-checks mentioned in section 2. He may visit the field at random a given number of times. If the labourer is never there, the landlord will conclude (perhaps wrongly) that his effort level has been zero. Providing the labourer is there at least once, the landlord will conclude (again perhaps wrongly) that effort level *e* has been forthcoming. Satisfying this crude spot-check test will yield a reward of $+ \delta_e$ and not satisfying it will incur a penalty of $- \delta_0$. Might such an arrangement be agreeable to both principal and agent?

Ignore for the present the problem of how the labourer is to know whether the landlord is telling the truth when the latter claims to have seen neither hide nor hair of the former. This is an important issue which will be taken up later in Chapter 6 on hierarchies. Assuming that the landlord monitors in the way described, the labourer will be able to calculate the probability that he is observed hard at work when in fact he has been idle, as well as the probability that he is observed to be idle when in fact he has been hard at work and so forth.

Let q_{0e} = probability that landlord observes zero effort when actual effort is *e*;

q_{ee} = probability that landlord observes effort *e* when actual effort is *e*;

q_{e0} = probability that landlord observes effort *e* when actual effort is zero;

q_{00} = probability that landlord observes zero effort when actual effort is zero.

With these probabilities we can construct a number of new gambles which we might call 'monitoring gambles'. Consider, for example, the following prospects:

$$m_{1A} = (q_{e0}, \Pi_{1A}^{*} + \delta_e; \; q_{00}, \Pi_{1A}^{*} - \delta_0),$$

and

$$m_{2A} = (q_{e0}, \Pi_{2A}^{*} + \delta_e; \; q_{00}, \Pi_{2A}^{*} - \delta_0).$$

These are the gambles the labourer would face if his effort level were zero. They depend upon the harvest. If the harvest turned out to be good and the labourer had agreed to be monitored he would then face gamble m_{1A}. Similarly, if the harvest was bad, the labourer would then face gamble m_{2A}. By agreeing to be monitored, therefore, the *idle* labourer would change the original gamble *G* into the complex gamble

$$G_m = (P_1, m_{1A};\ 1 - P_1, m_{2A})$$

Suppose now that $q_{00} > q_{e0}$, that is, the landlord is more likely to observe 'correctly' than 'incorrectly'. If the labourer is idle it is more likely that he will be observed as such than that he will be observed exerting effort e. This is our minimal requirement for the landlord's monitoring to be 'informative'. If $q_{00} = q_{e0}$ the spot-checks would produce a signal that was all 'noise' and no information. If $q_{00} > q_{e0}$ the signal would be positively misleading. Further, assume that $\delta_e < \delta_0$.

Clearly, if $q_{00} > q_{e0}$, and $\delta_0 > \delta_e$, gambles m_{1A} and m_{2A} are statistically 'unfair'. The labourer would prefer Π_{1A}^* to the gamble m_{1A}, and Π_{2A}^* to the gamble m_{2A}, assuming that he is risk averse. Thus we deduce that the idle labourer will not want to be monitored and that he will prefer G to G_m.

For the industrious labourer the situation is rather different, however. He will face the 'monitoring gambles':

$$m_{1A}^e = (q_{ee}, \Pi_{1A}^{*e} +\ \delta_e;\ q_{0e}, \Pi_{1A}^{*e} - \delta_0)$$

and $\quad m_{2A}^e = (q_{ee}, \Pi_{2A}^{*e} + \delta_e;\ q_{0e}, \Pi_{2A}^{*e} - \delta_0)$.

If he consents to be monitored the original gamble G^e will change to the more complex gamble

$$G_m^e = (P_1^e, m_{1A}^e;\ 1 - P_1^e, m_{2A}^e).$$

Again suppose that the monitoring of the landlord is 'informative' so that $q_{ee} > q_{0e}$ and that the industrious labourer is more likely to be seen as industrious than idle. Further assume that the reward δ_e and the penalty δ_0 are set such that $\delta_e < \delta_0$ as above, but also $q_{ee}\delta_e = q_{0e}\delta_0$. Gambles m_{1A}^e and m_{2A}^e will then both be 'fair' gambles.

As was seen in section 3, a risk-averse labourer will reject a fair bet. However, we also saw in section 3 that as the 'stakes' were reduced a risk-averse person would approach indifference between taking and not taking a fair bet. People are risk neutral 'in the limit'. Thus we might imagine δ_e and δ_0 being reduced in size whilst always maintaining the ratio $\delta_e/\delta_0 = q_{0e}/q_{ee}$. In the limit the industrious labourer will be indifferent between G_m^e and G^e. Because the 'monitoring gambles' m_{1A} and m_{2A} are statistically unfavourable the idle labourer, on the other hand, will always strictly prefer G to G_m and can never be brought to indifference no matter how tiny the stakes.

At point x, therefore, we have the following results as $\delta_e, \delta_0 \rightarrow 0$ with $\delta_e/\delta_0 = q_{oe}/q_{ee}$,

(i) $G_m^e \mathrm{I}\ G^e$.

(ii) GPG_m

(iii) GIG^e (by original assumption).

Thus, $G_m^e PG_m$. *Without* the monitor the labourer at x is just indifferent between effort and no effort. *With* the monitor and an 'informative signal' we can construct a situation in which the labourer *strictly prefers* effort to no effort at x and is no worse off in his own estimation than he was in the absence of the monitor ($G_m^e IG^e IG$).

Consider now how the principal is affected by these arrangements. We continue to assume that the signal is costlessly observed. Providing the monitoring gambles m_{1A}^e, m_{2A}^e are 'fair', the risk-neutral principal will be prepared to offer them to the agent whatever the absolute sizes of δ_e and δ_0. But even if the principal were risk averse we could apply the same argument used above for the agent to show that he would approach indifference as the stakes declined. Thus, in the limit neither principal nor agent will be any worse off from a risk-bearing point of view, as a result of the 'monitoring gambles'. But work incentives have changed, as we have seen, and the benefits from this enhanced work incentive can be used to increase the utility index of either the principal or agent.

The argument is illustrated diagrammatically in Figure 5.7. The locus rr' represents, as before, points at which the agent is indifferent between effort and no effort, when no information about effort is used in the contract. Monitoring, as described in the earlier paragraphs of this section, using noisy but informative signals, results in effort being strictly preferred by the agent at x. It will therefore be possible to find another point such as y at which the agent is once more indifferent between effort and no effort even in the context of monitoring.[7] The locus of all such points might be represented by the curve mm'. At y, the utility of the industrious labourer will be the same as at x, but the utility of the landlord will be greater than at x. Monitoring, by providing a source of additional effort incentives, enables risk-sharing benefits to be achieved without reducing the amount of effort forthcoming. In effect,

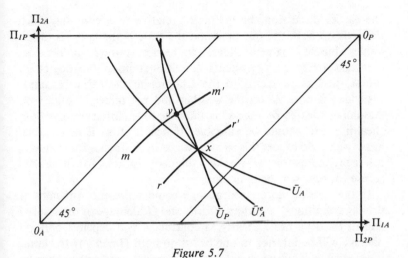

Figure 5.7

monitoring is being used as a substitute for a more inefficient
distribution of risk as a means of inducing effort.

6. EXAMPLES OF INCENTIVE CONTRACTS

The principles which have been outlined in the first five sections of
this chapter have applications which are more wide ranging than
the sharecropping case which we have thus far been using for illustrative purposes. Harris and Raviv (1978) provide a number of
interesting examples.

(a) Health and Motor Insurance

Moral hazard in insurance markets is a classic problem, as was seen
in Chapter 2. In terms of the content of Chapter 5, however, what
kind of insurance contracts are likely to be observed and in what
situations? Let θ, the state of the world, stand for 'degree of illness'
instead of weather conditions. Let e stand for 'health effort' for
example not smoking, taking safety precautions in dangerous tasks
and so forth. Finally, let Π represent 'amount of health care used',
that is, the outcome.

A contract which depends on the outcome alone (i.e. simply on
the amount of health care someone consumes) will, according to

the earlier discussion, be inefficient relative to a contract which depends on both the outcome and the state if the latter is observable. Thus, if 'degree of illness' can be observed we would expect contracts to specify payments conditional upon the degree of illness, just as payments to the labourer in the earlier example depended if possible on the weather and not merely the harvest. Assuming 'degree of illness' is unobservable, information about 'health effort' should be valuable. If health effort is observable, again we would expect this to be reflected in contracts, for example, lower premiums for non-smokers, higher premiums for those who refuse to wear seat belts in cars, etc.

In the case of motor insurance, θ could represent 'difficulty of driving conditions', e 'safety effort', and Π 'damage to the insured and to third parties'. Clearly, a contract which depends only on damage will be inferior to one based on both Π and θ if the latter is observable. Thus we might expect insurance contracts to vary by geographical area if 'driving conditions' differ. If θ is not observable, information on safety effort will be valuable. This too may be very difficult to observe, but if driving care is perfectly correlated with age, for example, we would expect to see insurance contracts varying with the age of the insured.

(b) Law Enforcement

Here the principal is seen as the political representative of the general public, while the agent is the policeman whose task it is to detect and punish crime. Suppose the outcome Π in this case is 'revenue generated by fines'. Effort e will be 'policing effort' such as patrols, observations and whatever other activities compatible with the law raise the total of fines collected. θ represents the 'state of crime'. If reflects the type and seriousness of crimes committed and, to fit into the principal–agent framework of this chapter, it is assumed that this 'state of crime' is independent of policing effort e.

Applying the sharecropping results to this new situation, an efficient contract would be expected to involve both the outcome, 'fines generated', and the 'state of crime'. The government would receive a payment from the police which depended only on the state of crime and the police would keep the residual fines. Risk could then be distributed in accordance with the principles of section 3. If the government was risk neutral and the police were risk averse, the residual fines in each 'state of crime' given that the standard policing effort had been applied would ideally be constant. On the other hand, if the police were risk neutral, no information about effort or state would be necessary for the efficient contract. The police would pay a flat fee to the government independent of the state of crime and would keep whatever revenue in excess of this fee they succeeded in generating. Effectively, the police would be paying a certain sum for the 'policing franchise' of an area and would be rewarded by their success in levying fines. Unsettling though such arrangements undoubtedly appear, there seems little doubt that they are well designed to produce a dedicated police force (dedicated, that is, to collecting fines). A more detailed discussion of 'franchising' as an incentive device occurs in section 7.

Assuming that the state of crime is unobservable, information on effort is valuable if the police are risk averse. Even if the information is 'noisy' it may be used to improve incentives, as we have seen in section 5. A policeman's contract might, for example, be designed so that effectively he 'posted a bond' which would be returned to him providing that malfeasance remained undetected over a specified period. Corruption or negligence would result, if observed, in the loss of the value of the bond. In other words, loss of the bond would be equivalent to the term $-\delta_0$ which appears in the monitoring gambles of section 5.

(c) Employment contracts

Consider first a case in which the employee's output is observable, whilst effort and state are unobservable. This case is identical with the sharecropping example discussed in section 4. The employee must take some risk if effort is to be induced, and this will involve inefficient risk sharing unless the employee is risk neutral. In the latter case we once more observe the 'franchising' solution, with the 'employee' paying a fee to the 'employer' for permission to use specified resources for a given period of time.

Where employees are risk averse a contract involving both outcome *and* state will be preferred to a contract involving just the outcome. The state variable θ might represent 'market conditions', in which case, if these were 'observable', contracts might be expected to link remuneration to some economic indicators of these conditions. Employees could be envisaged to pay a fee to the employer conditional only upon the state. This fee would presumably be lower in times of depression and higher in times of prosperity if workers were risk averse. The employer effectively offers insurance to the workers and takes the brunt of economic fluctuations. In the extreme case of a perfectly observable state variable θ, and a known function $\Pi = \Pi \ (\theta, \ e)$, the worker's remuneration would be constant in both prosperity and depression. Although practical examples of contracts *explicitly* written in this way are not easy to find, it has been argued that many contracts of employment are implicit.[8] The employer accepts an implicit unwritten obligation to insure the workforce against fluctuations in the way described. It is suggested that this *implicit* obligation helps to explain the 'stickiness' or 'inflexibility' of wage rates over the business cycle. Along with supplementary assumptions about the type of social security system operating, or the nature of information about θ (it may be asymmetrically distributed and available to employers but not employees), the implicit contracts literature has attempted to explain the existence of levels of employment greater than or less than would be observed under symmetric information. We shall discuss some of the ideas of the implicit contracts literature in a little more detail in Chapter 6.

Another application of the principal–agent results to employment contracts concerns the use of educational qualifications. Suppose that output depended not only on effort e but also on 'native ability' (Harris and Raviv, 1978). The state variable θ would now refer to the 'native ability' of the worker. Clearly this is not easy to observe, but if employers believed that 'native ability' was reflected in educational attainment we would expect remuneration to depend on qualifications and not just on the outcome. According to this view of things, education does not necessarily equip people with specific skills, but provides them through a series of tests, no matter how pointless in other respects, with evidence about their 'native ability'. Education is a 'screening procedure'[9] which tests for a particular type of attribute. This evidence can then be used by employers when contracting with employees.

Where the state variable is unobservable and workers are risk averse, information about effort is valuable. Perfect observability of the employees effort by the employer would simply result, of course, in a contract dependent on effort alone. The risk-averse employee would again be assured of the outcome, and the risk-neutral employer would take the risk. This, it will be recalled, is the result considered in Chapter 4 where the 'single proprietorship' was discussed. There, however, it was assumed that monitoring was costly and there was no presumption that effort was perfectly observable. It is worth while remembering, therefore, why it was that, even with costly monitoring, the contract did not involve the outcome and depended on effort alone. Conditions of team production implied that output could not be ascribed to particular members of the team, and the incentive effects of linking individual rewards to the collective outcome are minimal for large teams. In terms of our discussion of this chapter, therefore, contracts dependent upon the outcome will not induce effort under conditions of team production, because the probability of a preferred outcome is perceived to be only very weakly related to individual effort. A large individual effort (distance $\theta\alpha$ in Figure 5.4) will not greatly affect the slope of the indifference curves so that the set of contracts xyw in Figure 5.5 disappears and there are no *Pareto* improvements on θ. From an individual point of view the 'efficiency of effort' is small, even though jointly it may be very high.

The individual employer under conditions of team production must therefore rely on monitoring to induce effort. We have already surmised in Chapter 4 that the proprietorship will be viable only if the returns to monitoring are 'sufficiently great'. Again, to reinterpret this observation in the light of the analysis of Chapter 5 may be useful. Assume, as above, that there are only two effort levels, zero and e, which employees can choose. Assume further that if *everyone* chooses effort e the probability of outcome Π_1 will increase to P_1^e from P_1, otherwise the probability of Π_1 will remain at P_1.[10] Figure 5.5 can be reinterpreted to apply to the employer P and the 'typical employee' A, with indifference curves $\bar{U}_A^e$ now reflecting the utility index of the employee when the whole team is exerting effort e. If the employer could be *absolutely certain* of every employee's effort simply by monitoring at a given level of intensity the team would obviously be viable providing the potential benefits, distance αt multiplied by the number of employees, exceeded the costs to the employer of the critical level of monitoring required. Each employee would have a contract at α and would be monitored sufficiently intensely to determine with certainty that effort e was forthcoming. Providing the average monitoring cost per employee fell short of αt, both employer and employee are capable of becoming better off than remaining at θ.

A natural extension of this analysis is to consider what would happen if the employer could observe the employee's effort only with some accompanying error. In section 5 it was shown how even a very 'noisy' signal could in principle improve the positions of both principal and agent. However, in that section we were considering a case in which there existed a contract x involving the outcome alone which was *Pareto* preferred to the original position at θ in Figure 5.5. The addition of any informative, though noisy, signal could be used to improve further on such a contract. In the case here, however, we have assumed that no contract based on the outcome alone is viable, and our point of departure is from θ. Clearly, from this inauspicious starting point the principal's information about the agent's effort will have to be reasonably good if it is going to make much difference. Some signals may simply not be 'informative enough' to be capable of providing opportunities for mutual benefit. On the other hand intuition suggests that *perfect* information may not be necessary, and that a 'sufficiently informative' signal which was nevertheless subject to error might be useful.

That such a possibility exists can be seen by considering once more the monitoring gambles of section 5. There we saw that the labourer could, providing the monitor was more likely to observe 'correctly' than 'incorrectly', be presented with a reward structure which implied that an idle labourer would be taking an 'unfavourable' gamble while an industrious labourer would be taking a 'fair' one. Now unlike the labourer at point x in section 5, this will not be sufficient, in itself, to ensure that the labourer at a point such as α will prefer effort to no effort. The idle labourer at α will not like having to take an unfavourable gamble if he is monitored, but he does not like exerting effort e either, and the 'effort price' of avoiding the unfavourable gamble may be too high for him. (By contrast it will be recalled that at point x in the example of section 5, the labourer was indifferent between effort and no effort, so that there was no 'effort price' of avoiding the unfavourable gamble.)

Although the prospect of *any* unfavourable gamble will not automatically induce effort at point α, it is clearly possible that the prospect of an *extremely unfavourable* gamble might do the trick. At point α, the employee or agent would face the 'monitoring gamble:

$$m_A^\alpha = (q_{e0}, \Pi^1 + \delta_e; q_{00}, \Pi^1 - \delta_0)$$

assuming that effort zero were chosen. If the principal's information is very good so that both q_{e0} (i.e. the probability of being observed working when the agent is in fact idle) and q_{0e} (the probability of being observed shirking when the agent is really working) are very small, the gamble m_A^α will be extremely unfavourable. Thus, the more *reliable* the information of the principal, the more *adverse* is the monitoring gamble taken by the shirker. It is at least possible to envisage a point at which work becomes more attractive than the monitoring gamble associated with idleness.

We cannot appeal to the limit theorem used in section 5 to prove this proposition, since it is clear that the 'stakes' cannot be infinitesimally small if the jump in effort from zero to e is to be forthcoming. The employee, or agent, will have to face values of δ_e and δ_0 sufficiently large to induce effort e whilst the value of Π must be chosen so as to leave him as well off as he was at α. It is not therefore sufficient for the industrious labourer to be offered a 'fair' monitoring gamble at α, since risk-averse people will be made worse off by non-infinitesimal fair bets. The monitoring gamble will have to be favourable at α, or, if it is fair, the contract point must be to the right of α along A's certainty line. In the latter case, providing a point exists to the left of t (say point β) where the agent is as well off exerting effort and taking a fair monitoring gamble as he was at θ, and providing the monitoring gambles are so constructed that effort is preferred to idleness at β, the use of the principal's less than completely reliable information may permit *Pareto* improvements on θ. Distance $\alpha\beta$ in Figure 5.5 represents the cost to the risk-averse agent of taking the fair monitoring bet. Clearly, other things constant, the bigger are δ_0 and δ_e the bigger will be the distance $\alpha\beta$. But the more reliable the principal's information the more adverse is the monitoring gamble of the shirker and the smaller can be the value of δ_0 and δ_e compatible with making effort the preferred option on the part of the agent. Thus, more reliable information will be associated with a smaller distance $\alpha\beta$.

Figure 5.8 may help to illustrate the relationship between effort costs $\alpha\theta$, risk-bearing costs $\alpha\beta$, and the monitoring gambles. At point β the agent receives Π_1 with certainty. This gives no incentive

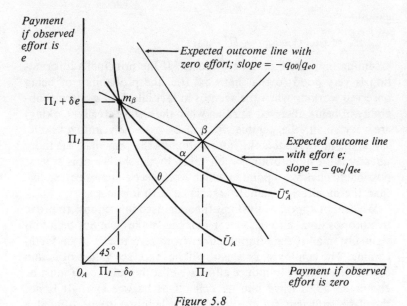

Figure 5.8

to exert effort. Now offer the agent a monitoring gamble, $\Pi_1 + \delta_e$, conditional upon being observed working, and $\Pi_1 - \delta_0$, conditional upon being observed idle. Further, ensure that this monitoring gamble is 'fair' so that $q_{ee} \; \delta_e = q_{0e} \; \delta_0$ with $q_{ee} > q_{0e}$. Call this monitoring gamble point m_β. Clearly the agent will be worse of at m_β than at β. The cost of bearing the uncertainty of the fair monitoring gamble is $\alpha\beta$. For the idle labourer, however, fair gambles occur along the line through β slope $-q_{00}/q_{e0}$ and hence the gamble at m_β is clearly unfavourable. Draw the idle labourer's indifference curve through m_β and let it cut the certainty line at θ. If distance $\theta\alpha$ is the cost to the agent of exerting effort level e, the agent will be indifferent at m_β between effort and no effort. m_β will represent the least costly monitoring gamble which is 'fair' to the industrious labourer and is just able to induce effort e.

The effect of more reliable information can now be deduced from the figure. An increase in q_{00}/q_{e0} (i.e. better information about the shirker) will steepen A's indifference curve through θ. It follows that at m_β A's utility index will be lower than before if he shirks, and he will strictly prefer effort to no effort. Thus a less costly monitoring gamble between m_β and β can be found. Even perfect information about the shirker will not remove risk-bearing costs entirely, however, if there is a chance of perceiving an industrious labourer as idle. Zero risk-bearing costs would require perfect information about the industrious worker, that is $q_{0e}/q_{ee} = 0$.

If we now introduce the complication that reliability of information may depend upon the monitoring costs incurred by the principal, we see that the distance βt in Figure 5.5 will exaggerate the gains to be had from monitoring by the amount of these costs. This suggests that there may be some efficient amount of monitoring effort on the part of the principal. At very *low* levels of monitoring effort, the information may be so unreliable that β lies to the right of point t and no *Pareto* improvement on θ is possible. At very *high* levels of monitoring effort, point β may lie close to point α. The risk-bearing costs associated with the monitoring gamble are low because information is very reliable. But in this case the monitoring costs may be so big that they more than absorb the potential benefits βt, and there is still no *Pareto* improvement on θ. If monitoring is to be viable there must be a point at which the distance βt minus total monitoring costs is positive, and the efficient amount of monitoring effort will be that at which distance βt minus costs of monitoring is maximised. This gives us a new perspective on Figure 4.2 in Chapter 4. There we argued that monitoring effort would be applied to the point at which marginal benefits and costs were equal. Here we are looking behind the MB_1 schedule. The benefit of additional monitoring in this framework is more reliable information. A given amount of effort e can thus be induced from each employee using monitoring gambles involving lower risk-bearing costs.

7. INCENTIVE CONTRACTS AND THE FIRM

In this chapter our primary task has been to consider in some detail the contractual problems which face two parties when outcomes are uncertain, and when information cannot be observed, or is costly to observe and subject to error. It is appropriate at this point to discuss explicitly the significance for the theory of the firm of the issues covered in the first six sections. Sharecropping, franchising, insurance contracts, police incentives, and even some of the employment contracts discussed earlier, may at first appear rather specialised and peripheral concerns rather than of central importance. Yet, as has been emphasised from the very outset, the firm is a particular type of contractual environment, and its characteristics would be expected therefore to be moulded by the sorts of considerations which formed the basis of our discussion above. In Chapter 1 the firm was rationalised as a device for coping with uncertainty and the passage of time, in Chapter 2 it was seen as a response to 'opportunistic behaviour' resulting from 'information asymmetry', in Chapter 4 the firm evolved to permit policing and monitoring of cooperating inputs in conditions of 'team production'. All these ideas are closely interrelated. They all reduce ultimately to the firm as an institutional consequence of imperfect information. And they all have in common the idea of the firm as a *nexus of contracts* with a central agent.

Within the nexus of contracts called the firm, however, there is scope for considerable variety. The nature of the contracts is not absolutely standard and will vary as conditions vary. As we saw in Chapter 2, Coase (1937) stressed the *direction* of resources and the employment or 'authority' relation as characterising the typical contract. No doubt there are particular cases in which this is descriptively not unrealistic, but labour is not the only type of input used by the firm and, as pointed out at the end of Chapter 2, positive monitoring costs associated with less than perfect 'observability' (Williamson would say 'information asymmetry') will usually mean that employer–employee relationships have attributes similar to those of principal and agent. The sections above have indicated, however, that there are many possible 'solutions' to the principal–agent problem, depending on assumptions about what is and what is not observable, the risk preferences of the parties, the costs of monitoring and so forth.

In some firms people will be closely monitored whereas in others they may have wider discretion. Some will be paid according to their own particular *output* (for example by piece rates), others in 'team' environments (in the sense of Alchian and Demsetz) may be paid according to their *effort*. Payment according to effort will involve 'monitoring gambles' as described above, and the nature of these may also vary between firms. If monitoring of effort is very efficient and reliable the risk involved in being monitored may be small, perhaps involving small bonuses or other prizes. Where monitoring is less reliable, the gamble may be substantial, as when promotion to a higher grade involves a considerable pay rise. Thus the structure of a hierarchy can be seen as being closely related to the provision of incentives through what we have called 'monitoring gambles' and this is a topic which will be taken further in Chapter 6.

It is important to remember also that *within a single firm* different people will have different types of contract. A senior manager whose performance is difficult to monitor by shareholders may have a contract which links remuneration to the outcome through stock options or bonuses linked to profits. The pay of Mr Ian MacGregor at the British Steel Corporation, for example, depended on the performance of the company over the contractual period. Similarly a travelling salesman for the company may depend heavily on his particular sales record, the difficulty of monitoring implying that the salesman has to tolerate considerable risks. The professional designers of the product, on the other hand, are also difficult to monitor. But because individual 'output' may be impossible to measure, 'effort' may be monitored and incentives given by means of promotion through a hierarchy. At least a design team is likely to be concentrated in a particular geographical location, and members may thus be assessed by more senior leaders of the team. The people who actually fabricate the product could have quite different contracts again, depending on the technological context and its implications for monitoring. To take just one example, a simple production line process involving little chance for 'shirking', with the line speed predetermined by the manager, could result in a standard payment per 'shift'. Providing the number of 'shifts' worked per week does not vary, the employee would be relieved of all risk. For a risk-averse employee this would be preferred to a contract dependent upon output, since output would vary with technical problems such as 'breakdowns' or poor components. Where, as is almost invariably the case in practice, the chance of a breakdown or the quality of the final product depends to some degree on the alertness, concentration, or dexterity of the employee, however, incentives via the possibility of promotion may still be used even on production lines.

Where monitoring is very costly, and effort and state of the world are effectively 'unobservable', contracts will depend upon the outcome alone. A particular example of this arrangement is the franchise contract, and we have discussed some of its properties in an earlier section. In the present context, however, the franchise contract warrants closer inspection because it represents a relationship which leaves the franchisee with a large area of discretion as to how affairs should be conducted. It is thus far distant from the 'authority relation' discussed by Coase, or the exercise of 'conscious power' mentioned by Robertson. From the point of view of economic principle, however, a franchise chain would seem to have the major characteristic required to make it a single 'firm'. A franchise chain is a 'nexus of contracts' in which each franchisee has a contract with a single contractual agent or franchisor. Legally, these contractual arrangements exist between separate 'firms', yet economically the transactions might be regarded as taking place within a single firm. This is the essence of a contribution by Rubin (1978) which emphasises the somewhat arbitrary distinction between interfirm and intrafirm transactions and argues that 'the economic concept of a 'firm' does not have clear boundaries' (p. 225).

In a typical franchise contract the franchisee pays a fee to the franchisor for the right to market a particular 'branded' product or service. The franchisee agrees to run the business in the manner stipulated so that product, price, hours of operation, personnel policies, etc. may be standard throughout the chain. The franchisor may provide assistance in the form of managerial training or site selection, and the franchisee will usually pay a royalty in the form of a percentage of sales. Rubin notes that a common explanation for these arrangements is that outside capital is attracted, and that franchising is a method of tapping the capital provided by the franchisee. However, the explanation is clearly suspect since, if the franchisee is risk averse, he would prefer a 'share' in the profits of the entire franchise chain rather than the right to the return from a single outlet in the chain. Risk-spreading considerations would therefore work against the franchise as an efficient form of economic organisation unless franchisees are all risk neutral. Yet the success of franchising in particular areas suggests that it has its advantages. The explanation favoured by Rubin is in terms of monitoring and control within the firm. Usually the franchisee is physically removed from the franchisor (as for example in a fastfood chain) and detailed monitoring would be extremely costly. Incentives can be provided instead by paying a franchise fee for the right to run the business for some period of time.

If the franchise chain is an institutional response to the incentives problem why do not franchisees keep *all* the profits attributable to their business? Why does the franchisor typically receive a royalty? Rubin argues that the franchisor also requires incentives. The profitability of a given outlet does not depend *exclusively* on how that particular outlet is managed. It also depends on the image of the product generally with potential customers, and this 'goodwill' is the primary responsibility of the franchisor. The franchisor is responsible for policing quality, and ensuring that each franchisee maintains the correct standards. Through advertising the franchisor also attempts to keep the distinctive features of the product known to the consuming public. Without the royalty, the franchisor would have a smaller incentive to pay attention to these activities. Thus, Rubin concludes that:

in those businesses where there is much managerial discretion, we would expect a higher percentage of the revenue of the franchisor to come from the initial fee and a relatively lower percentage to come from royalties.... Second, where the trademark is more valuable we would expect more of the franchisor's revenue to come from royalties, for this would create an incentive for him to be efficient in policing and maintaining value (p. 230).

Our discussion of the many different forms which the firm can take within the 'nexus of contracts' conception, and the inevitable fuzziness accompanying the econonic as distinct from the strictly legal view of the firm, leads to some important implications concerning the place of the entrepreneur and hence the relevance of Chapter 3 in the theoretical framework of principal and agent. The results stated in sections 1 and 2, especially as illustrated in the figures of sections 3, 4 and 5, may give a rather misleading impression of 'determinateness' about the whole problem. It must be remembered that the theoretical apparatus developed above is not intended to convey the conclusion that there is an 'answer' to the principal–agent problem for any given set of circumstances, and that therefore this 'answer' will be recognised by everyone and implemented. Such a conclusion would no more follow from the analysis of Chapter 5 than it would follow from the analysis of the gains from trade in Chapter 1. All that has been shown in this chapter is that *once the conditions are correctly recognised and interpreted* there may in principle be efficiency gains to be derived from an appropriately specified contract. Noticing the availability of these gains (Kirzner), developing entirely new institutional forms incorporating different incentive structures (Schumpeter), making 'judgemental decisions' about what form of contract would be best for a particular activity of the firm (Casson): these are entrepreneurial functions.

Impressions about risk preferences; judgements about what can be observed, how, and at what cost; guesses about the probability distribution of various states of the world: these are the forces which mould contractual relations, and in so doing throw up the institutional structures which are observed at any one time. There is nothing immutable about these structures. They change as continually as the 'shifting sands of industrial structure' described by Robertson and Dennison at the beginning of Part II. New or modified institutional forms embodying differing contractual relations compete in a continuing process of trial and error. A chain of restaurants run by professional managers suddenly faces competition from a chain of restaurants run by franchisees. The franchise chain switches to professional managers in large cities where the proximity of many outlets makes monitoring less costly. This is, however, anticipating some of the discussion of Chapters 7 and 8, where the nature of the competitive process is considered in more detail. Before then it will be useful to investigate more carefully some of the internal structural features of the firm.

NOTES

1. *Wealth of Nations*, book 1, pp. 9–12. Edwin Cannan Edition.
2. Smith's views concerning the degree of application exhibited by people undertaking a variety of jobs seem strange to modern ways of thinking. 'A man commonly saunters a little in turning his hand from one sort of employment to another. When he first begins the new work he is seldom very keen and hearty...and for some time he rather trifles than applies to good purpose. The habit of sauntering and of indolent careless application...renders (the country workman) almost always slothful and lazy...' (p. 10). From this quote it appears that Smith associates division of labour with *greater* diligence presumably because, in his example of pin making, monitoring costs would be relatively low. Smith does not, however, seem to distinguish between the effects of division of labour *per se* and the consequences for the costs of monitoring. It is plausible that in eighteenth-century conditions a country workman asked to perform a whole range of tasks in different places would be difficult to monitor. But an independent

craftsman (such as a blacksmith) would presumably have had a smaller incentive to be careless since he would personally bear the costs.
3. Towle and Co. v. White (1873).
4. Holmstrom (1979).
5. The Von Neumann–Morgenstern axioms extend the standard axioms of consumer theory to take account of uncertainty. It is assumed that:
   (i) Each person can order the basic outcomes (Π_i) which go to make up the gambles (G_i). A gamble is simply a probability distribution of outcomes. Thus $G_1 = (P_1\Pi_1; 1 - P_1\Pi_2)$ is a simple gamble involving two possible outcomes Π_1 and Π_2 with probabilities P_1 and $1 - P_1$ respectively. This is the form which the 'monitoring gambles' are assumed to take in section 5.
   (ii) Each person can order the gambles G_i transitively. Thus, when confronted with any two gambles the chooser will state either that G_1RG_2, G_2RG_1, or both, where R means 'is at least as preferred as'. Further if G_1RG_2 and G_2RG_3 than by transitivity G_1RG_3.
   (iii) The axiom of continuity states that for all outcomes. Π_i there exists a probability v_i such that $\Pi_i I[v_i\Pi_b, 1 - v_i\Pi_w]$ where Π_b and Π_w are the 'best' and 'worst' outcomes respectively. If the best outcome were 100 and the worst were zero, the axiom means that for any outcome between these figures (say 80) the chooser can be made indifferent between the certainty of 80 and a gamble involving 100 with probability v_i and zero with probability $1 - v_i$. Clearly as v_i approaches unity we will eventually prefer the gamble. As it approaches zero we prefer the sure prospect. At some point in between we can be made indifferent.
   (iv) In any gamble G_i it is possible to substitute for a basic outcome Π_i another gamble g_i where $\Pi_i I g_i$. Thus the components of a gamble can be other gambles, and this will make no difference to the consumer providing he is indifferent between the sure prospect and the gamble g_i which replaces it.
   (v) The complexity of a gamble is of no consequence. All gambles are eventually reducible to a probability distribution over outcomes, and this is always the choice perceived by the consumer. The consumer attaches the same utility number to all gambles representing the same probability distribution. Notice that this axiom puts considerable strain on the information-processing capacity of individuals. In the case of extremely complex gambles it could fall foul of the 'bounded rationality' problem mentioned in Chapters 1 and 2.
   (vi) If G_1 and G_2 are two gambles involving the same two outcomes Π_1 and Π_2 with $\Pi_1 P\Pi_2$, the consumer will prefer the gamble involving the greater probability of Π_1. A proof that a utility function may be derived from these axioms may be found in Hey (1979) pp. 30–3. The classic reference in this field is J. von Neumann and O. Morgenstern, *The Theory of Games and Economic Behaviour* (1944).

6. Hey (1979).
7. The locus of such points must lie to the left of rr'. Only if GPG^e, that is, if idleness is preferred to effort in the absence of monitoring, can we construct an example in which $G_mIG_m^e$, that is, the agent is indifferent between effort and idleness in the presence of monitoring.
8. Early papers on implicit contracts were those of Baily (1974) and Azariadis (1975). Okun (1981) has termed the implicit contract 'the invisible handshake'.
9. *See* K. Arrow (1973), 'Higher education as a filter', *Journal of Public Economics* July Vol. 2, No. 3, pp. 193–216.
10. The predicament of the team here resembles that analysed by Hirshleifer (1983). The payoff to each member depends upon the 'weakest link'. Hirshleifer gives the example of an island inhabited by a group of people, where each person is responsible for a portion of the sea defences. The land is flat so that the probability of inundation is dependent upon the strength of the weakest portion of the sea defences and hence the effort of the person responsible for the poorest section. This contrasts with a 'best shot' collective outcome in which everything depends upon the best effort forthcoming. The example given here is of an incoming missile which will damage all members of the group but which can be destroyed by any *single* member with a well-aimed shot.

6 Hierarchies

I polished that handle so carefully,
That now I am the ruler of the Queen's Navy.

W. S. Gilbert
HMS Pinafore

1. INTRODUCTION

The firm in conventional neoclassical economics is a curiously underdeveloped concept, an 'empty box', to use Clapham's (1922) phrase. As will be seen in more detail in Chapter 7 the firm of the standard textbook is no more than a 'production function', a mathematical abstraction indicating the relationship between 'inputs' and 'outputs'. The firm's operations are therefore defined technologically, the outcome of physical laws defined by a given state of the arts and known to everyone. For some purposes, this approach to the firm may serve well enough, and it is not intended to discuss explicitly the purely methodological issues which permeate disputes in this area. But an approach which abstracts from the information problem abstracts from institutions (Chapter 1), and an institution-free analysis is simply not very useful if our purpose is to consider the structure of institutions such as firms. In this chapter, therefore, an attempt is made to outline some more recent developments (still mainly within the neoclassical tradition) which specifically concern information problems, incentives and internal structure.

If economists have become interested in the application of their techniques to institutional issues relatively recently, other social scientists have been concerned with them for many years. It is to the literature of 'organisation theory' and 'management science'

151

that we must turn for early attempts to add substance to the firm and to analyse its internal structure.[1] Much of this work, however, was normative, and represented a desire to discover 'ideal' arrangements for manufacturing operations, rather than a desire simply to explain observed structures or analyse the causes of differences between structures. Taylor (1911), for example, was imbued with an almost messianic desire to rid the world of shirking ('underworking') through the establishment of 'work study' techniques and scientific management. His name has therefore become associated with systems of remorseless drudgery which pay scant attention to the individual characteristics of employees. Urwick (1943) was likewise concerned 'to establish a general set of principles or laws for designing organisational structures' (Jackson, 1982, p. 21). Principles were sought for establishing the correct division of labour, instituting the appropriate 'span of control' (number of subordinates per supervisor), defining a clear command structure and so forth. The result was a somewhat impersonal, mechanistic approach to organisations, which was criticised for overlooking more human and social factors. These factors such as 'management style', establishing friendly personal relationships and mutual respect, peer group constraints and effective communication were emphasised in the celebrated 'Hawthorne Studies'[2] and led to the development of the 'human relations school'. The approach was still normative, however, either because good human relations were seen as ends in themselves, or because a satisfying work environment was regarded as automatically conducive to physical productivity.

This chapter draws on a rather different tradition. The aim is not to be prescriptive but simply to make sense of the varying institutional arrangements which are observed in practice. Our starting point is an appreciation of transactions costs (Chapter 2) and the problems of contract enforcement to which they give rise (Chapter 5). In the tradition pioneered by Coase the firm is seen as a response to these problems, and we show how various theorists have attempted to explain basic hierarchical characteristics by reference to the theory of principal and agent. From the early work of Weber (1947) onwards, bureaucracies or hierarchies have been recognised as having certain standard features.

(a) The organisation is made up of people assigned to the various layers in the hierarchy. These layers may be defined in terms of 'authority' so that those assigned to a higher rank supervise those in the subordinate layer. In this case the number of layers in the organisation will depend upon the size of the base and the 'span of control' exercised by supervisors. Clearly the bigger the 'span of control' the flatter is the pyramid and the fewer the layers in the organisation for any given size of base. Williamson (1967), for example, used the idea of a fixed 'span of control' combined with the concept of 'control loss' (only a certain fraction of a supervisor's intentions are effectively implemented at each stage) to discuss the profit-maximising number of layers in a hierarchical organisation.[3] Hierarchical layers do not necessarily have to be defined by authority and supervision however. The organisation may be purely a 'wage hierarchy' with positions in some layers paid more than positions in others. Of course the two types of hierarchy may go together, as when supervisors are paid more than the people they supervise. It is not obvious, however, why this is usually so. Further, more senior posts do not always imply supervision. In British universities senior lecturers do not monitor lecturers. They often do essentially the same job even though the former are paid more than the latter.

(b) The number of people in higher positions in a hierarchy is fewer than the number in the immediately subordinate position. This is a rather mechanical implication of a hierarchy based on authority with an assumed 'span of control' greater than one. But in a wage hierarchy it is not immediately clear why there should be fewer people in higher paid positions than in lower paid ones. Why, for example, do we not tend to observe departments in universities in which every member of staff is a full professor?

(c) Positions higher up a hierarchy are filled predominantly by promoting people from lower positions in the hierarchy. To use Williamson's (1976b) terminology the 'ports of entry' into the hierarchy are mainly at lower levels. Promotion is often associated with a fixed retirement date so that people cannot linger too long in the most senior posts.

(d) Hierarchies are characterised by Weber's quality of 'impersonality'. People are treated alike once they have been assigned to a position in the hierarchy. Williamson sees this 'impersonality' in the lack of scope for individual bargaining and the necessity of accepting 'standard' terms and conditions of employment applicable to a particular hierarchical level (see section 8). When a hierarchy offers 'advancement' to a person, it is not tailored to that person's special circumstances but takes the form of a change from one standard contract to another.

These broad characteristics of hierarchies have attracted considerable attention from economists in recent years, and much of the later part of this chapter is concerned with them. As a preliminary exercise, however, we reformulate the analysis of incentive contracts to show how it relates to the choice of methods of payment adopted by the firm.

2. PIECE RATES AND TIME RATES

Although employment contracts were discussed at various points in Chapter 5, it will be useful to reinterpret some of the principal–agent results in terms of more conventional concepts. Our analysis thus far has been conducted with the aid of a simple box diagram with each point in the box representing a 'contract'. Implicitly therefore each point represents a primitive 'payment schedule' or 'incentive structure'. It determines what contractually accrues to the agent or employee in given circumstances. Suppose, as we did initially in section 4 of Chapter 5, that only the final outcome of the employees' effort is observable, then each point in the box diagram can be interpreted as implying a payment schedule made up of a time rate and a piece rate. Consider Figure 6.1 in which we reproduce a box diagram with the risk-neutral employer's indifference curve $\bar{U}_p^e$. Along $\bar{U}_p^e$ we identify four possible contractual positions labelled a, b, c and d respectively. The locus rr' which will just induce effort e from the risk-averse employee is drawn through point b. Point c lies on a diagonal drawn through the principal's origin and the agent's origin. Point a and point d are on the agent's certainty line and the principal's certainty line respectively.

Each of the identified contracts can be illustrated in a different way in Figure 6.2. Along the horizontal axis in Figure 6.2 is measured the actual outcome and along the vertical axis the payment to the employee. Since there are only two possible outcomes

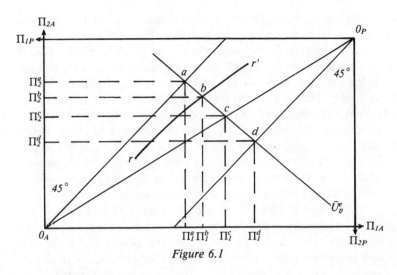

Figure 6.1

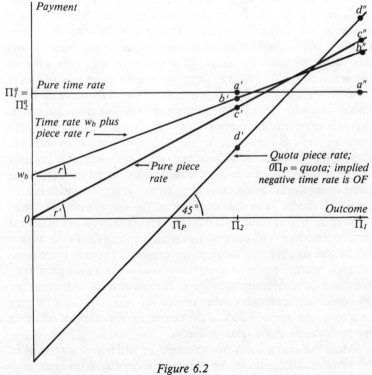

Figure 6.2

in our simple formulation, each contract point in Figure 6.1 is represented by *two* points in Figure 6.2. Thus contract *a* in Figure 6.1 is equivalent to the two points *a'* and *a"* in Figure 6.2. A straight line drawn through these two points is horizontal, indicating that the payment to the employee is independent of the outcome. This can therefore be regarded as a pure time-rate system. The employee receives a *certain* payment $\Pi_1^q = \Pi_2^q$. Interpreting the 'outcomes' measured by the dimensions of the box as referring to particular intervals of time (in Chapter 5 it might have been a year since there we were discussing the size of the harvest, but here we could regard the outcomes as applying to weekly intervals), $\Pi_1^q = \Pi_2^q$ would represent a weekly wage.

As was seen in Chapter 5, a weekly wage in the context of total lack of observability of effort would not produce the required work incentives. To induce effort the employee had to take some risk, and in the present context this implies an element of piece-rate payment. Point *b* in Figure 6.1 transfers to the two points *b'*, *b"* in Figure 6.2. A straight line through these points cuts the vertical axis at w_b. It is therefore possible to interpret the contract at *b* in Figure 6.1 as a combination of a time-rate or weekly wage w_b and a payment per unit of outcome or piece rate given by the slope of the line through *b'* and *b"*. Designate the slope of this line as *r*, then the payment to the employee $\Pi_A = w_b + r\Pi$ where Π is the actual outcome. This payment schedule will just induce the risk-averse employee to exert effort *e*, as was seen in Chapter 5. A contract at point *c* in Figure 6.1, it will be recalled, would involve risk-sharing losses relative to point *b* and (given the assumption of only two effort levels, zero and *e*) would result in no compensating increase in effort. The contract at *c* lies on the diagonal through the origins of the box and thus implies that the agent is paid the same proportion of the outcome, whichever outcome occurs. There is thus no time rate at all but just a pure piece rate, as shown in Figure 6.2 by the straight line through the origin. Of course there is no reason in principle why a contract at *c*, and hence a pure piece rate, might not be an efficient solution to the contractual problem given the right circumstances (the degree of risk aversion of the employee, the cost of effort to the employee, the effect of effort on the probability of Π_1, and so forth).

Indeed, although a risk-averse employee will never, according to the results of Chapter 5, be observed accepting a contract at *d* (since another contract will exist preferred by both employer and employee, see p. 130), a risk-neutral employee may do so. The resulting payment schedule is shown as the straight line through $d'd''$ in Figure 6.2. Note that the implied time rate is now negative and represents the 'franchise fee' discussed in the last chapter. It should not be concluded, however, that this fee has actually to be paid to the employer in the form of cash for the incentive structure to be operating. The fee can be paid 'implicitly' by effectively forgoing any reward over a certain range of outcomes, and hence paying the fee 'in kind' to the employer. Thus a piece-rate system can involve a 'quota' below which the employee receives nothing. In the case of the contract at d the employee receives whatever is produced,[4] but only above the quota Π_p.

The fact that only two outcomes were assumed to be possible meant that the various incentive structures could be represented by points lying along the straight lines in Figure 6.2. In the general case where any number of outcomes might occur and effort levels can vary continuously there is absolutely no reason to suppose that the efficient contract will imply a linear incentive structure. Indeed the informational and computational requirements involved in 'calculating' the best contract will be formidable and the result could be a highly complex structure. Once more therefore we are led back to the basic arguments of Chapters 1 and 2 and the proposition that bounded rationality and other information problems will imply continual experiment rather than perfectly stable 'solutions'. Stiglitz (1975) recognises this point and argues in terms reminiscent of Alchian (1950) or even Hayek (1948) that:

If there are large and significant advantages of one contractual arrangement over another, firms that 'discover' (this) will find they can increase profits and the particular contractual arrangement will be imitated. Thus, it might be argued that there is an evolutionary tendency of the economy to gravitate to the contractual arrangements analysed here (p. 556).

Stiglitz proceeds to investigate the properties of linear payment schedules where employees are risk averse and employers are risk neutral, and derives results which may be intuitively understood in the context of the model presented in Chapter 5: 'The piece rate is higher the smaller the risk, the lower the risk aversion, and the higher the supply elasticity of effort (the greater the incentive effects)' (p. 560).

In other words, if output is very closely related to effort and only weakly influenced by chance elements (the risk is small) the payment schedule will emphasise the piece rate, and the time rate will be low. By opting for piece rates, the employee does not expose himself to great risk but there is a clear advantage in providing incentives to effort. The impact of risk aversion also accords with a priori expectations. Where, as in Stiglitz's model, the outcome alone is observable, contracts which induce effort will involve the employee in *some* risk (unless of course $\Pi = \Pi(e)$). As we saw in Chapter 5, the risk-sharing losses were worth incurring provided that the incentive effects were big enough. There we were considering a case in which effort could take only two values, but where effort can vary continuously the efficient contract will be so adjusted that the *additional* risk-sharing losses associated with inducing an extra unit of effort from the employee are just equal to the marginal benefits derivable from the extra effort. Clearly, the more risk averse the employee the greater will be the risk-sharing losses involved in any given modifications of the incentive structure away from time rates towards piece rates. Marginal risk-sharing losses will exceed marginal benefits from greater effort sooner as the importance of piece rates is increased, and higher risk aversion is therefore expected to favour the time rate. By a similar process of reasoning it is clear that for any *given* degree of risk aversion the marginal benefits of a move towards piece rates will be higher the greater the resulting incentive effects, and thus large incentive effects favour the piece rate. A final conclusion from Stiglitz's analysis also accords with the results of our simple framework: 'If individuals are perfectly well informed about their own abilities' (i.e. they know the cost of effort and the effect on the probability distribution of outcomes) 'and there are no other sources of risk' (or people are risk neutral) 'then equilibrium will entail... auctioning off the jobs to the highest bidder, i.e. a non-positive time rate' (p. 563). This corresponds, of course, to our conclusion that with risk-neutral employees the incentive structure $d'd''$ in Figure 6.2 will be efficient.

3. THE ROLE OF THE MONITOR

The linear incentive structures of section 2 do not imply hierarchical relationships; they are simply a reformulation of the contractual issues discussed in Chapter 5 sections 3 and 4. We saw in section 5 of Chapter 5, however, how monitoring could result in both parties to a contract becoming better off. It is this use of a monitor or supervisor which is the distinguishing mark of what Williamson (1975) terms a 'simple hierarchy'. One person or group of people does the work, and another person monitors and assesses performance, as discussed in Chapter 4 in the context of Alchian and Demsetz's view of the firm. In fact monitoring can be considered as having too conceptually distinct roles.

(a) Monitoring is a response to the problem of 'moral hazard'. Because people, by assumption, cannot be relied upon to keep a promise to exert effort *e*, 'direct incentives' via piece rates are required to ensure compliance. The risk-sharing losses involved are the result of moral hazard, but they may be reduced by monitoring. As Stiglitz (1975) puts it 'workers voluntarily undertake to be supervised.... They submit to being compelled to work harder than direct incentives provide for because the consequence is a higher expected utility' (p. 571). Against these potential benefits it is necessary to set the costs of monitoring, as we saw in Chapter 5. It may also be that individuals will resent the presence of a monitor and extra costs (utility losses) will result from working in a less pleasant 'atmosphere'.[5]

(b) Monitoring may also be required to cope with a quite separate problem, that of 'adverse selection' (see Chapter 2 pp. 26–7). Thus far our theoretical discussion has been based on a single principal and a single agent. Where the possibility of several agents or employees was considered, the same framework was used by the expedient of using a 'typical' or 'representative' agent (Chapter 5 pp. 139–43). In other words all potential employees were assumed identical. Suppose now, however, that there are two groups of employees with two different skill levels and that the principal cannot by simple observation determine which person belongs to which group. The problem may be illustrated in Figure 6.3. The indifference curve $\bar{U}_{AS} = \bar{U}_{AU}$ indicates the locus of prospects yielding the same utility index to the skilled person *S* and the unskilled person *U* when neither is exerting effort. Thus we are assuming that both skilled and unskilled persons have the same risk preferences. When the skilled person exerts effort *e*, his indifference curve becomes $\bar{U}_{AS}^{e}$ through point α. As usual $\alpha\theta$ represents the cost of effort to the skilled person. For the unskilled person, however, greater effort may be required to change the probability of outcome

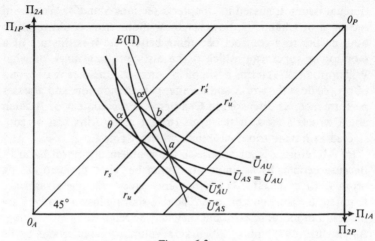

Figure 6.3

1 from P_I to P_I^e and his indifference curve is therefore labelled $\bar{U}_{AU}^{e'}$. Distance $\alpha'\theta$ is the cost of effort to the unskilled person. The upshot is that efficient contracts involving skilled people will lie along $r_s r_s'$ while contracts involving unskilled people will lie along $r_u r_u'$. Indifference curve $E(\Pi)$ represents the constant expected profits line for the risk-neutral principal assuming that the required effort is being exerted. The firm or principal can therefore offer a contract at a to the unskilled, or, compatible with maintaining the same expected profit, a contract at b to the skilled. If we assume for the moment that $E(\Pi)$ represents some competitive level of profits we would expect firms to sort themselves into groups: one group specialising in employing the skilled, the other group specialising in the unskilled.

This process of sorting employees into groups, however, requires that ability is observable, and we have assumed that ability cannot be observed. Of course unobservability would not matter if people could be trusted to declare accurately their level of skill assuming that they, at least, know what it is. But Figure 6.3 illustrates that the unskilled will have an incentive to lie about their ability. An unskilled person will have a higher utility index if he can obtain a contract at b ($\bar{\bar{U}}_{AU}$) than he would have at a ($\bar{U}_{AU}$). Thus, like the craftsmen in their dealings with person A in Chapter 2, unskilled people may misrepresent their skill level and attempt to 'contaminate' high skill level firms. In response to this problem the firm may employ screening devices or skill indicators, as was briefly mentioned in Chapter 5. But clearly another mechanism is to monitor performance and allocate employees to skill categories within the firm.

4. WAGES, MORAL HAZARD AND ADVERSE SELECTION

The transactions-based view of the firm provides a rationalisation of simple hierarchy (interpreted loosely as the use of monitors) based upon an attempt to cope with moral hazard and adverse selection. As yet, however, we have no explanation of why the monitors in the hierarchy should be paid more than the people they are monitoring, why the people being monitored should have 'standard' contracts with the terms specified collectively rather than subject to individual bargaining, why recruitment into the hierarchy will occur at the lower levels, and so forth. These matters will be considered in later sections. For the moment it is possible to lead into these areas by investigating another fundamental problem. Monitoring employees will be useless unless the monitor can apply some sanctions in the event of shirking being detected. The 'monitoring gambles' of chapter 5 had to involve the employee in the risk of loss if observed effort were below standard. The precise mechanism involved in these monitoring gambles was not discussed in detail, however.

Suppose that a 'team' enterprise requires a monitor to ensure effort e is forthcoming from all its members. If effort is satisfactory a certain payment (or wage) will be paid. Where shirking is observed a penalty is exacted. The nature of this penalty is important. A reduction in the wage paid for bad service would create moral hazard problems of its own. The employee would have to trust that the firm would not deliberately 'observe' a low effort and penalise him dishonestly. Later we will discuss mechanisms which may help to mitigate this problem. For the present, let us assume that the objection to relying on the 'observations' of only *one* of the contracting parties is overwhelming and consider the consequences. How is a firm to penalise an employee observed shirking? The obvious answer, and one which we encountered in Chaper 4, is that the firm can simply fire the shirker and not use his services henceforth. This was the rationale behind the necessity of making Alchian and Demsetz's monitor a central contractual agent with the power to hire and fire. But, as Shapiro and Stiglitz (1984) recognise, the theoretical objection to this mechanism as it stands is that the 'penalty' depends upon general labour market conditions outside the firm. To take an extreme case, suppose that full employment prevailed and that any fired worker could *immediately* be re-employed elsewhere at the going competitive wage. The so-called penalty for being observed shirking is in fact completely absent and with it the incentive effects of monitoring.

It is tempting to object that people fired for shirking will not find re-employment easy. But this is to confuse the two separate problems of moral hazard and adverse selection. Employers may use indicators such as employment history to counter adverse selection, but Shapiro and Stiglitz explicitly assume that all workers are identical in order to abstract from this problem. Thus, firms in this situation *know* that there is no reason to prefer one person over another on grounds of differential skill or propensity to shirk. If a fired person comes to them for a job they will conclude either that the person was wrongly fired, as is always a possibility with monitoring gambles, as we saw in Chaper 5, or that the previous employer was not clever enough in setting the appropriate incentive structure and that *anyone* would have shirked in the same circumstances.

In the conditions specified, being fired *will* be a penalty to an employee if the firm pays a wage higher than that paid by other firms. Being a 'good employer' and paying higher wages can therefore be seen as part of the process of constructing monitoring gambles which will induce effort. Employees wish to avoid being fired because this will involve taking a lower wage elsewhere. Unfortunately, all firms can play the same game, and if each acts independently their common policy of raising wages above the 'norm' will sabotage any incentive effects from differential wages. All will end up paying higher wages and each will find the incentive effects much smaller than expected. If the differential wage mechanism fails to produce incentives, however, the overall result of a *general* increase in the wage level is to produce monitoring incentives from a different source. As the wage level rises with each firm's efforts to attach a penalty to being fired, the higher price of labour reduces the quantity demanded and increases the quantity supplied. An unemployment pool is the result. It is this unemployment pool, in Shapiro and Stiglitz's framework, which provides the 'penalty' required if monitoring is to be viable within the firm. With a pool of unemployment a fired worker will not be able to find new employment immediately. The expected length of time unemployed will be directly related to the size of the pool. Thus, if x workers are fired per period of time and x workers are hired and if the pool of unemployed is $10x$, there will be ten potential applicants for each available job per period, and hence a one in ten chance of gaining employment. The expected duration of unemployment will be ten periods. [6]

Shapiro and Stiglitz thus provide us with a model which predicts unemployment not as a short-term aberration, nor as a result of 'voluntary' job search along the lines of Stigler's approach to information acquisition discussed in Chapter 3, but as the outcome of attempts by firms to provide effort incentives through monitoring. [7] The resulting unemployment is clearly 'involuntary' in the sense that all the unemployed are prepared to accept jobs at the proferred wage level, but wage reductions will not occur because of each firm's desire to maintain an appropriate 'penalty' associated with terminating the contract of employment. As we saw in Chapter 5, not all monitoring gambles will be the same, and firms facing differing monitoring costs or differing consequences of shirking may construct different gambles. If monitoring costs are high, and the adverse consequences of shirking on the team are severe, a firm may wish to have a particularly substantial penalty associated with being fired. This will result in some firms paying higher wages for the same labour than other firms, and continuing to do so as a deliberate policy over time. Clearly this approach to unemployment is of considerable interest to macroeconomists, and the formal model can be manipulated to show how the size of the unemployment pool is expected to depend on factors such as unemployment pay. [8] Our purpose in discussing it here, however, is to show how it relates to the moral hazard problem and the internal monitoring environment of the firm.

The payment of wages above the market norm can also be seen as a response to the adverse selection problem in certain circumstances. If firms cannot tell skilled from unskilled workers and simply pick at random from a group of applicants, they will wish to increase the proportion of skilled applicants to total applicants. Where the 'reservation wage' of people (i.e. the wage below which they simply will not apply for the job) is positively related to their level of skill, the firms can persuade more skilled people to offer themselves for employment by setting a higher wage (Malcolmson, 1981). The use of this kind of mechanism implies, however, that internal monitoring of effort or skill is ineffective either for technical reasons or for the moral hazard reasons mentioned earlier. It also assumes that 'screening' devices are not available.[9]

Our discussion of incentives thus far has proceeded on the assumption that moral hazard prevents agreements which use the observations of the monitor to determine rewards. The result has been a system which uses the threat of terminating the agreement to induce effort, a threat which requires unemployment if it is to be effective. Implicitly, therefore, the 'hierarchy' under consideration is a very simple one in which monitors observe employees and fire those observed shirking. This incentive mechanism would not involve the necessity of a pool of unemployment if the employee could be brought to trust the integrity of the firm. As in the example of police incentives in Chapter 5, each employee could then 'post a bond' which he would forfeit if discovered shirking. 'Posting a bond' does not have to be interpreted literally in this context. An equivalent incentive is provided if the employee agrees to receive his remuneration not in a constant stream over time but in a stream which starts lower and rises through time. The employer gains at first by paying a relatively low wage but will have to repay the employee later when the wage is relatively high. Clearly the employee will have an incentive to avoid being fired, and monitoring will therefore involve a credible threat (Lazear, 1979, 1981). Working for a relatively low wage early on implies that the employee provides a 'hostage to fortune', and demonstrates in so doing a serious commitment to the firm. This brings us at last to the important question of what induces the firm to demonstrate a serious commitment to the employee? What induces the firm to monitor honestly and to refrain from firing the employee as soon as his wage reaches a level which implies repayment of his bond? As with the second-hand car salesman of Chapter 2 the answer to this question revolves around the value to the firm of a 'reputation' for honesty.

Although there are obvious short-term gains to cheating the

employee, firing people dishonestly is not costless for the firm. If people begin to doubt the firm's integrity they will no longer be willing to enter a long-term relationship involving bond posting, and hence the incentive effects of this system will no longer be available to the firm. The firm will have to pay higher wages to new entrants, the value of the bond will be lower or zero, and monitoring more costly and less effective. Thus an agreement between firm and employee is not something which can be considered as a single isolated event. If each bargain represented the outcome of a game between the two parties and was never to be repeated, the firm would have a clear incentive to cheat the employee if the latter agreed to the bond-posting scheme. But of course, in such circumstances no employee would do so. It is the fact that the game is repeated continuously and that cheating by the firm will have serious consequences for future agreements which induces the firm to comply, and gives the employee the confidence to enter this kind of implicit contract (Radner, 1981). We cannot conclude that the firm will never cheat, however. Clearly, there would be circumstances in which the gains from reneging on the implicit contract are so great that they outweigh the future costs. Thus, as Lazear (1979) puts it 'minimising cheating costs. . . will therefore trade off reduced worker cheating against increased firm cheating as (the time profile of wages) becomes more end weighted' (p. 1271).

'Reputation' or 'goodwill' are clearly central to the problem of establishing the viability of implicit contracts. These concepts can appear somewhat abstract at first, and they are certainly difficult to observe and measure objectively. This does not mean, however, that we have to accept them as exogenous and mysterious forces out of the reach of economic analysis. Building a reputation amounts to thinking of ways of making implicit agreements enforceable. An important factor will therefore involve demonstrating to potential employees that the firm is fulfilling its implicit obligations. In the case of the rising time profile of wages discussed by Lazear, how are the employees to know whether any workers fired were honestly considered by the firm to be shirking? What is required, it might be argued, is some *observable* signal which induces this type of confidence in employees. Malcolmson (1984) suggests that the mechanism of promotion through a hierarchy is capable of generating just this kind of confidence. Instead of promising to pay everyone a higher wage later conditional upon their avoiding being fired by exerting 'sufficient' effort the firm offers to pay a specified proportion of the workforce a higher wage later. The firm gives assurances that it will promote to higher-paid positions a certain fraction of its employees and that those people promoted will be the ones observed to be exerting the greatest effort. Such a scheme offers a number of advantages. First, it does not require any attempt to define what is a 'sufficient' level of effort to achieve promotion, although such an effort level may be implicit in the scheme. Second, implementation of the policy gives rise to an observable signal (the number of people actually promoted), which acts as an assurance that the firm is indeed sticking to its side of the bargain. Of course, it could be questioned whether those promoted really were those who were observed to have the highest productivity. The firm might economise on monitoring costs by promoting the required proportion at random. Once again, if it did so, all the incentive properties of the scheme would disappear and it will therefore be important to the firm to convince the workforce of its monitoring integrity. Effort devoted to monitoring by the firm is observable by the employees, however, and this observability of monitoring effort combined with the promotions commitment provides an assurance of the firm's honesty, unless there is some perverse reason for the firm to promote those who appear the least productive. [10]

5. THE RANK-ORDER TOURNAMENT

This suggestion that a proportion of the workforce be offered a 'prize' (promotion) is an application of the incentive structure underlying the rank-order tournament. In a tournament, compensation is based not on the absolute level of individual output, but simply on the rank order of contestants. Prizes are fixed in advance, and then allocated to contestants according to their position in the ranking. As in a sporting contest, the 'closeness' of the match in no way determines the rewards. Some contestants may be so evenly matched that separating them in the final may be a matter of the merest chance, and yet the ultimate winner may receive many times the reward of the runner-up. This type of incentive structure has been analysed by Lazear and Rosen (1981). They show that 'under certain conditions, a scheme which rewards rank yields an allocation of resources identical to that generated by the efficient piece rate' (p. 863). Here we present a very simple special case of Lazear and Rosen's result in order to illustrate in more detail how the tournament works.

Suppose that employees are risk neutral. Using the results of Chapter 5, it was indicated in section 2 of this chapter (p. 157) that if individual output is perfectly observable, a piece rate by which each employee receives his full marginal product will be efficient. The analysis up to that point had assumed only two effort levels, zero and *e*, but the efficiency property of the piece rate under risk neutrality is maintained even when effort can take on a continuum of values. Since the person exerting additional effort receives the entire extra output produced under this piece-rate scheme, effort will be applied until the marginal costs incurred just equal the output which results. To make the example more concrete let person *j*'s output be directly related to his effort as follows:

$$\Pi_j = e_j + \theta_j$$

where Π_j = person *j*'s output, e_j = person *j*'s level of effort, θ_j is a random element with mean zero.

Further, let person *j* face a quadratic cost of effort function:

$$C(e_j) = \tfrac{1}{2}ae_j^2.$$

Maximising expected output net of effort costs will result in the simple first-order condition:

$$1 = ae_j \quad \text{or} \quad e_j = 1/a. \tag{6.1}$$

Now consider the case of a tournament. We will assume that two people are involved, persons *j* and *k*, and that their individual outputs are impossible to observe. Thus, although they are both risk neutral, a piece-rate scheme cannot be devised and they will be rewarded on the basis of observed effort. Even the observation of effort is subject to error, however, and we suppose for the sake of the illustrations that the distribution of this error is uniform. Two prizes are set in advance (Π_1 and Π_2 with $\Pi_1 > \Pi_2$). The person with the highest observed effort will receive Π_1; the other will receive Π_2. How will the behaviour of person *j* be affected by this scheme?

The expected outcome for person *j* may be written as:

$$E_j(\Pi) = P[\Pi_1 - C(e_j)] + (1 - P)[\Pi_2 - C(e_j)] \tag{6.2}$$

where P is the probability of winning the tournament and hence the prize Π_1. As a risk-neutral individual, person j will choose an effort level which maximises the value of this expected outcome. Effort will have two effects on expression 6.2. It will increase the costs incurred ($C'(e_j) > 0$) but it will also increase the probability of winning the prize Π_1 ($\partial P/\partial e_j > 0$). As usual the first-order condition for maximisation will ensure that marginal benefits and costs of effort are equated. Marginal expected benefits of extra effort are simply $(\Pi_1 - \Pi_2)\ \partial P/\partial e_j$ thus; [11]

$$(\Pi_1 - \Pi_2)\ \frac{\partial P}{\partial e_j} = C'(e_j). \qquad (6.3)$$

The dependence of P on j's effort now requires closer investigation. Let e_j^* be the monitor's *observation* of j's effort. As we have set up the problem this will be subject to an error θ_j, once more with mean zero. Thus:

$$e_j^* = e_j + \theta_j.$$

Person j wins the prize Π_1 if $e_j^* > e_k^*$ where e_k^* is the monitor's observation of person k's effort. We suppose that the error associated with observation of person k, θ_k, is distributed in exactly the same way as that associated with observing person j. Thus:

$$e_j^* - e_k^* = (e_j + \theta_j) - (e_k + \theta_k) = (e_j - e_k) - (\theta_k - \theta_j)$$

and

$$P(e_j^* > e_k^*) = P(\theta_k - \theta_j < e_j - e_k). \qquad (6.4)$$

The probability that j will be observed to work harder than k therefore depends upon how hard he really does work relative to k. The larger is $e_j - e_k$ the less likely it is that observational errors will be big enough to cause a perverse result to the tournament. This is what gives person j the incentive to exert effort.

To make the example still more specific the uniform (rectangular) distribution of θ_k and θ_j is sketched in Figure 6.4. The distribution $f(\theta)$ is assumed to range from $-\frac{1}{2}$ to $+\frac{1}{2}$. Thus it is possible, though very unlikely, that person j may be observed to have exerted effort $e_j + \frac{1}{2}$ or $e_j - \frac{1}{2}$. The probability is 0.5 that person j will be observed working harder than he does in fact work, and 0.5 that he will be observed working less hard. From (6.4), however, we see that the matter of most interest to person j will be the distribution

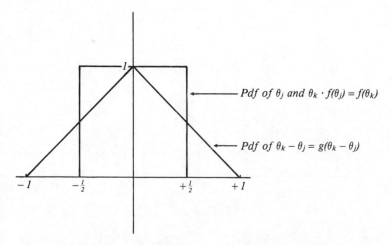

Figure 6.4: Distribution of observational errors

of $(\theta_k - \theta_j)$, that is, the *difference* in observational errors. Clearly person j will not mind if the monitor underestimates how hard he is working if the monitor also underestimates how hard person k is working by an equivalent or bigger amount. The distribution $g(\theta_k - \theta_j)$ is shown in Figure 6.4. Its shape may be intuitively understood by taking a discrete example and assuming that the monitor's errors will be either $-\frac{1}{2}$, 0, or $+\frac{1}{2}$ with equal probabilities. Clearly, if $\theta_k = \frac{1}{2}$ and $\theta_j = -\frac{1}{2}$, $\theta_k - \theta_j = 1$. This is the biggest value that $\theta_k - \theta_j$ can take, and is very unlikely since there is only one way it can happen. A value of $\theta_k - \theta_j = \frac{1}{2}$ is more likely since there are two ways this might occur ($\theta_k = \frac{1}{2}$, $\theta_j = 0$; and $\theta_k = 0$, $\theta_j = -\frac{1}{2}$). Finally, there are three ways $\theta_k - \theta_j = 0$ can occur (the monitor makes the same or no error for both persons j and k, $\theta_k = -\frac{1}{2}$, $\theta_j = -\frac{1}{2}$, etc.).

Figure 6.5 sketches the cumulative distribution function $G(\theta_k - \theta_j)$, that is, it indicates the probability of $\theta_k - \theta_j$ being less than or equal to the specified value. Clearly $\theta_k - \theta_j$ is certain to be less than or equal to $+1$ and cannot fall below -1. The function cuts the vertical axis at $P = \frac{1}{2}$ since $P(\theta_k - \theta_j < 0) = \frac{1}{2}$. Suppose now that person k exerts no effort ($e_k = 0$), what should person j do? Clearly, if person j also remains idle ($e_j = 0$), the probability that he will win the tournament will be $\frac{1}{2}$. But by working harder $e_j > 0$ the probability of winning rises above $\frac{1}{2}$. Indeed, if $e_j = 1$, person j would

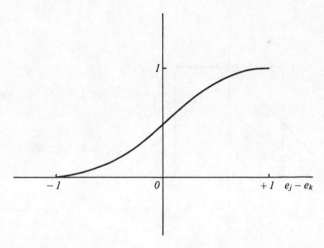

Figure 6.5: Cumulative distribution function of $\theta_k - \theta_j \cdot G(\theta_k - \theta_j)$

be certain of winning the tournament even in the unluckiest circumstances. He will not go this far, however, but as expression 6.3 indicates, will equate marginal benefits and costs of effort. Figure 6.6 shows the utility-maximising effort levels $\bar{e}_j$ of person j for three different effort levels of person k. Where $\bar{e}_k = 0$ the marginal benefit curve

$$\Pi^* \frac{\partial P}{\partial e_j} = \Pi^* g(e_j)$$

cuts the marginal cost curve at $\bar{e}_j = \Pi^*/(\Pi^* + a)$ with $\Pi^* = \Pi_1 - \Pi_2$. Where $\bar{e}_k = \Pi^*/a$ the marginal benefit curve becomes $\Pi^* g(e_j - \Pi^*/a)$ and $\bar{e}_j = \Pi^*/a$. Yet higher levels of effort on the part of person k cause j to reduce his effort until where $\bar{e}_k = 1$ the marginal cost of effort is everywhere above the marginal benefit and $\bar{e}_j = 0$. From the figure it is seen that we have assumed $a > \Pi^*$. This is to ensure that the second-order conditions are always fulfilled (the marginal benefit curves always cut the marginal cost curve from above).

By plotting utility-maximising values of e_j for different values of e_k, person j's 'reaction curve' is traced out. Figure 6.6 is enough to deduce its general shape, but it is a simple matter in this specific example to determine the exact expression. Substituting the explicit

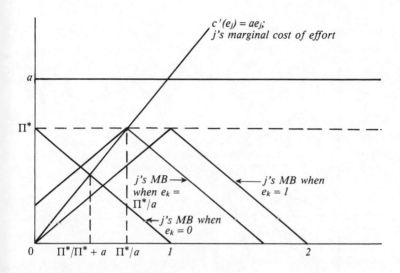

j's marginal benefit curve when $e_k = 0$ is $\Pi^* g(e_j)$.
When $e_k = \Pi^*/a$, j's marginal benefit curve is $\Pi^* g(e_j - \Pi^*/a)$
When $e_k = 1$, j's marginal benefit curve is $\Pi_g^* (e_j - 1)$.

Figure 6.6

functional expressions for the general form of (6.3) we obtain:

$$\Pi^*[1 - (e_j - e_k)] = ae_j, \ (e_k \leqslant \Pi^*/a),$$

and

$$\Pi^*[1 + (e_j - e_k)] = ae_j, \ (e_k \geqslant \Pi^*/a).$$

Hence

$$e_j = [\Pi^*/(a + \Pi^*)] + [\Pi^*/a + \Pi^*]e_k, \ (e_k \leqslant \Pi^*/a)$$

and

$$e_j = [\Pi^*/(a - \Pi^*)] - [\Pi^*/(a - \Pi^*)]e_k, \ (e_k \geqslant \Pi^*/a). \quad (6.5)$$

As we would expect, these expressions confirm that, for any given value of e_k, a bigger value of Π^* (i.e. a large spread between the prizes) will induce greater effort from person j. Further, for given e_k and Π^* a smaller value of a will increase j's effort (marginal costs of effort are rising less steeply). Figure 6.7 illustrates person j's reaction curve labelled jcj'. Symmetrical reasoning establishes

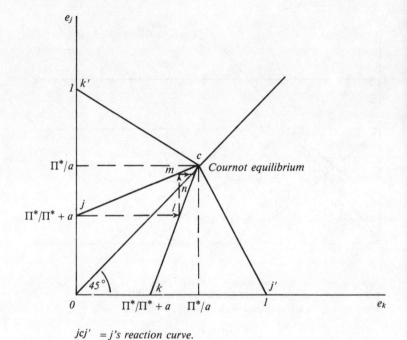

jcj' = *j*'s reaction curve.
kck' = *k*'s reaction curve.

Figure 6.7

person *k*'s reaction curve as *kck'* . For any given value of e_j it gives us *k*'s utility-maximising response.

The reaction curves of persons *j* and *k* intersect at point *c*. This point is called a Cournot or Nash equilibrium. Given *k*'s effort, person *j* is maximising his utility; and given *j*'s effort, person *k* is maximising his. Neither person *j* nor person *k* will wish to move away from point *c* therefore. We might envisage the approach to point *c* in dynamic terms with each person responding to the moves of the other along a path such as *j,l,m,n*, in the diagram. Given the symmetry of the two reaction curves, it is seen that point *c* lies on a 45° line and hence that both persons *j* and *k* end up working equally hard.

Notice that this result is a distinctive feature of the 'rat race'. If both individuals could arrange to limit their efforts, both would be better off. With $e_k = e_j = 0$ each person will still have a 0.5 probability of winning the tournament and will have saved all the effort costs. The two persons could agree never to turn up to work early in the morning or to leave late at night, never to take less than an hour and a half for lunch, never to work at home, never to flatter the boss, and so forth. But if this type of agreement cannot be enforced and policed, or if we envisage each individual as competing against large numbers of other people whose behaviour is taken as largely beyond any personal influence, the efforts of each person to 'get ahead' will be mutually frustrating. All people finish the week tired out from their efforts to win the tournament, and no one is any more likely to do so than they would have been had everyone stayed in bed.

As seen from expression (6.5) the amount of effort stimulated by the tournament depends upon Π^*, the difference between the two prizes. If Π^* were set equal to 1, the Cournot equilibrium would involve each person exerting effort equal to $1/a$. But this level of effort is precisely that forthcoming under the efficient piece-rate scheme outlined at the beginning of this section (expression 6.1). Thus the two prizes $\Pi_1 = (1/a) + \frac{1}{2}$, and $\Pi_2 = (1/a) - \frac{1}{2}$ will induce the same effort from the two contestants as the efficient piece rate. Because the contestants are risk neutral they will be equally happy under a piece-rate scheme or competing in a tournament with the prizes set so as to induce the same level of effort. Unlike the piece-rate scheme, however, the tournament does not require us to be able to measure on a cardinal scale each person's output: it merely requires that we can rank their performance in terms of more or less, better or worse. On the other hand, the tournament does require that the 'correct' prizes are set, and here we may once again imagine a competitive process of trial and error at work. A firm which sets $\Pi^* > 1$ will obtain greater effort from the contestants. The extra output generated by this additional effort will fall short of the costs incurred by the employees, however, and their expected utility $E(\Pi)$ will fall (expression 6.2). Thus a firm which hits upon the 'correct' structure of prizes will be able to attract contestants from firms who encourage 'too much' or 'too little' effort.

Notice the similarity between the 'monitoring gambles' discussed in Chapter 5, the 'bond-posting' incentive structure discussed in section 4 of this chapter, and the tournament. In the tournament the employee receives $(1/a) + \frac{1}{2}$ if he is lucky and $(1/a) - \frac{1}{2}$ if he is unlucky. Thus it looks similar to any other monitoring gamble. The only difference is that receiving the bigger prize does not depend upon achieving any particular satisfactory level of performance. It depends entirely on how a person performs relative to others. With the monitoring gambles of Chapter 5 all employees *might* have been observed working, and hence all would have their bond returned. Indeed if a worker could never be mistaken for an idler ($q_{0e} = 0$) all people putting in the required effort *would* certainly receive the larger reward. In the case of the tournament discussed above, however, one person wins and the other loses even though they are both predicted to exert the same level of effort.

It is important to remember that our exposition of the tournament assumed that employees were risk neutral. The fact that piece rates and tournaments can be made equivalent under these conditions does not mean that they can *always* be made equivalent. Risk aversion will obviously complicate matters considerably, and everything will depend upon the risks associated with piece rates compared with the risks associated with the best constructed tournament. The tournament replaces a whole distribution of possible outcomes with just two prizes. In so doing it removes many possible outcomes in the 'middle' of the distribution (in our example around $1/a$). This will clearly not be attractive to a risk-averse person. On the other hand, the two prizes set a limit on the range of possible outcomes and may rule out extremely disastrous or very favourable occurrences, and this is obviously attractive in the context of risk aversion.[12] A direct comparison between piece rates and tournaments is not of central concern here, however. The important point is that tournaments may be a viable form of incentive structure in circumstances where piece rates are not feasible because individual marginal products cannot be observed.

Lazear and Rosen's analysis of the tournament helps to make sense of many features of hierarchical firms which would otherwise be very perplexing. The high salaries of top corporate executives often draw adverse comment from people who correctly observe that these salaries can hardly be explained on the basis of very high productivity. But 'productivity' is not objectively measurable in many circumstances, and it seems reasonable to suppose that the observed salary structure represents a set of tournament prizes: 'This interpretation suggests that presidents of large corporations do not necessarily earn high wages because they are more productive as presidents but because this particular type of payment structure makes them more productive over their entire working lives' (p. 847). Reward at any one time will not reflect actual or even expected product. In our example both people worked equally hard and produced the same output $1/a$, yet their rewards differed, with one person getting more and the other less than their product. Monitoring costs will play a crucial role in determining whether or not tournaments are used. Tournaments require that each person's performance is compared qualitatively with that of everyone else, whereas with piece rates each person can be rewarded without reference to other people. Thus 'salesmen, whose output level is easily observed, typically are paid by piece rates, whereas corporate executives, whose output is more difficult to observe, engage in contests' (p. 848). A similar observation was made at the end of Chapter 5 (p. 145), but there promotion through a hierarchy was seen as dependent upon achieving satisfactory effort, whereas here we are perceiving it as a prize in a tournament.

6. IDIOSYNCRATIC EXCHANGE

The analysis of sections 3 to 5 helps us to rationalise some of the characteristics of hierarchical structures. Even in the context of *identical* employees performing *identical* tasks it is possible to understand the development of recognisable hierarchies. We have seen that the provision of effort incentives where individual output cannot be identified or where employees are risk averse may involve the use of monitoring gambles and hence:

(a) the use of monitors to measure effort:

(b) wages rising faster than productivity over time (Lazear) with mandatory retirement after a certain point, or;

(c) the use of 'tournament-like' incentive schemes whereby the firm undertakes to pronounce a certain fraction of its employees as 'winners' by promoting them to higher-paid positions (Lazear and Rosen, 1981, Malcolmson, 1984).

These ideas depend simply on the existence of moral hazard and the assumed propensity of people to shirk if they are not being monitored. They thus relate most closely to the discussion of 'team production' in Chapter 4. The fact that certain hierarchical features are explicable on this basis alone is significant, since theorists usually prefer their work to depend upon the weakest assumptions possible. Yet is has to be admitted that the models discussed so far produce only the barest outlines of a hierarchy, stripped of the complexity associated with the organisation of large firms. For a less austere approach, richer in its implications for internal structure, we now return to the work of Williamson (1975).

It will be recalled from Chapter 2 that person *A*, in his attempts to extend his house, faced many transactional problems other than the simple inability to observe the effort of the workmen involved. It was of the essence of person *A*'s problem that potential craftsmen were *not* of identical ability, that the different people in the team had *different* jobs to do, and that person *A* was not, and could not become, apprised of the best way of performing the different tasks involved. Certain information and certain types of skill were inevitably associated with the actual business of performing the job in question and would not be available on equal terms to person *A*. This type of knowledge was considered also in Chapter 3, where the scope for entrepreneurial reward from Hayek's 'knowledge of time and place' was discussed. Further, *A* confronted the 'bounded rationality' problem, the plain incapacity to calculate all possible best responses to every conceivable set of contingencies. Williamson's approach to hierarchies is rooted in an appreciation of these more varied but very fundamental transactional difficulties.

All people have their own special skills and attributes, and all tasks are idiosyncratic to some degree. As Doeringer and Piore (1971) put it: 'almost every job involves some specific skills.... The apparently routine operation of standard machines can be importantly aided by familiarity with the particular piece of operating equipment.... Moreover... a critical skill is the ability to operate effectively with the given members of the team.' (p. 15). At the risk of repetition, note again the difference between this observation as the starting point for analysis, and the models of sections 4 and 5 which assume away task idiosyncracy and differential skills. If, as a matter of observation, people and jobs are all special to some degree, transactions cannot be regarded as 'standard'. Each transaction has its own features which are unique, and the central agent or firm will find itself bargaining continually in a situation of bilateral monopoly and with asymmetrically distributed information. The possibilties available to the employee in these circumstances for 'opportunistic behaviour' were discussed in detail in Chapter 2. As Williamson defines it (1975b, pp. 258–9): 'opportunism is an effort to realise individual gains through a lack of candour or honesty in transactions. It is a somewhat deeper variety of self-interest seeking assumption than is ordinarily employed in economics; opportunism is self-interest seeking with guile'. Employees enter the firm and gradually become skilled and adept at specific tasks. This specialised knowledge gives the incumbent employee 'first-mover advantages' over potential replacements from outside and thus places the employee in a bargaining position which he may try to exploit in negotiations with the firm. Essentially Williamson sees most of the characteristics of employment hierarchies as a response to the transactional difficulties posed by 'small-numbers bargaining' and 'opportunistic behaviour'. Before proceeding to outline the mechanisms which are supposed to cope with 'opportunism', it will be useful to reflect in more detail on its nature and in particular on its relationship to the subject matter of Chapter 3—'entrepreneurship'.

7. RENT SEEKING, ENTREPRENEURSHIP AND OPPORTUNISM

The entrepreneur is nothing if not an opportunist. Without the ability to perceive opportunities and to make use of them while they last, resource reallocation and the efficiency gains which accompany them could not occur. From the hero of Chapter 3 however, the opportunist has unaccountably become the villain of Chapter 6, whose fiendish unreliability the whole paraphernalia of hierarchical organisations are designed to counteract. How are we to explain this unexpected change of view? The answer is basically simple in outline although often extraordinarily complex in detail. It revolves around the distinction between rent seeking and entrepreneurship. Entrepreneurship, as we saw at length in Chapter 3, produces efficiency gains. It extends our knowledge of the available possibilities for division of labour and exchange. The entrepreneur trades in property rights and, if successful, receives an entrepreneurial profit from the efficiency gains he has created. Rent seeking is behaviour aimed at acquiring or asserting property rights other than by voluntary exchange. Resources are expended in efforts merely to redistribute income.

Tullock (1980a) defines rent seeking as follows: 'an individual who invests in something that will not actually improve productivity or will actually lower it, but that does raise his income because it gives him some special position or monopoly power, is 'rent seeking' and the 'rent' is the income derived' (p. 17). The idea grew initially out of dissatisfaction with the conventional approach to measuring social losses due to monopoly. Monopoly profits in received theory are not part of the social costs of monopoly. They merely represent transfers from consumers who are worse off, to monopoly producers who are better off. Tullock argued, however, that if it were possible to receive profits by creating monopolies, people would invest resources in 'monopoly-creating activities'. Further, the resources 'invested' in total could equal or even on occasions far exceed (Tullock, 1980b) the monopoly profits obtained by the eventual holder of the monopoly. Thus the profits of monopolists attract attempts to gain monopoly privileges, and the resources expended in these attempts to gain monopoly privileges, and the resources expended in these attempts are part of the 'efficiency loss' associated with monopoly. A similar argument applies in cases where tariff protection is sought. Consumers lose and protected producers gain from measures to restrict foreign trade, but if these producer 'gains' are available, producers will expend effort and resources in lobbying and pressuring politicians to grant them protection. These political efforts are 'rent seeking' and represent social losses.

The archetypal form of rent seeking is theft. Theft involves a simple redistribution of resources and diverts activity from production and exchange to either thieving itself or protection from thieving. Burglar alarms, locks and other security devices use up scarce resources and are a response to a purely redistributional activity. To quote Tullock again: 'as a successful theft will stimulate other thieves to greater industry and require greater investment in protective measures, so each successful establishment of a monopoly or creation of a tariff will stimulate greater diversion of resources to attempts to organise further transfers of income' (1980c, pp. 48–9). The contrast between gaining from theft and gaining from the encouragement of fully voluntary exchange is the essential contrast between rent seeking and entrepreneurship. Readers should be aware that this use of the terms 'rent seeking' and 'entrepreneurship' is not fully agreed upon. Rent seeking is sometimes broken down into different types and an entrepreneur is often simply viewed as any rent seeker. Entrepreneurs do seek, and if successful receive, a form of rent (the efficiency gains created) and thus it is understandable that they should be seen as rent seekers. But the term 'rent seeking' is now so closely associated with the pursuit of income transfers, and the theory of entrepreneurship so intimately associated with the pursuit of efficiency gains, that the suggested distinction between rent seeking and entrepreneurship seems both useful and tenable.

When presented as the difference between theft and voluntary exchange, nothing might seem more clear-cut than the difference between rent seeking and entrepreneurship.[13] Yet detailed cases can give rise to conceptual problems. These problems will ultimately derive from ambiguities about property rights. If rent seeking involves a form of theft it must, as Sisk (1985) emphasises, imply the infringement of someone's property rights: 'Rent-seeking emerges when rights are challengeable' (p. 96). In the case of monopoly, considered above, the right of people to use resources in the monopolised trade was restricted by government decree. Thus, people's rights to use their resources (their property rights, see Chapter 4) have been restricted by the activities of the rent seeker, and the result is an uncompensated transfer. Similarly, if person A pays another to do some shopping and the shopper (an opportunist) lies about the price of the items purchased, a theft has taken place. The fact that person A may not know with certainty that he has been robbed does not affect the issue. His property rights have been infringed by the rent seeker and the knowledge that he is vulnerable to this type of rent seeking will presumably reduce his use of the shopper, or restrict it to items for which receipts (somehow made tamper proof) can be obtained.

Consider now the case of the artistically inclined entrepreneur of Chapter 3 who notices a valuable picture hanging in the house of an unsuspecting old lady. He offers her a sum sufficient to acquire the picture and makes a fortune. Has the old lady been robbed? Most of us would be inclined initially to say that she had, and that this action was rent seeking. Yet in principle this is clearly not the case. No uncompensated transfer took place and no property rights were infringed. Our trader with knowledge of the art market was an entrepreneur. There is no economic principle which says that entrepreneurs, even as we have defined them, will be generous to old ladies (which is not to say, of course, that they *ought* not to be).

Suppose, however, that we change the story so that the old lady shrewdly suspects that her picture is valuable and approaches an expert with an offer to pay for his professional advice. The professional adviser lies to her, purchases the item, and again makes a fortune by reselling at a huge profit. This is rent seeking because it involves the adviser implicitly challenging the old lady's right to the information for which she had paid. Trade in information gives rise to many problems, but the most fundamental is that of establishing clear and policeable property rights. It would, no doubt, be difficult to *prove* that the adviser had abridged the lady's property rights: 'I really had no idea at the time that the picture would prove to be so valuable'. But this is simply to reiterate the basic point that the lower the cost of challenging a person's property rights, the more likely they are to be challenged, and hence the greater will be the amount of rent seeking. Property rights in information are eminently challengeable.

The use of the word 'theft' in the context of rent seeking requires care. It is clearly a useful analogy, but the more neutral 'uncompensated transfer' is a less value-loaded term. If a group of businessmen lobby the politicians and receive a subsidy for their industry they are rent seeking. The tax mechanism is used to transfer resources from one group of people to another. An uncompensated transfer occurs and with it the attenuation of the taxpayer's property rights. But although some of us are apt to declaim on occasions that 'all taxation is theft', from a legal point of view this is obviously not so, and to avoid confusion it is better that theft be considered the archetypal case rather than the defining characteristic of rent seeking.[14]

A case closer to the problem of employer and employee is that of the plumber and person A in Chapter 2. A plumber who installs a system of unnecessary technical sophistication to heat a customer's house is a rent seeker. The resources expended are pure waste and the customer's rights to the information possessed by the plumber have been implicitly challenged. Contrast this with a plumber who, after finalising an agreement with person A, perceives new opportunities which will enable the same objectives to be achieved at much lower cost. He returns to person A and renegotiates the agreement. In the process he deliberately understates the cost-reducing characteristics of his discovery and succeeds in making a large profit. Is he a rent seeker or an entrepreneur? Everything depends upon our understanding of the contractual relationship between the plumber and person *A*. If the plumber had signed a contract saying 'I undertake to serve person *A* in the capacity of plumber over the following period and faithfully promise to use all the information at my disposal during this period in the interests of person *A*', the activities of the plumber in attempting to mislead person *A* could be construed as rent seeking. The plumber is renouncing the provisions of a contract. This is, of course, precisely what happens when a person paid by time rate shirks. But if the plumber's contract merely states 'I undertake to install a heating system which meets the following specifications', the use of new information to achieve this end at lower cost is pure entrepreneurship. If the contract actually specifics the exact equipment to be installed so that renegotiation is necessary before the new information can be used, the plumber may be less than candid about the cost advantages of the new system and vastly underestimate them, but no one has ever claimed that entrepreneurs must be frank. They merely fulfil their contractual obligations. A person paid by piece rate who discovers methods of improving his output is an entrepreneur, and may not be required contractually to inform his employer of these developments.[15]

Our discussion of principal and agent in Chapter 5 can thus be recast in terms of rent seeking and entrepreneurship. The contractual problem was to find mechanisms which would reduce rent seeking and channel attention away from attempts to challenge property rights towards attempts to achieve more effective coordination of resources. For Williamson this is also the function of hierarchical organisations. Both rent seekers and entrepreneurs are opportunists. But institutional structures determine the returns available from opportunist contract breaking and opportunist contract making and contract fulfilment. The baby of entrepreneurship sits, if we can adapt a popular metaphor, in the bathwater of rent seeking, and the function of hierarchies is to jettison the latter whilst somehow retaining the former. This extraordinary manoeuvre is beset with difficulty, and it is even rumoured that attempts have ended with the baby ousted and the performer drenched with the bathwater. In the next section we consider Williamson's observations on the procedures which make this result less likely.

8. INTERNAL LABOUR MARKETS

A description of the major 'contracting modes' (the spot contract, the state-contingent contract and the authority relation) has already been presented at the end of Chapter 2, along with a brief outline of Williamson's criticism of these modes (pp. 38–41). Bounded rationality and opportunistic behaviour deriving from task idiosyncracy imply, he argues, that alternative contractual arrangements have advantages over each of these forms of contract. As has been recognised at many points in this book, contracting in circumstances of asymmetrically distributed information is facilitated by 'reputation' and 'trust'. But it is fundamental to our approach to the firm that instead of *assuming* the existence of this 'reputation' and 'trust', institutional mechanisms are seen as the means by which confidence in the integrity of others can be encouraged. In Williamson's view the internal labour market represents an institutional response to the problem of opportunism, and elicits more cooperative behaviour from employees than would be possible under spot or state-contingent contracting.

Consider yet again the problem faced by the firm. If requires a person to perform some task. This task involves skills which are not general and cannot be used to aid performance in other lines of activity. They are *specific* skills (to use Becker's (1964) terminology). They are useful in the highly particular context of the firm, and some may be acquired only by on-the-job training, as in the case of 'knowledge of time and place' mentioned in section 6. Human capital theory concludes that the costs of *general* training, which increases the productivity of people in lines of activity both inside and outside the firm, will be borne by the individual concerned, whereas the costs of *specific* training will be borne by the firm. This argument depends on the idea that the firm will not pay for the general training of employees because they may then be enticed away to higher-paid jobs elsewhere and the firm will lose its investment. The firm cannot trust the employee. On the other hand, the employee will not pay the cost of specific training because this implies accepting a lower reward than could be obtained elsewhere during the training period. Higher rewards would be forthcoming *after* the training period, but this implies that the employee must trust the firm, and the traditional argument of human capital theory assumes this will not happen. Instead the firm pays for the specific training.

As we saw in section 6, however, a firm which pays for *specific* training might still itself be the victim of opportunism. An employee, by threatening to leave, is capable of inflicting large costs on the firm which would face the prospect of having to invest more resources in the training of another outsider. In the context of full employment the threat would be costless and hence credible (see section 4). Thus the conventional distinction between types of training, general and specific, and the conclusion that these are financed by the individual and the firm respectively, depends upon the assumption that employees do not trust firms but that in the realm of *specific* training firms have to trust employees. [16] Note that the opportunism of the employee is here a form of rent seeking and that the implicit challenge is to the employer's property rights in the 'specific human capital' he has financed. Just as with property rights in information, property rights in human capital [17] are difficult to establish and police for obvious reasons, and are therefore challengeable.

Unlike the conclusions of human capital theory, the upshot of Williamson's approach is a greater emphasis on the employee trusting the firm. The primary characteristic of the 'internal labour market' is that employees do not bargain individually over terms and conditions with the employer. Instead, a person joining a firm will be assigned to a certain grade in the hierarchy and will receive whatever remuneration attaches to that grade: 'The internal labour market achieves a fundamental transformation by shifting to a system where wage rates attach mainly to jobs rather than to workers' (1975b, p. 270). By 'job' here, Williamson *et al.* are not referring to a single idiosyncratic task but to a broad category of tasks attached to which are standard terms of employment. Because individual bargaining is ruled out 'the incentives to behave opportunistically...are correspondingly attenuated' (p. 271). The employee voluntarily accepts these constraints on his own freedom of action in the knowledge that others will be similarly constrained. Of course, while this procedure mitigates the problem of rent seeking through attempts to mislead the employer in an unending bargaining process, it does not in itself prevent shirking. Willliamson argues, however, that the promotion ladder is designed to counter this form of rent seeking and to encourage 'consummate' instead of 'perfunctory' cooperation. 'Consummate cooperation is an affirmative job attitude—to include the use of judgement, filling gaps, and taking initiative in an instrumental way. Perfunctory cooperation, by contrast, involves job performance of a minimally acceptable sort' (1975b, p. 266). Thus Williamson's approach is very closely related to the ideas of Lazear and others (sections 4 and 5) on the incentive effects of a rising profile of earnings over time. The additional element is an explanation of the hierarchical characteristic that each individual is not treated as a special case but is, at any one time, the holder of a 'standard' contract applying to a particular grade. From this perspective it no longer follows therefore that firms will finance specific training. If the worker accepts a lower wage at first which reflects his lower productivity as he gradually becomes acquainted with the idiosyncracies of the task, he effectively 'posts a bond' as discussed at length earlier. In so doing he is forced to trust the firm. But why should we expect the employee to trust the firm rather than the other way around?

For any exchange transaction to take place, even of the most basic 'bread for beer' variety, someone has to trust someone else. At the end of section 4 it was shown that the firm's 'reputation' would suffer in the long run if it cheated on its implicit agreements. A strand in the argument was missing at that stage, however. In principle, the same 'reputation-protecting' argument could be applied to employees to show that *they* might lose in the long run if the firm trusted them and they cheated. Clearly 'reputations' in the labour market may be important, and we shall see later that some writers have used this possibility as a limiting factor to managerial cheating of shareholders (Fama, 1980). However, it is usual to argue that, for most types of employee, 'reputations' are difficult, that is, costly to create. As Klein (1984) puts it 'A firm generally has lower costs of creating brand name capital and hence contract fulfilment credibility because of its increased repeat purchase frequency' (p. 333). In other words a single firm's integrity is tested each period in its dealings with each of its employees. Because it is a 'central contractual agent' it is party to many contracts, whereas each employee is party to only one. Further the working lifetime of a joint-stock firm is not limited in the same way as the working lifetime of employees (although bankruptcy can 'terminate' a firm's life). Thus 'cheating firms are likely to become known more quickly than cheating workers, reducing the short-run cheating potential of firms relative to workers' (p. 333). Note that this is an application of Stigler's (1964a) idea that firms themselves are more likely to cheat on Cartel arrangements by price shading if there are only a few customers than if there are very many, because detection is less likely in the former case. A single employee may only serve a few customers (employers) in a lifetime, and although a good 'track record' of reliability is not worthless, the difficulties of communicating such a record to potential employers (the source of the adverse selection problem) imply high costs of creating this type of 'brand name capital' as Klein calls it. Contrary to conventional human capital theory, therefore, 'the worker can be expected to make much of the specific investment and the firm guarantee that it will not hold up [18] the worker by reducing his wage below the value of his marginal product' (Klein, 1984, p. 333).

The internal labour market reduces the return to opportunism and encourages cooperation by replacing individual bargaining with a set of standard contracts and the promise of promotion. These standard contracts, concerning as they do the relationship of employer and employee over a substantial period of time, cannot be comprehensive in their provisions because of the problem of bounded rationality. As time advances, therefore, disputes will arise concerning the precise interpretation of the vague terminology of the standard contract. In my own case, for example, a contract requires that as a reader in economics I 'perform the duties which are customary for such posts in universities in Great Britain and shall include teaching, research, examining, and if so directed administration'. Whether a daily chore of making the tea for the vice-chancellor could be considered as 'administration' or 'research' would have to be settled by arbitration procedures. The establishment of these arbitration and grievance procedures is thus an integral part of the internal labour market, and is closely associated with the role of trade unions or other associations of employees. Trade unions can be seen as monitoring the firm's commitment to its implicit obligations (Malcolmson, 1982), making 'shirking' by the firm less likely and increasing the confidence of employees in the working of the internal labour market.

9. THE FIRM AS A 'GOVERNANCE STRUCTURE'

Moral hazard, adverse selection and bounded rationality imply that all transactions must involve trust, and that all transactions involve problems of policing and enforcement. The firm can be seen as a highly developed mechanism of contract enforcement, a 'governance structure' (Williamson, 1979). Enforcement mechanisms will vary with the type of contract involved and the hazards to which it gives rise. Some transactions are highly standardised and involve limited problems of moral hazard. In Chapter 2 we discussed Alchian's (1979) rationalisation of money as a device to 'standardise' transactions through the use of a medium about which everyone was well informed. Thus traditional markets are a form of governance structure appropriate for the exchange of money and other standard products. As Williamson (1979) puts it: 'highly standardised transactions are not apt to require a specialised governance structure' (p. 248). Where very idiosyncratic transactions are concerned and knowledge is asymmetrically distributed, exchange may be inhibited unless confidence can be established. This confidence requires a continuing association between the transactors and where recurrent transactions are possible to arrange a 'highly specialised governance structure' (p. 248) called the firm can develop.

Before leaving the subject of hierarchies and the internal labour market it is necessary to suppress any impression that the firm 'solves' the transactional problems we have been considering. Examples of rent seeking in hierarchical organisations are hardly unknown, and a cooperative attitude is clearly not the same as an entrepreneurial one. Williamson, as we have seen, includes as a type of 'cooperation' the use of 'judgement' which is for Casson (Chapter 3) the defining characteristic of the entrepreneur. Yet cooperative people are not always those who take initiative and use judgement, and those who use their judgement are not always very cooperative. Cooperative people 'tow the line' instead of confusing matters by suggesting different lines to tow or arguing that everyone should be pulling in a different direction. The internal labour market may encourage cooperation, but it is much less clear that it encourages initiative. In a hierarchical organisation the returns to 'consummate cooperation' have long been recognised. Sir Joseph Porter KBE was certainly very cooperative. Indeed, it would be difficult to imagine cooperation more consummate than was Sir Joseph's:

> I always voted at my party's call,
> I never thought of thinking for myself at all,
> I thought so little they rewarded me,
> And now I an the ruler of the Queen's Navy.

The baby certainly seems to have disappeared with the bathwater here. But perhaps this is not what Williamson has in mind.

NOTES

1. For an excellent overview for the uninitiated *see* Jackson (1982) Chapter 2. The chapter is specifically designed as a means of giving the economist some background information on the organisation theory literature.
2. Studies undertaken at the Hawthorne works of the Western Electric Company in the late 1920s and 1930s.
3. This approach has been developed more recently by Calvo and Wellisz (1978, 1979).
4. Note that all through this section the outcome is perfectly observable and hence the usual objection to piece rates, that quality will suffer, does not follow. Where output is not perfectly observable and is subject to quality variations the quota piece rate has obvious disadvantages and requires costly quality control procedures. If customers are well informed about quality, however, and franchise arrangements can be instituted, observability will not present a problem, as we saw in Chapter 5. Workers will have an incentive to maintain quality.
5. Williamson (1975, pp. 37–8) argues that 'atmosphere' and 'supplying a satisfying exchange relation' are part of the economic problem. There are close parallels here with the 'human relations school' of organisation theory mentioned briefly in section 1. The British system of relying on voluntary blood donors is a much discussed example of the importance of establishing emotionally satisfying arrangements. A market in blood could be established, but would affect the individual's perception of the act of supplying blood. Titmus (1970) argues that the gift relationship is not only a worthy ideal in itself, but may also produce in certain circumstances a more effective system. The argument is of far wider significance than the blood example alone suggests. Akerlof (1982, 1984) applies the idea of 'gift exchange' to the whole area of labour contracts. Employers pay workers more than market clearing wages (a gift) and in return they hope for a gift of greater loyalty and effort than would otherwise be forthcoming. He cites evidence from social psychology (Adams 1965) indicating that people regarding themselves as 'overpaid' are more productive than those merely receiving 'the rate for the job'. The approach is thus a variety of the 'efficiency wage' theory (section 4 and footnote 9 below). Although of considerable interest and importance we cannot hope to do justice to this approach here.
6. Duration of unemployment will have a geometric distribution with mean $1/p$ where p is the probability of finding a job in a given period.

7. 'The type of unemployment we have characterised here is very different from search unemployment. Here, all workers and firms are identical. There is perfect information about job availability. There is a different information problem: firms are assumed (quite reasonably in our view) not to be able to monitor the activities of their employees costlessly and perfectly' (p. 439).

8. Higher unemployment pay will reduce the incentive effects of a given wage level. Firms will raise wages in order to maintain incentives and a larger unemployment pool will result (*see* Shapiro and Stiglitz, 1984, p. 439).

9. The class of models discussed in this section relies on what is termed the 'efficiency wage' hypothesis. This idea originated in the development economics literature where it was observed that higher wages by improving nutrition and health might increase the productivity of the worker. Thus physical productivity and wages are not independent and the 'efficiency wage' might fall after an increase in the real wage rate. In the context of developed economies the argument is still that effort (and hence productivity) is not independent of the wage. Another version is that of Salop (1979) who argues that higher wages reduce labour turnover and reduce recruitment and training costs to the firm. For a review see Yellen, 1984.

10. Anecdotal evidence suggests that this is not impossible in certain circumstances as when a bureaucracy promotes someone to reduce the damage they are inflicting in their present job. Presumably this is more likely in a non-competitive environment.

11. The second-order condition

$$(\Pi_1 - \Pi_2)\partial^2 P \, \partial e_j^2 < c''(e_j)$$

must also be satisfied for a maximum.

12. In the case of a uniform distribution of θ with risk-neutral employees the tournament involves setting the prizes at either end of the distribution (in our case $1/a + \frac{1}{2}, 1/a - \frac{1}{2}$). But in the more general case the prizes will not necessarily be right at the extremities. *See* Lazear and Rosen (1981) for a discussion of the tournament with risk-averse contestants.

13. It is worth emphasising that this concept of rent seeking as the pursuit of transfers by challenging of property rights is not intended to be normative. It in no way follows that entrepreneurship is desirable and rent seeking undesirable by definition. To take an obvious example, a slave who challenges his master's rights by running away is a rent seeker, while the trader in slaves could be an entrepreneur. Clearly, the desirability of a given system of property rights is a conceptually separate issue to that of determining whether someone is attempting to undermine them or is accepting them as a framework for his transactions. The identification of rent seeking does require, however, that the status quo is well defined, and this may not always be the case.

14. In his article (1980a), Tullock gives as an example of rent seeking the

investment of time and effort in passing the examination to enter the civil service in Imperial China. It is not clear, however, that this is a true case of rent seeking as we have conceived it, although it is perfectly consistent with Tullock's definition quoted in the text. The problem is that the investment of resources in exam passing challenges no one's property rights. Imperial China ran a tournament of the type which we investigated in section 5. The prizes were arranged such that the spread encouraged, no doubt, enormous 'overinvestment' in exam-passing effort. Passing the exam meant (so Tullock informs us) a passport to power and status in a society offering few alternative routes. This may not have been efficient, and some competition among institutional arrangements might have revealed this and ultimately produced more efficient screening and a different distribution of prizes. But if we assume that the structure of government in China was not in dispute then individual maximising behaviour given the incentive structure prevailing, while possibly socially inefficient, would not count as rent seeking as we have defined it. The fact that a society is inefficient or full of monopolists does not *necessarily* mean that it is full of rent seekers. To take another example, suppose that the government announces that henceforth no more monopoly privileges will be granted. Suppose further that the government is actually believed (the example is not intended to be realistic). Monopoly rent seeking would then cease. If I wished to become a monopolist it would be of no avail my trying to persuade the government to infringe other people's existing rights. Instead I would just have to purchase my monopoly from an existing holder at a price freely negotiated between us. Effort is transferred from rent seeking to exchange. Of course I am in a sense 'seeking the monopolist's rents', but this merely comes down to the conventional economic assertion that we are all maximisers. Rent seeking is something different from any old maximising behaviour or it would not be worth discussing. Similar comments apply to another of Tullock's examples, the purchasing of commissions in the British Army in the first half of the nineteenth century. Tullock argues that buying government jobs is not always inefficient and quotes Niskanen's suggestion that purchasing a commission is like 'posting a bond' and could be regarded as a pledge of good performance which acts as an incentive device. From our earlier comments, however, it is not even clear in principle whether purchasing government jobs is a form of rent seeking, whatever the efficiency or incentive properties of the system. If people do not challenge the system, and the government merely auctions off jobs to the highest bidders, no rent seeking is involved. The case would be entirely equivalent to the 'franchise' solution to motivating the police force discussed in Chapter 5. Of course, entirely different considerations come into play if the right of people to purchase jobs in this way is disputed. Suppose that all jobs were allocated in accordance with performance in an examination. Attempts at bribery would then represent rent seeking. They would imply a challenge to the rights of the examination winners.

15. There is an analogy here with the problem of public sector contracts. 'Cost plus' agreements run the risk of encouraging rent seeking. 'Fixed price' agreements imply greater risks for the contractor and require the product to be closely specified, but they encourage entrepreneurship.
16. This statement requires qualification. Becker (1965, p. 154) recognises that certain features of employment contracts suggest that firms hedge their bets. Thus 'incompletely vested pension plans may be used because they help to insure firms against a loss on their specific investment'. But this represents a method of binding the employee to the firm as a long-term commitment with remuneration rising over time (*see* Lazear section 4). It is thus really a way of making employees pay for specific training by posting a bond to be repaid later.
17. It is important to remember that property rights are not dependent entirely on legislation. Property rights 'are to be construed as supported by the force of etiquette, social custom, ostracism, and formal, legally enacted laws supported by the state's power of violence or punishment' (Alchian, 1965, p. 129).
18. 'Hold-up' is another expresssion for the sort of opportunism discussed by Williamson. The possibility of 'hold-up' exists wherever very 'specific investments are made by one of the parties to a transaction' (Klein, 1984, p. 332). In an illuminating example Klein points out that 'one would not build a house on land rented for a short term'. Similarly firms will not make specific investments in training employees who are not committed over a sufficiently long time span.

7 Integration and the Visible Hand

The forces determining the shape and size and activities of industrial organisations do not hammer them out like the Brigade of Guards.

R. S. Edwards and H. Townsend

1. THE VARIETY OF BUSINESS ENTERPRISE

The firm investigated in Chapter 6 was beginning to take on some of the characteristics of hierarchical organisations and to reflect a few of the structural features associated with modern business enterprise. But our discussion of internal structure is hardly complete. We have presented various attempts at rationalising *employment* hierarchies, yet many other characteristics of the firm remain to be considered. In this chapter we consider explicitly the question of the determinants of the size and scope of firms. Firms, as was noted at the very beginning of Chapter 1, vary greatly in size from organisations of tens of thousands of employees which generate income for those involved equivalent to the national income of some independent nation states, to small local business enterprises, one-man businesses and partnerships—why the variety? If hierarchies have the incentive properties noted in Chapter 6, why not organise the whole economy as one gigantic hierarchy? What forces determine the limits of the firm and at what point do alternative contractual arrangements begin to reassert themselves?

Pure size is not the only matter of interest. Size is related to, and perhaps even the outcome of, decisions concerning the scope of the firm. Some firms are highly specialised while others undertake an apparently diverse set of activities. This diversity of activity is usually reflected in three dimensions—vertical, lateral and geographical.

(a)　The degree of 'vertical integration'

Production of final output usually requires materials to be transformed through many intermediate stages. In some instances a single firm will attempt to integrate these stages, even where quite different technical problems may be encountered at each stage. Historically well-known examples of 'spectacular' backward vertical integration are the acquisition by Lever in the early twentieth century of raw material investments in West Africa in order to supply his requirements for vegetable oils used in soap and margarine manufacture. Dunlop also integrated backwards into rubber plantations, Guest Keen and Nettlefolds and Tube Investments the engineering companies into steel production in the 1950s, and General Motors in the US into the production of motor car bodies and other components (1929). The last case was mirrored later in the UK by the acquisition of Briggs Motor Bodies Ltd, by Ford, and Fisher and Ludlow Ltd by the British Motor Corporation in 1952, and has been the focus of some theoretical interest in recent years (section 5c). Examples of forward vertical integration include the ownership by brewers of public houses ('tied houses'), or of petrol stations by oil refiners, or of special links between motor manufacturers and dealers.

Examples can be found, however, of companies that have not integrated backwards or forwards in this way, or at least have remained specialised at a particular stage for a substantial period of time. From the late eighteenth century to the 1950s, for example, Guinness specialised in what used to be called porter and is now known to most people only as 'Guinness'. In 1951 a director of Guinness could write[1] 'Nothing in the nature of either vertical or horizontal trustification was attempted'. Guinness produced only a little malt—'just enough to give them a clear insight into all the problems of barley and malt'. They owned no retail outlets. 'They have done just one thing and done it better than anyone else. That policy has been fixed at the top and has run right through at all levels.' Until recently therefore a deliberate business strategy of specialisation was adopted at Guinness. At the retail level a similar strategy appears to be pursued by most chain stores. Again in the mid 1950s Mr. A. J. Sainsbury wrote that[2] 'It has never been our policy to manufacture a considerable proportion of the goods we sell', while other famous stores in the UK such as Marks and Spencer also purchase their wares on the open market. The rise of 'own brands' by which Sainsburys, Tesco, or other chain stores, vouch for the quality of some item but arrange for its manufacture by an 'independent' firm is, however, an interesting form of 'integration' which highlights the difficulty of distinguishing where in the spectrum of contractual arrangements the boundary between market and firm is to be found.

(b) The degree of 'conglomerate' diversification
Some firms, vertically integrated or otherwise, still operate within a limited sphere. This may be defined technologically in terms of a specific limited type of *output*, or concentration on products all derived from a particular *input* or particular industrial process. Thus Edwards and Townsend (1967) write of the history of Pilkington Brothers up until the mid 1950s as follows: 'Pilkington Brothers have grown by stretching backwards into earlier stages of production, forwards into processing and distribution of glass, and sideways into the manufacture of additional glass products; their growth has taken them all over the world but it has always been concerned with glass' (p. 60). Other firms seem capable of undertaking operations in apparently 'distant' areas. Products may be quite different both in terms of the market served (with very low cross-price elasticities of demand) and of the technology and inputs required. The growth of these 'conglomerate' organisations has been a notable feature of the last four decades and the links between the component parts of such enterprises are not always very obvious. The history of Guinness is an interesting example of the changing patterns of recent business enterprise. From the textbook example of a specialised firm, strategy changed radically, and in 1985 Guinness has been attempting a takeover of Arthur Bell the whisky firm, and is reported to be extending its interests in a chain of newsagents shops. The goal has become the development of 'an international brand-orientated consumer products business'.[3]

The great variety of activities undertaken in a conglomerate does not imply that there is no underlying logic to its development, and the history of each enterprise usually reveals the sometimes surprising links between apparently quite different industrial processes. Technological developments and marketing skills clearly play an important role in moulding the modern conglomerate. Guinness, to pursue this example further, has always been celebrated for its advertising and its skill in marketing a 'branded' product. It may be that this expertise which can be applied in other areas, rather than detailed knowledge of the properties of stout or porter, is the more valuable under modern conditions and is to form the foundation for future developments. Knowledge not of a particular product but of how to develop and sell new ones must feature prominently in any attempt to make sense of the widely diversified corporation. An important objective of this chapter will be to discuss why firms rather than markets may be an appropriate institutional response to the problem of coordinating resources in a world of continual technical change.

(c) **International Integration**

Another form of integration which has developed rapidly in recent years is geographical integration, the combining in a single firm of operations in many different locations and often in different countries. Standard theory is hard pressed to explain this phenomenon. It may of course be a simple consequence of vertical integration if raw material supplies are derived from different countries. But many multinational enterprises are conglomerate enterprises, and once again it is to the problem of information which modern analysis has turned in an attempt to find the forces which encourage the development of this geographically dispersed type of corporation.

2. STRATEGY AND STRUCTURE

The degree of vertical, lateral, conglomerate or international integration reflects the firm's strategic development. Another important feature of the firm is its internal administrative structure. In Chapter 6 we investigated the incentive properties of simple hierarchies, but we did not consider in what ways administrative systems might differ and whether any differences between firms might be explicable using the framework of transactions costs. Just as, at the beginning of Chapter 6, it was to the literature on management science that we turned for the early analysis of hierarchies, so it is to the business history literature that we must refer for the first attempts to analyse developments of business structure and to consider possible links between changes in structure and changes in strategy.

Chandler (1977) considers the impact of the railroad and the telegraph on business organisation in the United States during the nineteenth century. Although economic historians have hardly overlooked the importance of the railroad, the purely adminis- trative achievement which they represented is not something which has been emphasised. Chandler points out that before the 1840s there were no business hierarchies in the United States and no middle managers. A railroad, however, requires a relatively com- plex administration to undertake the function of scheduling the trains, contracting for fuel and other supplies, maintaining rolling stock and track, selling tickets to passengers or arranging for the carriage of freight and so forth. In short 'the operational require- ments of the railroads demanded the creation of the first adminis- trative hierarchies in American business' (p. 87). The typical administrative solution adopted during the nineteenth century, both in the US and in the UK, to the problems encountered as the scale of operations grew was the so called 'functional' or 'unitary' (U)-form. Although the scale of business enterprise developed rapidly its scope remained limited. The improvements in com- munication brought about by the railroad and telegraph encour- aged forward vertical integration into wholesaling for some branded goods, and even into retailing with the development of 'new complex, high priced machines that required specialised marketing services—demonstration, installation, consumer credit, after-sales service and repair' (p. 288); but the typical firm was not highly diversified and the U-form was the standard corporate structure.

Figure 7.1 illustrates the structure of a U-form enterprise. It is centralised and divided into departments which specialise in certain enterprise-wide functions. For illustrative purposes the functions identified are the conventional production, sales and finance; but we might also have added other possible functions depending upon the character of the enterprise such as research and development, personnel and distribution. This U-form structure reflects the

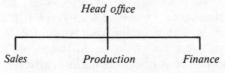

Figure 7.1: The unitary form

advantages of arranging both for managers to specialise in the problems of a particular function, and for communication to be established mainly along functional lines. Production managers communicate primarily with other production workers and do not require, for the most part, detailed information about finance or marketing. Given the bounds which exist to the individual's information-processing capacity each manager is left to concentrate on specific links which are expected to be most important for his particular purpose or function.

For enterprises with a limited scope this system had (and has) definite advantages. Problems were encountered only when the firm began to undertake an increasing variety of activities and operate in many different geographical locations. The production and marketing problems arising in the field of one product may have very little connection with the production and marketing problems arising in another. Functional managers begin therefore to become overloaded, attempting to make sense of flows of information which do not have many links between them. A firm manufacturing products such as shampoo, hair dyes and ethical drugs may find, for example, that the sales effort needs to be 'divisionalised'. Ethical drugs may be marketed by visits to doctors and hospitals by a specialised staff of trained representatives. Shampoo requires large-scale advertising and may be sold through thousands of retail outlets. The same management team will find it difficult to cope with the problems of both sectors simultaneously.

The gradually extending scope of the firm led during the 1920s and 1930s in the United States to experiments with different administrative structures and ultimately to what is now termed the multidivisional or M-form. Chandler traces these developments to a few major firms such as Du Pont and General Motors. The innovation consisted of a set of 'divisions' based upon products or geographical areas with a management organised within each division on functional lines to take responsibility for short-run operational decisions. Over these divisions was a 'general office' with the task of planning long-term strategy, and monitoring divisional performance. Figure 7.2 illustrates the 'pure' case of the multidivisional structure in the context of the 'conglomerate'. Many intermediate cases could be envisaged, of course, and it would be a mistake to consider the business history of the last fifty years simply as comprising the general gradual adoption of the

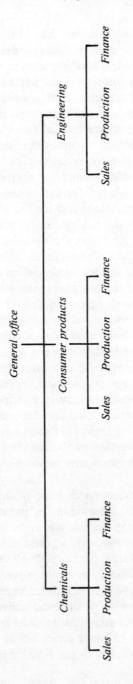

Figure 7.2: The multidivisional structure

'superior' M-form of organisation. The M-form structure is better adapted to a particular type of strategic development, especially conglomerate and multinational expansion, than is the U-form, and the diversified corporation could not have reached the stage that it has without this organisational innovation. But firms adopting a more specialised strategy will not necessarily be divisionalised, or may adopt a hybrid organisational form.

Underlying the choice of organisational structure are the same considerations which have proved important throughout this book. Information must be collected and deciphered, responses put into effect, and inputs policed. If information about the market in hair dyes, shampoos, setting lotions and the like is jointly produced, it is reasonable to prevent duplication and to attach responsibility for these products to a single office. On the other hand there may be almost no connection between the market in shampoo and that in cough mixture and even less with drugs which can be obtained only from a doctor. In these circumstances sales might be divisionalised into consumer products, patent medicines and ethical drugs. Research and development, on the other hand, might not be divisionalised and serve the entire organisation, depending upon perceptions about possible links between research into cough mixture and other drugs. Figure 7.3 illustrates the corporate structure of an entirely imaginary corporation, specialising in chemical products that are all more or less related to 'personal health'. If it were the case that the same production lines could be used to make and pack shampoo as could make and pack cough mixture, production would not be controlled by the divisions but would become 'functionalised', and the company would become increasingly U-form.

Economies in the collection and use of information therefore represent an important determinant of organisational structure. Kay (1982, 1984) presents an analysis of structure based squarely on informational links: 'Wherever a potential link exists it may give rise to a potential economy; for example by facilitating specialisation and division of labour, or by improved exploitation of an indivisible resource' (1984, p. 95). Information which may have consequences for a number of different activities is just such an 'indivisible' resource. Communicating information to others can present severe problems (a factor which will be of great importance in section 6), and this leads to the boundaries between decision

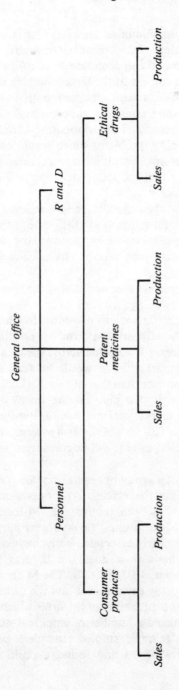

Figure 7.3: A hybrid form

units being drawn 'to minimise necessary exchanges of information' (p. 102). 'Strategy thus determines structure; the extent and content of links dictate the appropriate form of internal organisation' (p. 103). In the context of the large, complex corporation the M-form, in Williamson's words 'served both to economise on bounded rationality and attenuate opportunism' (1981, p. 1556). Kay (1984, Ch. 6) concentrates on information-handling economies and bounded rationality, problems which would exist even in the absence of opportunism, but Williamson's reference to opportunism is a reminder that corporate structure will also affect the ability to police inputs.

Because the staff at the general office are relieved of day-to-day operational responsibilities much of their time is spent in considering strategic alternatives and monitoring the divisions. Two significant theoretical propositions have flowed from this observation.

(a) If the general office is seen as charting the overall progress of the corporation it will have control over investment resources which it will allocate to the various divisions. In Chapter 6 we considered Williamson's idea of the firm as an 'internal labour market'. Here in Chapter 7 we come across the idea of the firm as an 'internal capital market'. The words 'allocation mechanism' might be more appropriate than that of 'market' in both instances, since the whole point is that pure market forms of contract are superceded by 'non-market' forms, but the terminology is now quite well established. This idea of the firm as a response to transactions costs in the capital market will be considered in greater detail in sections 4 and 6.

(b) The existence of a group of general managers monitoring the divisions may increase the efficiency of operations and induce greater effort. This has been termed the 'M-form hypothesis'. Organisation along M-form lines 'favours goal pursuit and least-cost behaviour more nearly associated with the neoclassical profit maximisation hypothesis than does the U-form organisational alternative' (Williamson, 1975, p. 150). The M-form represents a more efficient monitoring environment and the gains, it is argued, will be reflected in the profitability of the firms which adopt it. This hypothesis has stimulated a number of empirical studies. Armour and Teece (1978), for example, studied a sample of petroleum firms covering the period 1955–73 and found a positive relationship between M-form structure and profitability 'during the period in which the M-form innovation was being diffused' (p. 106). In the period 1969–73, however, differential performance between M-form organisation and other forms was not observed and the authors inferred that 'the sample firms were, in general, appropriately organised' (p. 118). Thus, there is no assumption that M-form organisations are more efficient under all circumstances, but merely that for certain types of firm the M-form innovation was profitable. Over time, imitation reduces the profits accruing to the innovating firms. Another study by Teece (1981) covered a wider range of industrial activities. It involved identifying the first firm in an industry (in the case of conglomerate enterprise this is, of course, not an easy concept to define) to adopt the M-form of organisation. This firm was tagged 'the leading firm' and its performance was compared with a second firm 'the control firm' as close to the leading firm as possible in terms of product range and size which adopted the M-form later. Performance was compared in two time periods. In the first, only the leading firm was organised in an M-form. In the second, both firms were M-form. The economic hypothesis was that the 'control' firm would improve its performance relative to the 'leading' firm in the second period. Two statistical tests rejected the 'null hypothesis' that there was no effect on performance of organisational form (i.e. that the probability of observing an 'improvement' in the second period was the same as the probability of observing a 'deterioration'on the part of the 'control' firm).[4]

In the UK, adoption of the M-form took place later than in the US (Channon 1979). ICI was evolving a divisionalised structure as early as the 1930s (Hannah, 1983, pp. 81–5) and this was fully established by the mid 1950s and was described in textbooks such as that by Edwards and Townsend (1967. p. 67). But this experience was not typical. Just as the UK lagged by several decades in the merger movement which established the framework of the 'corporate economy' at the end of the nineteenth century and very beginning of the twentieth century in the US, there was a similar lag in the development of managerial structures to cope. Between the two world wars in the UK many firms were 'loosely run confederations of subsidiaries with little central control' (Hannah, 1983, p. 87). As was reported in Chapter 4, Chandler identifies family management and the absence of a managerial class as reasons for UK backwardness. In the US adoption of the M-form of organisation and the rapid development of conglomerate and multinational enterprise were associated with the 1940s and 1950s. In the UK (and other European countries) these changes appear to have been delayed until the 1960s and 1970s. When they did arrive, the evidence of studies by Steer and Cable (1978) and Thompson (1981) is that the organisational changes had substantial effects which are consistent with the M-form hypothesis.

3. VISIBLE AND INVISIBLE HANDS

From sections 1 and 2 of this chapter we have seen that the 'visible hand' can guide the process of resource allocation and integrate vertical, lateral, conglomerate or international transactions using a variety of corporate structures. As has been remarked in earlier chapters, however, the distinction between visible and invisible hands is less clear than the terminology suggests. As Klein, Crawford and Alchian (1978) put it 'the conventional sharp distinction between markets and firms may have little general analytical importance' (p. 326). When thinking about the firm it is natural to envisage the factory and office buildings, the machines and equipment, the signs proclaiming the company name, and perhaps even the wrought iron gates confidently symbolising the idea that there is a clear boundary to be drawn between what goes on inside and what goes on outside. Begin to think in terms of the transactions involved, however, and the buildings and offices look increasingly 'open plan', the gate is perpetually ajar, and the evanescent firm appears to have all the substance of the residual grin on Alice's Cheshire cat. It would however, be prudent to avoid the fate of the unfortunate sheep-dog in Hardy's novel[5] who, concluding that he was employed to run after sheep, drove them over a precipice and was shot for his pains, a result 'which so often attends dogs and other philosophers who follow out a train of reasoning to its logical conclusion. . .'. Our aim is to pursue the firm in an attempt to learn more about it, not to hound it to extinction.

Nevertheless, a transactions cost approach to economics does make a clear definition of 'the firm' difficult, and theorists have avoided the problem by concentrating instead on the question of why contractual arrangements differ as circumstances differ. In some cases 'market-like' contracts are adopted and in other cases contracts are more 'firm-like'. 'Firm-like' contracts, it will be recalled, govern the transactions between the parties involved over a long period of time. They are also, because of bounded rationality, *incompletely specified* and leave many obligations implicit. 'Market-like' contracts, by contrast are (in the purest case) *completely specified* with obligations perfectly understood and explicit. Because of bounded rationality such contracts can involve only the simplest transactions and relatively short periods of time. So clearly is the contract specified and so easily is it policed that the identity of the buyer or seller is of no consequence and transactions can be almost 'anonymous', as when someone purchases a raw material such as copper of verifiable quality on a specialised market.

The first stage in the substitution of 'firm-like' for pure market relationships occurs, therefore, when the specific identity of buyers and sellers begins to matter. In a very stable, unchanging environment, information asymmetries and adverse selection might inhibit trade, but the development of specialised dealers in the various goods and services with a valuable 'reputation' to protect (as described by Alchian, see Chapter 2) will enable exchange to proceed. Any 'reputable dealer' will suffice for the purposes of buying or selling, and there will be no particular reason for always using the same one. Static conditions therefore greatly favour the use of markets and correspondingly restrict the scope of the firm. Where contractual requirements are complex and uncertain, bounded rationality leads both to implicit contracts and a much increased scope for moral hazard and the exercise of opportunism. It then becomes advantageous to develop a continuing trading relationship with particular suppliers. These suppliers (like the labour force in Chapter 6) gain in the experience of perceiving what the customer wants, satisfying a particular customer's changing requirements, and coping with the idiosyncracies of the tasks in hand. A continuing relationship is also central to the problem of policing the behaviour of suppliers. Thus, as Spence (1975) remarks 'many of the structural features of resource allocation problems appear similar in markets and in organisations' (p. 171).

The requirements of a continuing association able to respond flexibly to new circumstances, and capable of providing incentives leading to cooperation instead of opportunism, gives rise to 'the firm'. As we saw at the end of Chapter 6, Williamson (1979) refers to the firm as a governance structure. The boundaries of such a structure, and the boundaries of the firm as defined by the law, however, will not necessarily coincide. Continuing relationships embodying procedures for adjudicating in the event of disputes and including monitoring and incentive devices can evolve between legally quite separate firms. The governance structure idea has something in common with Edwards and Townsend's definition of the firm as 'an area of unified business planning' (p. 64) although it is important not to interpret this as implying that each firm is a miniature 'command economy'. Some firms may adopt procedures which are quite decentralised, as was seen in section 2.

To conclude this section on the problem of defining the boundaries of the firm, a few practical examples may be useful. A brewer known nationally for a particular brand of beer may permit this beer to be bottled locally by other independent brewers or bottlers. This type of agreement would normally entail rights of inspection and technical control by the national brewer whose reputation and brand image are at stake. Thus we might argue that the transaction involved is a market transaction between two independent companies and that this is the 'invisible' hand at work. We have seen, however, that the controlling hand can be quite 'visible' in this type of case, and that the dividing line is fine between a fully regionally integrated single brewery, and a set of 'market' contracts integrating the operations of a group of regional brewers. Conversely, the dealings between divisions or departments of a single firm may involve relationships which differ very little from those which might be expected in the market.

A further case of interest, which will be considered again in section 5, is a transaction which involves the buyer of an input providing the supplier with raw materials or important items of equipment necessary for its production. This has been termed *quasi-vertical integration*. Quasi-vertical integration has been defined by Monteverde and Teece (1982) as 'the ownership by a downstream firm of the specialised tools, dies, jigs and patterns used in the fabrication of components for larger systems' (p. 321). The buyer contracts 'in the market' for the supply of the desired input but has property rights in the equipment necessary for production to take place.

Another form of quasi-vertical integration, undertaken for rather different reasons, occurs when a company trains the specialist staff necessary to sell its goods effectively, but then uses the premises and other inputs of an independent retail store. In this case the company is attempting to gain greater control over the 'human' rather than the 'physical' capital. Examples would include the use of a particular area in a department store for the sale of glass, chinaware, or cosmetics, supplied by specialist companies and staffed by their trainees. A further option is the use of a franchise contract which gives the holder of the franchise an incentive to market a product with enthusiasm, if not always with the greatest care. The 'firm-like' features of this contract have already been discussed in detail at the end of Chapter 5.

Integration, whether horizontal, vertical, or geographical, may be effected therefore using a range of contractual mechanisms. The choice of contract will reflect the attempt to cope with the information problem. Earlier in this book it was found convenient to distinguish three facets to this problem and these will form the subject matter of the next three sections. There is first the problem of bounded rationality, the impossibility of predicting and specifying the appropriate response to every conceivable contingency. This leads to the firm as a *device for handling change*, for increasing flexibility and adaptability in the face of new circumstances. Here the firm is closely connected to the entrepreneurial function identified by Casson and Knight, the exercise of judgement in the face of environmental uncertainty. A second facet to the problem is that of establishing and enforcing property rights. Property rights are insecure and, in the extreme case, worthless, if they cannot be enforced and protected. Enforcement requires, however, that infringements are detected, and detection requires information. This leads to the firm as a *monitoring device* to cope with moral hazard and adverse selection. The focus of attention is on information concerning the behaviour and performance of the various parties to a contract. It was this conception of the firm which underlay much of the analysis of Chapters 5 and 6. The third facet is the problem of perceiving (Kirzner), creating (Shackle) or forcing through (Schumpeter) new opportunities and new information. This leads to the firm as *the instigator of change* and is most closely associated with the view of entrepreneurship espoused by Schumpeter. In sections 4, 5 and 6, each of these facets will be examined in turn to see how they are reflected in the structure of firms. We will attempt to show how modern theorists have linked the information problem to the organisational form adopted and especially to the extent of vertical, horizontal, conglomerate and geographical (especially multinational) integration.

4. INTEGRATION, COMPLEXITY AND ENVIRONMENTAL UNCERTAINTY

After reviewing the literature on corporate strategy and structure, Caves (1980) remarks that much of it seems implicitly to be concerned with the concept of an 'organisational production function'. The 'inputs' into this function, he argues, are resources devoted to collecting and analysing information and coordinating other factors of production. The 'output' is the ability to reallocate. . . in response to unexpected disturbances' (p. 89). The mode of expression betrays Cave's neoclassical standpoint, and in Chapter 3 it was seen that many would dispute the ability of the neoclassical paradigm to cope with the truly 'unexpected' as distinct from the statistically 'risky'. Nevertheless, Caves would not be alone in wishing to salvage as much as possible of neoclassical theory, and again in Chapter 3 the attempt of Casson to use a neoclassical framework to analyse what was effectively the market in the services of coordinators was described. Although Caves could not know (Casson's book had not been published) the inputs into his 'organisational production function' are Casson's entrepreneurs. Casson is quite clear that the entrepreneur can be an employee (pp. 213–15) and that the institutional setting of the firm will be one of the factors underlying the 'supply' and 'demand' curves of Figure 3.1.

(a)   Integration, Coordination and Complexity

Notwithstanding Williamson's view reported in Chapter 2 that the distinction between complexity and uncertainty is inessential since both give rise to the problem of bounded rationality, we will consider separately the influence of each on the firm. Very close and complex technical relationships between processes and products may imply high costs of transacting in the market because of bounded rationality, but it is not clear that coordinating these processes necessarily requires great *entrepreneurial* as distinct from *technical* judgement. It may be perfectly obvious what actions need to be taken in any given set of circumstances, even if the exhaustive enumeration of all the possibilities in a state-contingent market contract is not feasible.

This is the situation which underlies some of the 'conventional' explanations of integration within the firm. Within the neoclassical tradition of the 'firm as production function' mentioned at the beginning of Chapter 6, it is natural to look for explanations of horizontal integration in the pursuit of economies of scale; or of conglomerate integration in technical complementarities or economies of scope; or of vertical integration in the close technical connections between one stage of production and the next. The objections of the transactions cost school to this way of thinking are most succinctly summed up in Williamson's (1975) aphorism: 'technology is no bar to contracting' (p. 17). Let us interpret this point in more detail and consider its applications to horizontal and vertical integration.

(*i*) *Horizontal Integration.* This is the most familiar case considered in elementary textbooks. By integrating within a single firm the resources required to produce larger quantities of a single output, costs may decline if there are economies of scale. A falling average cost of production with higher output is ultimately traceable to 'indivisibilities' associated with the various inputs. A particular item of capital equipment, for example a ship for transporting cargo in bulk, will have associated with it a level of utilisation which minimises costs per tonne mile. If the ship is not fully laden, costs obviously will rise. On the other hand, tonne miles can be increased by reducing the time spent at ports or in maintenance. Such continuous operations may increase staff costs as crews, maintenance engineers, and administrative personnel are augmented. This example is therefore just a special case of the economist's familiar idea of increasing and then ultimately diminishing returns to a fixed factor.

Now suppose that there are five firms each shipping a particular type of cargo (let us say grain) between two countries. They each purchase the grain from suppliers, store it in warehouses, transport it in their own ships across the ocean, and distribute it to wholesalers at the other end. It is clear, however, that the actual process of shipping is unnecessarily costly with five crews and five small ships. A single large ship would enable advantages of scale to be achieved.[6] Does this imply that the five firms should merge their operations? 'Common sense' suggests that this would not be unreasonable, but there are other options open in principle. The most obvious alternative is that a new specialist ship-owner enters the market with a giant grain transporter, and the five grain buyers and distributors contract with the shipowner for cargo space on the larger ship. In a world of zero transactions costs, in other words, indivisibilities might just as reasonably lead to 'disintegration' and the entry of a new specialist firm as 'integration' and the creation of a *single* firm out of the five existing ones. The purely *technical* advantages associated with particular bits of equipment do not automatically *require* reduced numbers of firms for their realisation. They *may* lead to integration, but the hidden and unspoken assumption in the 'common sense' view is the (very often correct) one that transactions costs will inhibit the 'market-like' solution.

All 'economies of scale' involve an indivisibility of some form. Two further examples taken from Hay and Morris (1979), pp. 44–5) may be useful. Larger size, it has been argued, will lead to economies in the use of maintenance staff. If a breakdown in any particular item of equipment is a random variable with a certain probability distribution, the larger the number of items of such equipment the less is the variation in the average number of breakdowns per period.[7] It then turns out that a given standard of service (in terms of the probability that a breakdown will occur with no staff available to cope with it) can be achieved at lower cost per machine as the number of machines increases. Although technically flawless, we can not deduce from this that larger 'firm' size is encouraged. Many small firms could, in principle, use an independent maintenance firm to cope with breakdowns, just as coffee machines, domestic appliances and office equipment are frequently serviced and mended by outside contractors. This could either be done on the basis of a payment per visit; or each small firm could pay a retainer to the maintenance company which would effectively represent an insurance premium, and the company would pool the risks. Either way, economies in maintenance do not logically imply the amalgamation of small firms, though the transactions costs associated with contracting in the market may of course, produce such an effect.[8] Similar reasoning can be applied to the case of economies of purchasing inputs. If there is a fixed or overhead element associated with the cost of effecting each order, independent of the size of the order, it is clear that costs per unit will decline as the average size of purchase increases. This seems to favour large firms. But we should be absolutely clear why this is so. The overhead element independent of the size of the order is nothing other than a simple representation of a 'cost per transaction in the market'. If there are transactions costs associated with market exchange, reducing the number of such transactions will be encouraged. The economies thus identified are transactions cost economies. If, for example, this transaction cost were peculiar to the bulk order of supplies of a particular input and did not apply to the transactions between the purchasing firms, a set of small firms could band together and order in bulk, rather as a group of students might combine to order a magazine or newspaper. 'Integration' would then occur only at the single specific level of transactions with this particular supplier and not more generally.

(*ii*) *Vertical Integration.* Technological considerations have traditionally been seen as an important force leading to vertical integration in some industries. The case of the iron and steel industry is perhaps the most often cited. Thus 'the later stages of production are bound to the earlier by many specially close technological links. In particular a great waste of heat can be avoided...' (Robertson and Dennison, 1960, p. 27). From our discussion of horizontal integration the objection to the view that vertical integration is a purely technological phenomenon will be clear. The question is simply whether the close technological links should be coordinated within the firm or by market transactions. Contracts *might* be drawn up which would permit the process of steel making to proceed with the steel maker purchasing iron in molten form. So detailed is the coordination required, however, that this is clearly not going to be the favoured procedure, and the entire process is more conveniently brought under a single administration in the firm. In cases like the production of iron and steel the advantages of vertical integration are so obvious that it appears somewhat pedantic to drag transactions costs into the discussion. Yet logically, nothing can be deduced about the organisation of production without reference to transactions costs because the organisation of production concerns precisely the choice of contractual arrangements best suited to a particular set of technical circumstances.

(b)   Integration, Coordination and Uncertainty

In a continually changing environment entrepreneurs gather information, interpret it to discover the opportunities latent in it, and act upon it. Acting on the basis of entrepreneurial judgement requires command over resources. It does so because the market value of an entrepreneur's knowledge cannot itself be appropriated simply by trading it in the market. A buyer would require the information before an assessment of its value was possible, but once in possession of the information there would be no need to purchase it.[9] The firm responds to this problem by screening for entrepreneurial talent, placing entrepreneurs in circumstances likely to produce a flow of information suitable for the exercise of entrepreneurial judgement, providing them with resources to back their judgement, and instituting a reward system which enables those with a flair for these decisions to benefit from them. On this interpretation, the firm represents an internal capital market, a method of allocating scarce resources amongst competing uses on the basis of entrepreneurial judgement.[10] The job is done internally because of the problems associated with transactions in markets for information.

Integration of activities to take advantage of internally generated information would still seem to imply a fairly specialised firm. Vertical integration may be seen as a way of gaining from the improved communication of information from upstream to downstream firms. Arrow (1975) considers better information about the supply (and hence the future price) of an upstream good, leading to more appropriate input decisions by a downstream firm, as a motive for vertical integration. Integration into closely related products or processes may be favoured because information concerning markets or production is not totally specific, and may have wider-ranging implications. A useful example of integration both as a means of discovering and analysing information, and as a means of using information, is the chain store. Many chain stores have benefited from the development of knowledge concerning customer wants, and the identification of gaps in the market. This has not necessarily led to backward vertical integration into manufacturing, since the links between market information and production information may not be very important. The store concentrates on the entrepreneurial functions of identifying demands and then contracts with manufacturers directly to arrange supply. This, of course, implies that information about what is wanted can be cheaply and clearly communicated to potential suppliers. If the request is too innovative it may be difficult to arrange supply from independent contractors, and backward vertical integration may occur. In section 6 we will consider the relationship between integration and innovation in more detail.

Information generated within the firm about markets can therefore be used to contract with suppliers, and the benefits derivable from this entrepreneurial information can then be used in every branch of the chain. A similar point could be made about information concerning the actual operation of the stores, the handling of goods, layout, warehousing, pricing, and so forth. New information can be used quickly throughout the chain of stores. As Edwards and Townsend recognised in their explanation of the growth of the chain store 'the main advantage lies in the fact that there are large indivisibilities in knowledge', (p. 296).

The economics of the chain store leads conveniently to the problem of the multinational firm. In both cases the same fundamental phenomenon requires explanation—the integration of geographically dispersed operations in a single firm. Traditional theory has addressed the problem of explaining the geographical dispersion of production (Scherer, 1975). Essentially the analysis derives from the location theory of Weber (1929), Alonso (1964) and others, as well as the 'central place theory' associated with Christaller (1933) and Losch (1954). In this theory the advantages of concentration (mainly economies of scale) are traded off against the advantages of dispersion (mainly savings in transport costs), and a 'least cost' spatial pattern of establishments is derived for a given distribution of demand over the area. There is no clue here, however, as to why the establishments so distributed are integrated within a single firm in some instances but not in others. Similarly, in the international setting, static theory does not explain why production is undertaken by indigenous firms in some cases and by affiliates of a multinational corporation in others. Dunning (1973) surveys not only location theory but also traditional trade theory in an attempt to highlight the ultimate source of multinational enterprise. He concludes that neither have any relevance to the issue. If the affiliates of a foreign firm have advantages over indigenous firms, this must have something to do not with advantages associated with the country concerned but rather with advantages specific to the multinational enterprise. The character of these advantages is important: 'Essentially, they are enterprise-specific, that is they are not transferable between firms, and are a function of their character and ownership'. (p. 314). The multinational enterprise, according to this view, possesses a resource not available to the indigenous firms and for which there is no effective market so that acquisition of the resource through the process of exchange is ruled out. Special skills and technical 'know-how' clearly come into this category. Knowledge acquired by pure experience at doing the job is entrepreneurial in character and impossible to market. It is specific to the firm because it is generated by the entrepreneurial talent of the people who happen to be working in it. Use of this firm-specific information may then result in multinational expansion.

Conglomerate firms are much more difficult to explain on the basis of the use of internally generated information. Instead the emphasis switches to diversification as a means of coping with unexpected events. A neoclassical approach would see the firm as holding a portfolio of risky prospects so designed to maximise the value of expected wealth (in the case of risk neutrality) or, more generally, expected utility (in the case of risk aversion or risk loving). This 'portfolio' could involve the firm undertaking projects in many different product areas. A serious difficulty, however, is to understand why risks should be pooled within the firm instead of in the markets for financial claims. In a neoclassical world with low transactions costs, risks could be pooled as effectively by people holding claims to the returns from a variety of independent but specialised firms operating in different areas, as claims to the returns from a single suitably diversified firm. Thus individual people through their portfolio of *financial* assets could select a desired risk-return profile, and this could be done independently of any decisions concerning the appropriate administrative framework for coordinating the *physical* assets concerned. If the firm itself takes on a risk-pooling role it is once more to the transactional problems of the alternative institutional arrangements that we must turn for an explanation.

One obvious candidate for consideration is that people lack the information to take complex portfolio-building decisions, and that the transactions costs involved in holding a large number of different financial claims would prevent risk pooling. This problem, however, would appear to be met by developments within the financial markets themselves, developments such as the growth of unit and investment trusts which give people access to specialist information and, through the use of an intermediary, once more reduce transactions costs. A more persuasive explanation for diversification within the firm concerns the use of the physical assets, human capital and firm specific 'know-how'. As was seen in some detail in Chapter 6, within the firm information about members of the team is collected, inputs are monitored and complex hierarchiacal incentive structures are instituted. Many of the skills absorbed are firm specific rather than product specific and relate to the ability to communicate and to get on with colleagues. Further, incentives require that the firm is perceived as having effectively an indefinite 'life' and is unlikely to go bankrupt. At the same time they imply that, for a portion of a person's career, remuneration will exceed anything available on the 'open market'. In these circumstances the ability to relocate resources from stagnant to growing sectors is essential. Bankruptcy or stagnation and decline in a specialist firm are of no consequence in a neoclassical world of full information where laid-off resources are immediately reabsorbed elsewhere at the going market rate. But in the context of the analysis of Chapters 5 and 6 it is clear that the consequences of decline for the operation of the internal labour market or the tournament could be very severe and imply a renunciation of the firm's 'implicit' obligations.

Rapidly changing and uncertain conditions will therefore lead to conglomerate diversification and an M-form corporate structure. The head office monitors each division's performance and, through the internal capital and labour markets, reallocates resources to growing and away from declining areas. This strategy is not therefore simply a matter of pooling risks. If it works, it will do so because the firm's structure permits flexibility and encourages adaptation to conditions more correctly viewed in Knight's terms as 'uncertain'. Kay (1984) in his explanation for the conglomerate emphasises this point. The firm will make use of information flows from 'richly linked' product markets, but this implies that 'where links exists they may create mutual or common vulnerability' (p. 96). In very static environments this may not be of great concern[11] but in other areas the danger of 'technological mugging' may lead to conglomerate diversification. For Kay, neoclassical portfolio theory is not the appropriate tool for understanding this phenomenon: 'The decision maker faces a truly uncertain situation in which there is an asymmetric emphasis on the possibility of life cycle decline rather than life cycle growth.... All we assume the decision maker is able to do is to order the environment in terms of surprise potential' (p. 98).[12] Environments in which surprise potential is great will lead firms to diversify into areas which are not strongly linked, in order to reduce the damage which might result from a sudden mugging.

5. INTEGRATION, MORAL HAZARD AND ADVERSE SELECTION

In this section we consider integration as a response to information asymmetry. The analysis runs parallel to that of Chapter 6 on the policing of labour contracts, but here the emphasis is on the problem of contracting with buyers or of suppliers of non-labour inputs.

(a) Monitoring input quality

If the quality of inputs is observable at very low cost we could expect market transactions to be used for recurrent purchases of 'standard' items.[13] Even where quality is costly to monitor, full integration within the firm is only one of several options available. The continuing use of a particular supplier with a good 'reputation' to protect is a possible response to adverse selection. 'Cheating' on the part of such a supplier would be costly if discovered and 'the discipline of continuous dealings' with the implied threat of terminating the association following unsatisfactory performance may provide a 'solution' to the incentive problem. Clearly, this relatively simple response to adverse selection and moral hazard requires both the existence of 'reputable' suppliers, and at least some 'informative signal' about quality in order that a 'monitoring gamble' can be constructed. Obviously the more informative the signal used, the more effective the monitoring of the input will be. Information is valuable to the buyer and may be sought in a variety of ways depending upon the costs involved.

It may be, for example, that simple inspection of the input is sufficient to ascertain its quality and reliability and that staff with specialist knowledge can be employed simply to undertake this task. On the other hand, inspection of the input itself may not provide, at reasonable cost, information about quality. Knowledge of production conditions may be important. If this is so, a number of consequences follow. The first possibility is that detailed environmental circumstances, to which all producers are subject, may have important effects, and that these can be appreciated only by practical experience. This might result in a buyer integrating backwards into the production of an input simply to acquire this kind of information and thus to remove the information asymmetry associated with dealings with other suppliers. The objective is not to produce 100 per cent of requirements of the input, but to produce information. An example already quoted is that of the interest of Guinness in malt production. Similarly, the history of Sainsbury provides a number of cases: 'Before the war we were very large buyers of beef cattle in Aberdeenshire, through our Northern agent, and it was our desire to get direct experience of rearing and fattening costs...that led to our farming enterprise'.[14] A second possibility is that quality is determined primarily by the efficiency of the production operation run by the supplier. This might lead to arrangements for technical inspection and direct monitoring between independent firms. Finally, where the detailed specification of the input is continually subject to change, technical inspection may give way to full internal integration within a single firm.

Forward vertical integration of manufacturers into retailing involves a similar range of options. Where one manufacturer's product is indistinguishable from another's, the use of market contracts and an independent wholesaler is suggested. The wholesaler develops contacts with retail outlets and supplies them with a variety of products from his stock. The transactional economies involved in employing an intermediary are clear since the alternative is that each manufacturer must develop links with each retailer. Problems arise, however, when it is no longer a matter of indifference to the manufacturer *where* his goods are sold, *how* they are treated and how presented. Faulty handling or poor presentation in the wrong environment may affect the brand image of the manufacturer's product. Complex products or new products require that consumer confidence is established, and once again this involves the development of a 'reputation' which is attached to a brand name. Manufacturers may respond to this problem in a number of ways. The first option is to establish a sales force to sell direct to retailers and monitor performance, presentation and general quality of store. This is the policy adopted by Yardley and Co. the manufacturers of perfumery and cosmetics in the 1930s and 40s. Selling more complex commodities may require a knowledgeable person to communicate with each potential customer, and here forward integration by the manufacturer can range from the direct training of the sales force and the use of space in a department store or (more recently) 'shopping mall' through franchising, to full integration.

Etgar (1978) reports that full or 'partial' vertical integration (franchising) into retailing is common in the US. It is a system through which 'more than one-third of products and services is currently distributed' (p. 249). He argues that forward vertical integration is 'motivated by a desire *to achieve product differentiation in the ultimate market*' (emphasis in original). If a distributor represents several suppliers, all will benefit by better service, whereas exclusive distribution is required to tie a good image to a particular brand. Etgar therefore formulates the hypothesis that 'suppliers who forward integrate from a competitive level into a competitively structured distributive level will provide more services' (p. 251). This hypothesis is tested using data from the property and casualty insurance industry. In this industry the system of independent insurance agents has been challenged since the war in the US by the direct writing system (using either employees or franchisees). Etgar isolates twenty one service variables (such as degree of home inspection, and time taken to settle the majority of claims) and compares the performance of the vertically integrated and non-integrated distributors. Significant differences were detected in eleven of the service areas, and eight out of these eleven service variables showed a higher quality performance by vertically integrated distributors.

(b) Monitoring restrictive agreements

Integration in pursuit of monopoly profits has been considered a primary determinant of industrial structure for many years. Even in this familiar area, however, it is necessary to understand the implicit assumptions about transactions costs which underlie the conventional theory. The advantages to be gained from 'combinations' have been recognised in every age. In a famous passage, Adam Smith writes that 'people of the same trade seldom meet together, even for merriment and diversion, but the conversation ends in a conspiracy against the public, or in some contrivance to raise prices' (p. 130). But 'integration' can take many forms other than the creation of a single firm, and the choice of institutional arrangements will depend upon transactions costs. A voluntary agreement between all existing producers covering prices to be charged and quotas to be produced would fulfill the same objectives as a complete merger. In a world in which information were perfect and transactions costs zero there would be no reason for preferring one method of monopoly creation over another from the point of view of the producers. If integration within a single firm is the strategy followed, this will be because the costs of monitoring and hence of ensuring compliance in the market exceed the costs of internal organisation. As Stigler (1964) remarks 'no conspiracy can neglect the problem of enforcement' and he bases his theory of oligopoly squarely on the problem of acquiring information about the behaviour of other independent producers. A rapid and accurate flow of information about the compliance of others with the provisions of a restrictive agreement will render integration by merger less necessary as a means of securing monopoly advantages. It is interesting to note that economists have traditionally been sceptical about the stability of restrictive agreements and have noted the incentive to cheat on their provisions. This scepticism may explain the suspicion with which horizontal mergers are often regarded, internal control being substituted for external agreements.

The costs of monitoring restrictive agreements in the market are also reflected in some other 'conventional' explanations of internal integration. Consider the argument that an upstream monopolist will integrate vertically with a downstream buyer to correct for the tendency of the independent buyer to substitute other inputs for those supplied by the monopolist if there are technical opportunities for doing so (Vernon and Graham, 1971, Schmalensee, 1973). A vertically integrated concern would, it is argued, increase combined profits by using more of the internally supplied input in the downstream production process. Figure 7.4 illustrates the point using the traditional isoquant–isocost diagram of neoclassical theory. The input of the monopoly supplier is measured along the horizontal axis and 'other inputs' on the vertical axis. Given a monopoly price P_m the downstream producer will adopt the combination of inputs at a, where the line of constant outlay (slope $- P_m/P_n$) is tangential to the isoquant labelled $\bar{q}$. An integrated producer will be interested not in the monopoly price but in the marginal cost of production of input m labelled C_m. Clearly the cost of $\bar{q}$ will be lower at point b than at point a for the integrated producer, and more of input m will be used.

This argument is impeccable from the point of view of neo-classical theory but, once more, it does not address the question of why market alternatives to vertical integration are not adopted. If substitution against the monopolist is severe, why does the monopolist not adopt a two-part tariff? Under a two-part tarriff, the buyer would pay an initial lump sum and then a price per unit of the input purchased. The system is often used for such items as telephone, gas or electricity services with a 'quarterly rental' for the telephone in addition to a price per call. A sufficiently low price per unit would solve the problem of substitution of other inputs by the buyer, and an appropriate 'standing charge' would give the monopolist his profit. As Figure 7.4 indicates, the resource savings available from moving to point b imply that some two-part tariff arrangement could benefit both monopolist and buyer. Only the bargaining costs associated with implementing it would appear to stand in the way.

The main difficulty of the two-part tariff arrangement is in ensuring that the buyer does not purchase the product on behalf of others and then resell it. If this happened on a large scale, the monopolist would miss out on the lump sum payments which buyers would otherwise have to pay. This is, of course, a problem faced by any scheme of price discrimination. A price of P_m for the first m_2 units of the input purchased (Figure 7.4) and a price of C_m for any further purchases would, for example, be an alternative system which would increase the profits of the monopolist seller and not harm the buyer, whose total costs would remain unaltered. Once again, resale from one purchaser to another would completely undermine the monopolists's position.

Forward integration in this case, therefore, is really a method of policing a system of price discrimination which might otherwise not be possible in the market. Formally it involves the same reasoning as that used by Perry (1980) to explain the process of forward vertical integration by Alcoa in the years 1888–1930. The standard

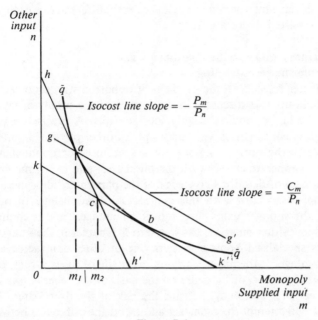

Figure 7.4

analysis of price discrimination tells us that if there are several different markets for a product with different price elasticities of demand, a profit-maximising monopolist will charge a higher price to the buyers with the relatively *inelastic* demand. Preventing arbitrage between the markets is the major problem and it is for this purpose that forward vertical integration may be undertaken. By integrating with the buyer with the most elastic demand the monopolist can charge a higher price to the other buyers without fear of resale. Perry identifies five major markets for aluminium— as a reducing agent used in the production of iron and steel, and as an input in the manufacture of cooking utensils, electric cable, automobile parts and aircraft. On the basis of the price-discrimination hypothesis 'we expect Alcoa to have been more extensively integrated into those downstream industries with relatively more elastic derived demands for primary aluminium' (p. 44), and this is the pattern which Alcoa apparently followed. The argument depends heavily on unstated assumptions about the transactions costs of alternatives to integration, however, and other theorists have interpreted the evidence very differently (e.g. Silver, 1984, reported in section 6).

(c)   Transaction specific investments and opportunistic recontracting

In Chapter 6 section 6 the problem of opportunistic recontracting and 'hold-up' was discussed in the context of the supply of labour when the latter acquired highly specific skills. A precisely equivalent problem can arise with the supply of other physical inputs or services to the firm. A supplier of a specialised component may have to cooperate closely with the purchaser, and over time gains a great deal of detailed knowledge of the particular 'idiosyncratic' problems associated with this contractual relationship. In other words the supplier gains 'first mover advantages' and a complex bargaining situation arises. As was seen in Chapter 6, the financing of this specialised know-how puts one or other contractor at a disadvantage. If the buyer, early on in the life of the contract, purchases the services of the seller on the basis of the seller's initial or pre-experience efficiency, he runs the risk of 'hold-up' later. The seller could attempt to recontract and extort the difference between the value of his services and those of the next best outsider. Assuming that this threat was lifted by the seller 'posting a bond' and accepting lower remuneration in the first pre-experience period, the buyer might then act opportunistically by refusing to repay the bond. Contractors wishing to protect a 'reputation' will have reasons not to act opportunistically in this way, as was seen in earlier chapters. Nevertheless, the greater the appropriable quasi rents available (that is, the greater the difference between the value of a particular supplier's services and the next best outsider) the greater is the incentive to act opportunistically and the bigger the contractual problem.

Monteverde and Teece (1982a) use this framework to formulate the following hypothesis in the context of the automobile industry: 'The greater is the application of engineering effort associated with the development of any given automobile component, the higher are the expected appropriable quasi rents and, therefore, the greater is the likelihood of vertical integration of production for that component' (p. 207). They measure 'engineering effort' by the cost of development of a component and also take account of 'the degree to which any given component's design affects the performance or packaging of other components' (p. 210). Each component is coded according to whether it is produced in-house or supplied by an outside contractor. Monteverde and Teece are then able to show that vertical integration and 'development effort' are statistically positively and significantly related for their sample of components.

The existence of 'appropriable quasi rents' is not a product only of acquired 'know-how'. It may also derive from transaction-specific *physical* investment. In order to supply a particular component to a firm, a producer may have to invest in equipment which is more or less *specific* to this transaction. Once more this gives rise to quasi rents because the value of the equipment in an alternative use may be well below its value in the manufacture of the component for which it was designed. In the extreme case the equipment may be totally specific to a given transaction, and the alternative to using it for this purpose is simply to sell it for scrap. An opportunist buyer, under these conditions, might attempt to recontract with the supplier and seize these quasi rents. Once the physical investment has been made, the supplier is 'locked-in' to a particular buyer and therefore faces the danger that the buyer will adjust the terms of the contract unfavourably.

This argument clearly relies for some of its force on the existence of changing, uncertain conditions. In a static world with contractual obligations closely specified over a long period of time, the possibility of 'recontracting' is ruled out. Property rights are clearly defined and obligations are spelled out as far into the future as is necessary. No problem of bargaining over quasi rents then arises. As has frequently been asserted, however, the existence of bounded rationality will usually prevent a comprehensive agreement of this type, and the terms must of necessity leave much that is 'implicit'. Explicit sanctions imposed by a third party in the event of some contravention of the provisions of a contract are often costly to arrange and require very simple, unambiguous contract terms. Most complex contracts rely on trust between the parties and the threat of termination and loss of reputation. In these circumstances, the possibility that a buyer will act opportunistically must be a matter of concern to the supplier.

Klein, Crawford and Alchian (1978) argue that the avoidance of opportunism deriving from specific investments will lead to vertical integration. They use the historical example of relations between

General Motors and the Fisher Body Corporation to illustrate the difficulties of market contracts and the tendency towards integration. In 1919 the Fisher Body Corporation agreed to supply General Motors with closed car bodies. To do this, Fisher Body had to undertake highly specific investments in body presses and dies. The contract specified a price for car bodies of cost plus 17.6 per cent (no capital costs were included). In 1926 the two companies merged their operations fully. Over the intervening years the demand for closed bodies had risen above expectations and General Motors felt the price they were paying was too high in the new conditions. Further, because capital costs were not included in the agreement, Fisher had an incentive to use techniques embodying as little capital as possible. Transport costs, on the other hand, were included and this gave Fisher little incentive to relocate their operations near General Motors, a move which the latter tried to encourage.

The case of General Motors and Fisher Body is a complex one and involves considerations other than the mere *specificity* of the capital investment required. Uncertain, changing conditions will favour full integration with a regular supplier, as was argued in section 4. Focusing down on the issue of transaction-specific capital alone, it is possible to argue that opportunistic behaviour can be overcome by quasi-vertical integration and that full integration is not necessary. Thus Monteverde and Teece (1982b) suggest that 'what Klein, Crawford and Alchian have offered is not a theory of vertical integration but a theory of quasi integration' (p. 323). If specific investment is required, opportunism can be prevented by making the *buyer* finance it. The buyer of the input acquires property rights in the equipment necessary for its manufacture and grants certain rights of use to the seller. A relationship similar to that of landlord and tenant described in Chapter 4 is established with respect to property rights in the equipment. The seller of the input supplies the resources which are less specific and can be turned quickly to other uses and are thus less subject to 'hold-up'.

It is worth noticing that, in the case of physical equipment, financing the investment does not subject the buyer to the risk of 'hold-up' as it did in the case of 'know-how'. A buyer that finances the acquisition of non-patentable special skills and 'know-how' may be threatened by a seller who then has first-mover advantages. But a buyer who finances *physical* equipment is not subject to this threat, assuming that property rights can be policed and enforced at relatively low cost. The use of the physical assets can be transferred to another supplier in the event of threats from an existing one: the use of non-patentable 'know-how' cannot. This is the essential difference between the two cases and explains why, in principle, transaction-specific capital leads to quasi-vertical integration.

In order to test the theory that specific capital encourages quasi-vertical integration, Monteverde and Teece (1982b) took a sample of components from two divisions of a US supplier of automotive products. Potential quasi rents were calculated by taking two measures—the simple dollar cost of specialised equipment and an 'estimate of the percentage of original tooling costs which would be required to convert the tooling to its next best use' (p. 325). They found a significant positive relationship between their measure of appropriable quasi rents and the occurrence of quasi-vertical integration, but the general explanatory power of their estimated equation was low.

(d) Enforcing inter-temporal commitments

Subsection (c) was concerned with the problem that the parties to a contract might attempt to 'renegotiate' it as time passed. A particularly extreme example would be that of a buyer who terminates the association and contracts with a *new* supplier after a certain period of time has elapsed. Considerable attention has been given to the incentive properties of terminating an agreement in earlier sections and chapters, and it may therefore come as a surprise that there are circumstances in which a buyer may wish voluntarily to 'disarm' and forgo this threat of termination. It may, in other words, be necessary for the buyer to 'tie himself down' and promise not to use alternative suppliers. Clearly, a buyer who does this will wish to monitor the operations of his supplier very closely and vertical integration is the likely result.

Goldberg (1976) argues that granting a producer the 'right to serve' a constituency may be in the interests of the buyers if uncertainty about the introduction of new technology and the possible obsolescence of specific capital equipment renders the producers unwilling to undertake the required investment in the absence of some assurance about continuing outlets. The problem is not that the buyer might attempt to capture the quasi rents associated with transaction-specific capital (as under subsection c), but that he might desert the supplier entirely in favour of a new entrant using superior technology. Although, in the short run, it will always be in the buyer's interests to maintain the freedom to contract with anyone who offers the most favourable terms, 'the effective achievement of their long-term interests requires that barriers be erected to their pursuit of short-run self-interest' (Goldberg, 1976, p. 433). Unfettered freedom to contract with anyone else at any time will not be in the buyer's interests if the supplier is thereby rendered unwilling to undertake the necessary investment.

These ideas were developed primarily as an approach to the theory of regulation and were elaborated more formally by Ekelund and Higgins (1982). Public regulation, particularly of 'natural monopoly' markets, often involves restrictions on new entrants, and this has been widely criticised by economists as suppressing competition and innovation. Goldberg does not dispute that giving the supplier a 'right to serve' could adversely affect incentives and suppress innovation, but in a very dynamic uncertain environment the total *absence* of such a right could also suppress innovation and prevent entry. He points out that private contractors will often voluntarily attempt to restrict their future options through long-term arrangements. Interpreted in this way, the firm operates like a 'thermal' type of nuclear reactor, increasing the chance that innovations will be 'captured' by using a 'moderator' to slow them down. Innovations which are, so to speak, 'uncontrolled' may be lost. It is a paradox that Schumpeter's 'gale of creative destruction' if too severe, could lay waste all plans to innovate.[15] The firm encourages change by simultaneously moderating its force, and assists new entry by restricting the scope for further entry.

That restrictions on future freedom of contract do not necessarily prevent entry can be seen by considering the problem faced by a firm wishing to encourage the production of a component at present being supplied by a monopolist. It could be argued that the downstream purchaser will have an incentive to produce the upstream component within the firm in order to obtain it more cheaply. The problem with such reasoning is that it is not clear why, if the downstream firm is capable of producing the component in this way, some other independent supplier cannot enter the market and compete with the monopolist. One possible answer is that the new entrant will take time to learn the techniques of production involved, and the established monopolist may have firm-specific cost advantages (i.e. there are barriers to entry). In this situation, faced with the monopolist's threat to retaliate by cutting price in the event of new competitors entering the market, a potential new supplier would look for assurances from the downstream buyer that a continuing outlet would be provided at agreed prices. 'Firm-like' long-term arrangements therefore emerge, and possibly full vertical integration.

6. INTEGRATION AND INNOVATION

The ideas of Goldberg and others on the role of long-term commitments in coping with specific capital investments in the context of technical change lead naturally to an appraisal of the firm as a device for initiating change. In subsection 4 our attention was focused on flexibility and adaptability in the face of an exogenously changing environment. Here we see the firm not as a passive response to the environment but an active determinant of the technical conditions prevailing.

Invention, the perception of new technological possibilities, is inevitably the product of personal insight and personal circumstances. Although it is possible to argue that invention may be stimulated by bringing together within the firm groups of ingenious people all with the characteristics of curiosity and technical knowledge, many of the inventive insights appear still to originate from people outside (Jewkes *et al.*, 1969). To go from a new concept and perhaps a working model to the launching of a commercially viable product or process, however, usually requires the close cooperation of many people over long periods and involves the exercise of entrepreneurship of the Schumpeterian variety. Innovation and the firm are therefore intimately associated. Perhaps the most famous historical example concerns the association between James Watt, who appears to have had a working model of his steam engine operating as early as 1765, and Matthew Boulton, whose entrepreneurial flair and financial assistance were required before the first commercial engine was installed in 1776. Development expenditures amounted to at least sixty man-years of skilled labour (Scherer, 1980, p. 412).

(a) Research and Development

Enormous institutional changes have occurred since those early years of the industrial revolution, and in the modern world research and development expenditure amounting to many billions of dollars is undertaken every year.[16] In fields such as chemicals, drugs, electronics, communications, instrumentation, aircraft, electrical and mechanical engineering, investment in research and development exceeded 3 per cent of sales revenue during 1975 in the United States. Other industrial groups such as food, textiles or paper undertake much less research and development as a percentage of sales revenue, but individual firms assigned to these industries may vary considerably in research effort.

The effects of continuing innovation within the firm on its size and structure have been debated fiercely for many years and a full review cannot be attempted here.[17] It has been argued that large firms are required for successful innovation either because innovation is now beyond the resources of smaller enterprises; or because there are 'economies of scale' associated with research and development (sophisticated scientific equipment is 'indivisible' as is the knowledge to which its use may give rise); or because large size permits the pooling of risks over many projects; or because market power is required to produce an environment sufficiently stable to provide the long-term confidence necessary for the innovator.[18] Others have pointed out that a flow of small- to medium-scale innovations well within the capacity of firms of moderate size to undertake continues from year to year, and that only in the 'spectacular' fields of nuclear power, weapons and space research (mostly government founded) is very large size a pre-requisite. Smaller firms may be more flexible and less prone to bureaucratic inertia, while the risks associated with innovation will vary widely and may, on many occasions, be perceived as not all that great. Most businessmen will try to ensure that most of the major technical problems have been satisfactorily resolved by relatively inexpensive research before the start of full-scale development.[19] Several smaller competing firms may provide an environment more stimulating to the pace of innovation than a single large firm by increasing the incremental reward attached to a more rapid completion of a project, but, as already noted in subsection 5, too many potential imitators or improvers may have an adverse effect and reduce the scope for profitable innovation.[20]

From the point of view of the transactions cost approach to the firm, the implications for firm structure of research and development expenditure depend upon the ability to trade in the information to which the research gives rise. Where the information is difficult to communicate simply, or where licensing the use of the information exposes the firm to opportunism, we would expect the firm to achieve its return by expanding internally. It is this reasoning which forms the basis of the theory of multinational enterprise associated with Dunning (1977), Buckley and Casson (1976), Hymer (1976) and Rugman (1980). Information, to quote Rugman 'is the oil that lubricates the engine of the multinational enterprise' (p. 368). It is, however, information which is product specific rather than merely firm specific. Innovations which improved the general operating efficiency of a firm, for example in its administration or marketing, could be used to expand in its home markets. Product-specific information which cannot be traded and which cannot be used to increase direct exports (perhaps because of tariffs, quotas, transport costs or other barriers to trade) will lead to geographical expansion.

Some link is therefore expected to exist between research and development expenditures and international and conglomerate expansion. Wolf (1977) for example, finds a statistically significant relationship between the extent of multinational operations and technical capability defined as the percentage of scientists and engineers in total employment.[21] Vaupel (1971) found for a sample of 491 US companies divided into national, transnational (operating in under six foreign countries) and multinational classes that research and development expenditure as a proportion of sales was 2.4 per cent for multinationals, 1.6 per cent for transnationals and 0.6 per cent for national enterprises. Similarly Dunning (1973) reports the results of his own study of US affiliates in the UK: US affiliates tend to be more concentrated in faster growing and export oriented industries. They are also attracted to the technologically advanced industries and to those where both capital and advertising expenditure is slightly above average'. (p. 322).

Evidence is less clear in the case of conglomerate diversification. Wolf (1977) again finds evidence that domestic diversification is related to technical capability as defined above, but as Scherer (1980) points out (p. 422) studies of very broad diversification (across two-digit industry groups) do not reveal a close positive relationship with research and development expenditure. This may indicate that most research and development is product or process specific and does not typically confer benefits on activities in many different product markets.[22] If this is so, conglomerate diversification cannot generally be explained in terms of economies in the use of research and development resources, and is better viewed, as in section 4, as a defensive response to the possibility of technological 'mugging'.

Another attempt to study the association between integration, this time *vertical* integration, and research, is that of Armour and Teece (1980). They hypothesise that vertical integration will increase the productivity of resources devoted to research, essentially because of improved flows of information between stages of production. In a sample of petroleum firms for the period 1954–75, vertical integration was measured by the number of primary production process stages undertaken (e.g. crude production, refining, transport and marketing). Other 'exogenous' variables included size, cash flow and diversity (the number of activities in which the firm was engaged, for example coal, uranium exploration/milling/mining, shale reserves, etc.). Their results indicated that 'vertical integration significantly influences.... basic and applied research expenditures' (p. 473). Thus the direction of 'causation' is seen by Armour and Teece as flowing from 'strategy' to research expenditure rather than from research expenditures to 'strategy'. In principle of course both factors will react on one another and it may be misleading to consider that one 'causes' the other.

(b)   Schumpeter's Entrepreneur

As was seen in Chapter 3, Schumpeter argued that large corporations 'ousted' the entrepreneur and technical progress developed a momentum of its own. Thus, the influence of research and development on firm structure and strategy can be seen as part of a theory of the development of these mature corporations which have managed to 'institutionalise' technical change. In this subsection, however, we return to the original Schumpeterian vision of the innovating entrepreneur forcing through technical developments. Some theorists, and especially Silver (1984), have used this view of the entrepeneurial process to explain vertical integration.

Firms integrate forwards or backwards not merely to protect the information at their disposal from alert opportunists (as under

subsection (a)) but to *force through* changes which others are insuf-
ficiently alert to appreciate and who steadfastly refuse to be convinced. The difficulties faced by an entrepreneur in convincing a
financier of his ability and judgement were mentioned in Chapter
3, and the advantages of the entrepreneur having access to private
resources were recognised. But this problem does not stop at the
stage of finance. An innovating entrepreneur will have to persuade
all the people playing a part in his plans that he has the skill and
expertise to carry them through, and that he can fulfil his promises
to suppliers and potential customers alike. Many of these may be
suspicious of new ideas and doubtful about the possibilities of
success. A supplier may be particularly reluctant to cooperate if
heavy transaction-specific investment is involved. This is not simply
because of the recontracting problem discussed earlier or the fear
of further technical change. Even abstracting from these problems,
the supplier would need to be reassured that the innovating entrepreneur had plans which were commercially viable.

Silver (1984) argues that much historical experience of integration is consistent with this view of the entrepreneurial process. New
ideas are implemented by aggressive forward or backward integration and, after they have become accepted, and information about
the new ways of doing things has become more widely available,
disintegration may occur and the 'invisible hand' may begin to reassert itself. Note that vertical integration, far from being designed
to *restrict* access to information, is, in this view, a device to
disseminate information which would otherwise simply not get
across.

When the meat packers of Chicago wished to transport meat to
the eastern cities of the USA they integrated forwards into retailing
and wholesaling. Local wholesalers were initially unwilling to risk
the introduction of refrigerated warehouses for handling large tran-
shipments of meat as they had no experience of what quality could
be expected or of consumers' reactions. Once markets had been
tested and established, independent wholesalers were willing to
enter the trade and the meat packers withdrew entirely from retailing. A similar story can be told concerning the forward integration
of oil refiners into the retailing of gasoline in the USA. We are so
familiar with the service station designed specifically for the
motorist it is easy to forget how novel the idea must have seemed
seventy years ago when petrol would have been purchased from a

general purpose store. Once the construction of a network of outlets was complete, a move towards disintegration could occur mainly through franchise arrangements.

A notable example from British economic history of the resistance to new ideas which Schumpeter's entrepreneur overcomes is provided by the introduction of Henry Bessemer's process for making steel. When first announced, unexpected difficulties were encountered because Bessemer had unwittingly used low-phosphorus iron in his experiments and the process turned out to be unsuitable for the high-phosphorus pig-iron used by most manufacturers. Bessemer discovered the source of the problem and by using non-phosphoric pig-iron imported from Sweden was able to reduce the cost of steel from £50 to £7 a ton. In spite of these technical developments: 'I was paralysed for the moment in the face of the stolid incredulity of all practical iron and steel manufacturers.... None of the large steel manufacturers of Sheffield would adopt my process, even under the very favourable conditions which I offered as regards licences, viz. £2 per ton'. Bessemer responded 'by adopting the only means open to me—namely, the establishment of a steel works of my own in the midst of the great steel industry of Sheffield'.[23]

Each of the examples cited thus far has concerned developments of some historic importance. The argument is applicable in many other areas, however. When efforts were made to redevelop a British watch industry in the decade after 1945 (apparently as part of the defence programme) manufacturers were forced to undertake the production of components and tools. As a result the structure of the industry was quite different from that found in Switzerland at the time, where many firms were highly specialised (see again note 11). A process of very gradual historical evolution may produce a complex pattern of market cooperation between independent firms. Rapid development is rarely compatible with such a structure, and integration is required to marshall the available technical knowledge and disseminate it. To quote Edwards and Townsend once more: 'an industry cannot be started by the integration of a large number of small firms across the market if few people have the necessary technical knowledge, organising knowledge and enterprise'. (p. 242). In another case study the managing director of Aero Research Ltd, a company mainly concerned with developing glue (and acquired in the 1950s by Ciba

Ltd), emphasised the importance of 'customer education'. Although full forward integration to overcome this problem did not take place, measures were required such as the installation at cost price of tanks and apparatus at customers' works to permit bulk delivery of the new materials, the production of a monthly technical bulletin, and the running of summer schools.[24]

A final example concerns the case of Alcoa, already discussed in section 5. There it was seen that Perry (1980) explains Alcoa's strategy of forward integration as a means of instituting a regime of price discrimination. Silver (1984) argues, however, that the evidence can be interpreted in a different light. Alcoa integrated forwards into those areas where they could assist in establishing new uses for aluminium. Perry dismissed this kind of explanation as 'naive' but, as Silver points out, Perry's evidence is not sufficient entirely to discredit it.

7. CONCLUSION

Firms differ. Even those selling in closely related markets may vary considerably in size and structure. Conventional theory is not well equipped to explain this variety and predicts instead that there will be convergence to some optimal size and scope, depending upon technical conditions and the resulting cost curves. The approach surveyed in this chapter suggests, in contrast, that firms differ because the information problems with which the visible hand is designed to cope will alter over time and vary between firms. Integration may reflect a desire to protect and restrict the flow of information to others, it may represent an attempt to disseminate new information to potential customers or suppliers, it may occur as a defensive response to technical change, or as a way of monitoring and enforcing contracts in the face of potential opportunism. Each of these possibilities has been discussed. They do not represent mutually exclusive and rival hypotheses, but may all play a part in making sense of the complex and changing patterns of integration observed in practice.

NOTES

1. Quoted in Edwards and Townsend (1967) pp. 45–6.
2. Edwards and Townsend (1967) p. 301,
3. *The Times* 12 July 1985 p. 19, report of an analysis by Hoare, Govett.
4. There are many interesting problems associated with this type of work — the identification of industries and firms, the suitability of the statistical tests, etc., but a detailed appraisal of the empirical work would take us too far from the main theoretical purposes of this chapter.
5. Thomas Hardy, *Far From the Madding Crowd*, Penguin.
6. Sometimes the technical economies here are linked to the fact that the volume of a container (such as a box or a cylinder) increases as a proportion of its surface area as the sides of the box or the radius of the cylinder are increased. If costs are proportionally related to surface area, while output is more closely related to volume, average costs will fall as dimensions increase.
7. This is simply an application of the 'law of large numbers'.
8. Geographical proximity may be important but again does not in principle preclude the use of markets.
9. This is sometimes called Arrow's paradox (*seee* Arrow, 1962). Kay (1984) links Arrow's paradox to the general phenomenon of 'closed loops'. Information is required to make a decision, but it is only by making the decision that we can find out the information required to guide our decision making (pp. 68–9).
10. Entrepreneurship within the firm has been increasingly recognised and has recently been given the name 'intrapreneurship'. *See* N. Macrae (1976) *The Economist*, also G. Pinchot III (1985).
11. Kay (1984) gives the example of the Swiss watch industry before the coming of electronics. Firms were highly specialised and vulnerable. Edwards and Townsend (1967) refer to the same case (pp. 237–40). The latter used the Swiss industry as an example of a case in which market transactions were important, and contrasted this with the British watch industry where operations were more integrated (pp. 240–2). This contrast suggested that the degree of integration was not merely a technological matter, but depended upon the process of development and 'maturity' of the industry, a point taken up further in section 6.
12. The use of a non-probabilistic approach to expectation and the concept of 'degree of surprise' is associated especially with G. L. S. Shackle (1970, Ch. 5).
13. This argument was used by Robertson and Dennison (1960) to explain the separation of spinning and weaving in the cotton industry in the UK but not in wool: 'The various kinds of cotton yarn are much more uniform and easily standardised products than those of 'woollen' yarn, and the cotton weaver is more certain of being able to satisfy his exact requirements in the open market, and has therefore less inducement to spin for himself.' (p. 27).

14. Edwards and Townsend (1967, p. 302).
15. This statement is perhaps a little strong. If capital fixity combined with a rapid flow of potential new innovations meant that no one was willing to adopt an innovation it would follow that each individual could then innovate, secure in the knowledge that no one else would. The situation is similar to the paradox of voting. Given the minute chance of affecting the outcome of an election it is easy to show that 'rational abstention' is the best policy for the individual who faces positive costs of becoming informed or casting a vote. But if *everyone* is in this position each will reason that, if no one else is going to vote, a trip to the voting booth would be well worth while since it will determine the outcome of the election. Owen and Grofman (1984) present a model in which individuals determine an optimal probability of voting to resolve this paradox.
16. In 1975 US industrial research and development expenditures were $23.5 billion.
17. Scherer (1980, Ch. 15) provides an overview and references to many of the fundamental contributions.
18. J. K. Galbraith (1952, 1967) is particularly associated with these views.
19. E. Mansfield *et al.* (1971)
20. Scherer (1980) calls this the 'market room' effect, which, he argues, works in the opposite direction to the 'stimulus' effect (pp. 426–30). It is possible to argue that innovation will be 'too fast', if it occurs at all, in circumstances of great rivalry. The situation is analogous to the rapid exploration of an area in the hunt for minerals. Mineral rights can be secured only when discovered, and this will cause resources to be expended in 'discovering' deposits of minerals in advance of the date which would have been the outcome of a development process based upon secure property rights.
21. One estimated equation is:

$$X + F = -0.15 + 0.171S + 0.603T$$
$$(3.019) \quad (6.152)$$

't' statistics in parenthesis $\quad R^2 = 0.453$

where X = US exports of ith industry as percentage of domestic production in 1963

F = foreign production propensity; sales of US foreign affiliates in ith industry as percentage of domestic production in the ith industry

S = average size of firm in ith industry

T = proportion of scientists and engineers in labour force.
22. Nelson (1959) advanced the hypothesis that conglomerates might have an advantage in basic research, that is, research which might throw up unexpected results of importance to different products or processes.
23. Bessemer's description of his problem is taken from his autobiography and quoted in Edwards and Townsend (1967, pp. 11–12).
24. Edwards and Townsend (1967, p. 110).

8 The Division of Ownership from Control

The stockholder is therefore left as a matter of law with little more than the loose expectation that a group of men, under a nominal duty to run the enterprise for his benefit and that of others like him, will actually observe this obligation. In almost no particular is he in a position to demand that they do or refrain from doing any given thing.

A. A. Berle and G. C. Means[1]

1. THE BERLE–MEANS HYPOTHESES

Throughout Part II of this book attention has been concentrated on the problem of principal and agent. Chapter 5 outlined some basic propositions about contractual arrangements under various hypothesised conditions. Chapter 6 looked specifically at labour contracts, and Chapter 7 at contracts involving certain non-labour intermediate inputs and other goods and services. At each stage we were concerned to discuss the institutional consequences of imperfect information. In this chapter we continue the story by surveying one of the most controversial areas in the theory of the firm—the so-called 'division of ownership from control', and the incentive problems to which it gives rise.

In Chapter 4 the development of the limited-liability joint-stock enterprise was described. This type of company enabled very large projects to be undertaken by using resources provided by many shareholders, resources coordinated by a specialised management under a board of directors. At the time of the Joint Stock Companies Act 1856 in the UK, it was by no means obvious that this form would come to dominate industrial and commercial life. Indeed the highly dispersed joint-stock company was considered by many to be fatally flawed as a structure of property rights suitable for pursuing a business enterprise. We have already quoted Adam Smith's opinions about the 'negligence and profusion' associated with the management of such enterprises. 'Private adventurers', he argued, had a great advantage over joint-stock companies in foreign trade (the only major area where limited liability joint-stock companies operated in Smith's time). Joint-stock companies 'very seldom succeeded without an exclusive privilege; and frequently have not succeeded with one', (Vol. 2, p. 233). The twentieth century seems conclusively to have refuted Smith's view, however, and the joint-stock company appears well able to withstand the competition from alternative institutional forms.

The growing importance of the joint-stock enterprise, the increasing size of many enterprises, and the wider dispersion of stock ownership in these enterprises were charted by Berle and Means (1930). By 1930, according to Berle and Means, the 200 largest corporations in the United States (other than banking corporations) controlled 49.2 per cent of corporate wealth, 38 per cent of business wealth and 22 per cent of national wealth (p. 33). The trend of increasing concentration had transformed the US economy in the early years of the twentieth century and seemed to show no sign of abating. By 1977, however, the share of the largest 200 corporations in corporate wealth had fallen to 38.3 per cent (Weiss, 1983, p. 453) mainly because of 'the collapse of the railroads, the municipalisation of transit, and the restructuring of the utilities'. In the absence of these developments, Weiss argues, aggregate concentration would have risen to 55.2 per cent. The UK saw a similar dramatic rise in aggregate concentration during the twentieth century. Prais (1976, p. 4) records the share of the hundred largest enterprises in *manufacturing* net output. This rose from around 16 per cent in 1909 to approximately 42 per cent by 1976, most of the increase occurring after 1949. Utton (1982, p. 22) remarks that 'the great increase in the relative growth of the largest enterprises in the UK in the last twenty five years has produced a manufacturing sector which is one of the most highly concentrated (if not *the* most highly concentrated) in the world'.

For our present purposes, the mechanisms which have been used by corporations to grow are not of central concern. Growth may occur through a process of merger (an explanation favoured by Hannah and Kay (1977)), or through internal growth. Some have argued that the growth of firms can be regarded as a process of 'spontaneous drift',[2] for example Prais (1976) and Marris and Mueller (1980). The whole of Chapter 7 was concerned with the forces moulding the size and scope of firms, and with the evolution of corporate strategies and structures after the coming of limited liability. Here, interest is focused on the position of the shareholder in the corporate economy—the holder of exchangeable, collective residual claims.

From the shareholder's point of view it is not the size of the corporation itself which presents special difficulties, but the phenomenon of highly *dispersed* shareholdings. These two factors, size of corporation and dispersion of shareholdings, are logically quite distinct. Unfortunately, the observation that in practice those corporations in the very largest size class have 'inevitably' a dispersed structure of shareholdings and the idea that dispersion has 'permitted' the growth of these giants makes it easy to confound the effects of each. The distinction is important, however, because many relatively small corporations may have dispersed shareholdings, and a few corporations which are in absolute terms large (even if not in the very top league in terms of sales or assets) may still have an identifiable interest with a significant proportion of the shares.

What constitutes a 'significant' proportion of the shares is clearly not easily settled. Berle and Means defined a stock interest as 'important' if it exceeded 20 per cent of the voting shares, and argued that corporations with a single holding of more than 20 per cent (and less than 50 per cent) and with otherwise dispersed shareholdings would be 'minority controlled'. Corporations with 'no single important stock interest' were labelled 'management controlled', or 'joint minority–management controlled' if the largest block of voting shares fell between 5 per cent and 20 per cent. 'Control' was defined (p. 66) as '. . . the actual power to select the board of directors (or its majority)'. Larner (1966), using the same criteria as Berle and Means, [3] investigated the top 200 non-financial corporations in the US in 1963 and compared the results with those of 1929. The results are recorded in table 8.1.

It is seen from the table that in 1929, 58 per cent of the assets of the 200 largest non-financial corporations were classified as under management control. By 1963, Larner calculated that this percentage had risen to 85 per cent. 'It would appear that Berle and Means in 1929 were observing a 'managerial revolution' in process. Now, thirty years later, that revolution seems close to complete, at least

Table 8.1: Assets of 200 largest non financial corporations

Type of 'control'	1929	1963
Private[4]	4	0
Majority	2	1
Minority	14	11
Legal device	22	3
Management	58	85

Source: taken from Larner (1966)

within the range of the two hundred largest non-financial corporations' (pp. 786–7).

The continued importance of 'private' limited companies in the UK until the years following the First World War (see again Chapter 4) suggests that the trend towards dispersion was slower than in the US. The interwar years, however, saw a substantial move towards 'public' companies and the diversification of shareholdings.[5] Between 1911 and 1960 'the minority of wealthy families no longer held their wealth in single companies in which they were also directors, choosing instead to spread their wealth over a wider range of assets'. (Hannah, 1983, p. 57).

By the middle of the twentieth century, therefore, the dispersed joint-stock corporation appeared to dominate many sectors of industry and commerce. For many observers the consequences were expected to be far-reaching. Berle and Means (p. 116) summarised their findings using allusions to a process of imperial expansion: 'The concentration of economic power separate from ownership has, in fact, created economic empires, and has delivered these empires into the hands of a new form of absolutism, relegating "owners" to the position of those who supply the means whereby the new princes may exercise their power'. The managers of joint-stock corporations were thus invested by Berle and Means with princely authority over vast dominions—authority which, the word 'absolutism' suggests, is untrammelled by consitutional or other restraints. Galbraith (1967) has been one of the most effective modern exponents of this thesis, and has termed the managerial elite which is said to govern much of industry 'the technostructure'.

Masters of new technologies and methods, members of the techno-structure have replaced the old landed gentry and the more recent Victorian capitalists as the ruling class.

The work of Berle and Means was very favourably, perhaps even uncritically,[6] received at the time of publication. Yet its influence on professional economists was not very great and the bulk of analysis continued to proceed on the assumption that firms were run in the interests of their shareholders—that is, on the assumption of 'profit maximisation'. It was not until the late 1950s and 1960s that 'managerial' models of the firm became influential (see section 6), but even then it was widely considered that such models were a refinement of the conventional theory, appropriate in conditions of monopoly or tight oligopoly, but largely irrelevant in competitive conditions. Two major factors therefore limited the impact of the Berle–Means observations on economic theory. First, traditional theory was, and is, a theory of price. The objective is simply to predict qualitatively what changes in price will occur in response to exogenous changes in conditions such as increases in income, alterations in factor prices, the imposition of taxes and so forth. A theory of equilibrium price, as was seen in Chapter 1, does not require a theory of the firm. Details of decision-making structures, descriptions of organisational design, the incorporation of hierarchies inhabited by scheming rent seekers, all simply clutter up the analysis to no particular advantage. As Machlup (1967, p. 13) put it 'Frankly, I cannot quite see what great difference organisational matters are supposed to make in the firm's price reactions to changes in conditions'. Second, even though it was accepted that in a monopolistic situation firms would have some freedom of manoeuvre and that hence 'the real existence of firms (that is, an empirical counterpart to the theoretical construct) is required...' (pp. 15–16), in practice, notwithstanding the continuing increase in aggregate concentration, conditions were assumed to be sufficiently competitive for the conventional theory to be generally though not universally, applicable.

It has been a primary purpose of this book, however, to argue that an understanding of economic processes *does* require a theory of the firm. Static or comparative static analysis of equilibrium prices is one thing, the analysis of resource allocation under conditions of uncertainty, complexity and bounded rationality is quite another. This is why so much attention has been given to organisational structure and relatively little to the conventional theory of price. The institutional developments which established the corporate economy in the twentieth century therefore require analysis and interpretation in the light of our earlier chapters. Were Berle and Means correct in their assertion that managers effectively 'controlled' modern joint-stock enterprises? How has the joint-stock company managed to overcome the glaring problem of managerial efficiency which many had considered would confine it to a limited sphere of operations? In sections 3 and 4 we consider these questions using the theoretical framework presented in Chapter 5. Before doing so, however, it is necessary to appreciate that the division of ownership from control is not a problem confined to the joint-stock enterprise.

2. PROPERTY RIGHTS AND THE DIVISION OF OWNERSHIP FROM CONTROL

From the material presented in Chapters 2 and 4, the first things to note about all transactions is that they involve the exchange of property rights in resources, that these rights are never totally unconstrained, and that all rights require to be enforced and protected from challengers (rent seekers). Thus, whatever the *legal* position, the economic concept of 'ownership' is not well defined. People hold property rights. A private, exchangeable, non-partitioned right in a resource comes closest to the popular conception of 'ownership', but even here rights of use may be restricted. On the other hand it is usual to talk of 'owning' shares in a company, and, as we have seen, these shares represent collective rather than private rights. It would seem safer, therefore, to avoid the concept of 'ownership' altogether and to adopt the terminology of property rights theory. Similarly, whatever the rights are that we hold, they are rarely completely unchallengeable, and our 'control' is therefore never perfect. This is clear enough from the analysis of Chapters 5 to 7. If shareholders do not 'control' managers, according to Berle and Means, it is by no means clear that managers can be said to 'control' workers, or that outside suppliers of components or other service inputs are perfectly under 'control'. The case of the shareholder's position in the firm is not therefore special, and the problem that shareholders face is not qualitatively different from that confronted by person A in Chapter 2 in his dealings with the architect, plumber and electrician.

A firm represents, according to the view developed in each of the earlier chapters, *a nexus of contracts*. These contracts establish an allocation of rights among the individuals who comprise the firm. The nature of these contracts and the difficulty of defining a boundary to the firm have been discussed in some detail elsewhere. Here it is necessary to consider whether the same conceptual framework is applicable to the relationship between the shareholder and the firm. The most systematic exposition of the idea of the firm as a 'legal fiction which serves as a nexus for contracting relationships' is to be found in Jensen and Meckling (1976, p. 311). Their discussion of 'ownership structure' in the corporation is based entirely on the concept of 'agency costs generated by the contractual arrangements between the owners and top management of the corporation' (p. 309). To a lawyer, however, the shareholder's relationship with the firm cannot be regarded as a contractual one. Neither is it true that shareholders have contracts with managers. Thus, to argue, as we did above, that the shareholder and the manager are in a similar relationship as person A and his architect is to ignore the fact that no *actual* contract exists in the former case while it does in the latter. This has led some theorists to argue that the principal-agent paradigm is not appropriate in the context of shareholder and manager. Clark (1985, p. 56), for example, objects to the use of the terms 'principal' and 'agent': 'The core legal concept implies a relationship in which the principal retains the power to control and direct the activities of the agent'. The shareholder's powers in a corporation are limited, however, and 'the officers and directors are "fiduciaries" with respect to the corporation and its stockholders'. They have various responsibilities and duties but they are not agents.

Supporters of the nexus of contracts approach recognise that the shareholder–manager relationship is not contractual from a legalistic point of view, but argue that it can be analysed as if it were. The contract is once again 'implicit'. Clark (1985, p. 61) replies that 'this extreme contractualist viewpoint is almost perverse. . . . I would insist that the use of the term contract in connection with "implicit contracts". . . is metaphorical, and. . . that the metaphor is seriously misleading'. In earlier chapters we have attempted consistently to present and elaborate upon the contractualist position, and Chapter 8 is no place to recant. That our use of terms such as 'contract' or 'agent' does not accord with legal definitions may be readily agreed. Perhaps this is unfortunate in that it invites misunderstanding and confusion in discussions between economists and lawyers. But use of these words in the context of the problem of managerial incentives is only likely to be 'seriously misleading' to those who see the principal as having 'the power to control and direct'. As was seen in Chapter 5, much of the *economic* analysis of principal and agent proceeds on the assumption of 'unobservability' of effort and state of the world, and hence this analysis presupposes the effective impossibility of direct control as distinct from indirect incentives based on the outcome. The principal may retain an entirely notional *legal* 'power' to direct the agent, but any principal in the conditions postulated would have no *effective* power to do any such thing. Conversely, the lower the monitoring costs faced by the principal, the greater his skills and technical knowledge about the tasks assigned to the agent, and hence the greater his *effective* power to direct, the less he needs an agent.

Accepting therefore that managers are not, legally speaking, agents of shareholders, it is still reasonable to argue that the manager does have a contract with the firm, that the provisions of this contract and the incentive devices built into it will crucially influence the willingness of people to hold shares in the company, and that in assessing the likely effectiveness of these contracts the shareholder will presumably have the same factors in mind as in an assessment of an agency contract. If it were objected that few shareholders would have detailed knowledge of managerial contracts in a firm, the defence must be similar to that advanced by Stiglitz in the context of the discussion of piece rates and time rates (Chapter 6, p. 157). Over time the competitive process selects those arrangements with survival value and these will look, in the end, like a 'solution' to an agency problem.

The principal–agent paradigm has further advantages. The incentive problem identified by Berle and Means is by no means peculiar to the joint-stock company, and it is possible to apply the same analytical framework in the context of alternative institutional forms.

(i) The Nationalised Firm
In the UK the years following the Second World War saw a substantial growth in the nationalised industry sector. Large and

important industries such as coal, gas, the railways and iron and steel were nationalised in the years 1946–9. The 1970s saw a further expansion of the state sector into shipbuilding (1977), aerospace (1977), and the development of interests in particular companies such as British Leyland (1976), Rolls Royce (1971) and the British National Oil Corporation (1976). Since 1980 there has been a reversal of this trend. The 'privatisation' of the British National Oil Corporation, British Aerospace, British Telecom and Jaguar Cars has already occurred, and further disposals are planned, most notably British Airways and parts of British Gas.[7]

The nationalised industries in the UK have usually taken the form of 'public corporations'.[8] These corporations have assets vested in a Board of Directors and the responsibilities of the board are set out in Acts of Parliament. For our purposes, however, the important characteristic is that there are no exchangeable residual claims held by members of the public. This would also apply to British Leyland (with only a very small private shareholding) and Rolls Royce. These companies are 'public companies' with the shares held by the state and are not classified as 'public corporations'. The public corporations alone were responsible for 16 per cent of gross domestic fixed capital formation and 10.8 per cent of gross domestic product in 1983. They also employed 1.6 million people.[9] A significant economic sector in terms of output, employment and capital investment thus comprises institutions in which no exchangeable residual claims exist, and a further group of companies have the great majority of their shares held by the state.

Public corporations illustrate very well the difficulty of using the term 'ownership'. No one 'owns' the assets of a public corporation although various individuals, directors, managers, or government ministers possess property rights. If the word 'taxpayer' were substituted for the word 'stockholder' in the quote from Berle and Means which heads this chapter, it would apply to the nationalised industries without further amendment (apart perhaps from the deletion of the word 'almost' in the second sentence). It is not surprising therefore that the policy problem of 'the control of the nationalised industries' has become of great importance and observers such as Millward (1978), Littlechild (1979) and Rees (1980) have presented the issues in terms of the theory of agency.

(ii) The Bureaucracy

Similar problems of control arise in the case of services supplied by a bureaucracy or government agency. In the fields of education, health, environmental and other social services, output is often not rationed by price but is distributed at zero price and rationed by non-price methods. These bureaucracies therefore do not receive revenue from sales of their products but are funded by government grants. They are similar to nationalised industries in that no exchangeable residual claims exist. The economic analysis of bureaucracy is particularly associated with Niskanen (1968, 1971, 1973, 1975). Niskanen regards the bureau as a monopoly supplier of a service facing a single customer (the government) which purchases on behalf of the rest of the citizens. In this bilateral bargaining situation the bureaucrat is assumed to be at an advantage because of his control over information flows. We will discuss the consequences of these assumptions in section 6 when the managerial approach to the firm is sketched in more detail. Clearly, however, the problem of monitoring and managerial incentives is a central one in the economics of bureaucracy, and some writers, for example Rowley and Elgin (1985) have argued that the principal–agent paradigm is as applicable to this case as to the joint-stock company.

(iii) Non-Profit Enterprises

Government bureaucracies are not alone in their provision of services such as health and education. In these and other fields they are accompanied by institutions which sell services in the market but cannot distribute residual profits. Once again there are no holders of residual claims. Non-profit enterprises have a board of trustees who are responsible for appointing managers to run the day-to-day administration, and for ensuring that the activities of the enterprises are compatible with the purposes for which they were established. Managers might be expected to have considerable discretionary power under these circumstances, and theories of the activities of non-profit institutions have been developed in this 'managerial' tradition. Nicols (1967) argues that mutual (i.e. non-profit) savings and loan associations in the US will behave differently from stock (i.e. for profit) associations. Depositors in mutuals receive 'shares' but 'typically surrender their proxies to management on opening an account' (p. 337). The result is a diffused 'ownership', but 'control' concentrated in management. Nicols describes management at one point as 'a self-perpetuating autocracy' (p. 337). Managers can divert the resources of mutuals for their own benefit, he argues, by inflating expenses. Where new entry is restricted managers may operate a policy of creating artificial shortages and then 'ration' loans to those who purchase insurance or other services from private companies in which they have a personal interest. Nepotism is likely to be higher in mutual than in stock associations, a proposition Nicols tested by the simple expedient of checking the names of chief executive officers and other officers to see how frequently officers had the 'same name'.

This approach is clearly in a direct line of descent from Berle and Means. A similar type of analysis is presented by Newhouse (1970) in his model of a non-profit hospital. Trustees, administrators and medical staff will inflate the quality of medical services provided in the interests of prestige. Expensive medical equipment will be underutilised, while Newhouse uses 'accreditation' as an index of quality and notes that 'there is a lower percentage of accreditation among the proprietaries than among the voluntaries' (p. 69). We will discuss Newhouse's model briefly again in section 6. For now it suffices to note that the view of non-profit institutions taken by Nicols and Newhouse suggests that they can survive only in a protected environment. Both are explicit about this: 'The mutual is an institution which can survive only at the cost of continued governmental restriction of competition' (Nicols, 1967, p. 346). Similarly, Newhouse explains the non-profit hospital by reference to legal barriers to entry and favourable tax status. Thus both writers take the same position with respect to non-profit enterprises as Adam Smith took with respect to the joint-stock form. They can survive only with an 'exclusive privilege'.

Recent work in the transactions costs tradition casts doubts on this conclusion, however, and suggests that it may be as mistaken as was Smith's assessment of the joint-stock company. Papers by Hansmann (1980), Easley and O'Hara (1983) and Holtmann (1983) explore the idea that non-profit enterprises are a response to particular kinds of information problem and thus 'contract failure'. If contractual problems deriving from bounded rationality and information asymmetry explain hierarchical structures and internal labour markets (Chapter 6), and if the same forces help to determine the scope of the firm (Chapter 7), it would be surprising if they had no influence on the allocation of rights to residual profits. This issue forms the subject matter of sections 3 to 5.

(iv) Labour-Managed Firms

Another case which illustrates the difficulty of using terms such as 'ownership' and 'control' is that of the labour-managed firm. In this type of firm each member of the team has a collective right to share in the residual and can, through a process of collective decision making, appoint those who will act as the day-to-day managers. If each person working in the enterprise has a 'share' then, in the legal sense used by Berle and Means, all members of the team are 'owners'. Often, however, the legal 'ownership' of the enterprise is vested in the state, as is the case for example in Yugoslavia. George (1982) suggest that the term 'cooperative' be used in the former case and 'labour-managed firm' in the latter. A more important issue concerns the exchangeability of rights. Usually, membership of the team and the collective rights which accompany it cannot be traded. Non-exchangeability of property rights is something cooperatives have in common with non-profit enterprises, and property rights theorists would expect the conduct of these enterprises to be affected in significant ways. The labour-managed enterprise has been studied extensively in recent years[10] and we will touch on some of the important findings in section 5.

Each of the institutional forms discussed in this section share with the joint-stock company one central problem; 'ownership' and 'control' are separated either because residual claims are widely dispersed, or because they are non-exchangeable, or both. This structure of property rights contradicts the idea that residual claims will become concentrated in the hands of a single monitor (see Chapter 4), and suggests that managerial 'shirking' will be a serious problem. Yet incentive problems have not prevented non-profit enterprises, cooperatives, joint-stock companies, and many other slight variants of these basic types from evolving. Non-profit-making nursing homes and other charitable foundations survive in competition with other forms, not exclusively because of tax advantages. The 'Rochdale Pioneers' of the cooperative movement in the mid nineteenth century were assisted by no coercive power. Buyers of IBM shares do not do so at gunpoint. In sections 3 to 5 we survey the available monitoring devices more carefully and investigate how institutional structures are related to the agency problem. As Fama and Jensen (1983, p. 345) express it, 'we explain the survival of organisational forms largely in terms of the comparative advantages of characteristics of residual claims in controlling the agency problems of an activity'.

3. INCENTIVE CONTRACTS

(a) Managerial Remuneration in the joint-stock company

When the provider of capital appoints a manager to decide how it should be used, an agency problem arises. In Chapter 5 it was seen that the nature of a contract between principal and agent will depend upon what can be observed, by whom, and at what cost. Let us suppose that the manager's effort and the environment or 'state of the world' in which he is operating are unobservable to outsiders. The contract will then depend upon the 'outcome' alone, and the provisions for sharing the outcome between the two parties will depend upon the risk preferences of each. In other words, if a manager is to be given an incentive his reward must depend upon the outcome, in this case the overall profit of the firm. Returning to Figure 5.5, the principal P can be regarded as the provider of capital and the agent A as the manager. If shareholdings are widely dispersed, P can be regarded as a 'typical shareholder' who is risk neutral so far as the operation of the firm is concerned. The shareholder is interested only in the expected value of his profits from the firm. The manager is risk averse and is, by assumption, unable to find insurance in the market because of the inability of insurers to observe states of the world any more easily than shareholders. There may then exist a contract along the locus xw which will induce effort e from the manager of the shareholders' funds. If managers are risk averse they will never take the entire risk, and hence we will not observe the manager effectively holding all residual claims and the provider of capital turning into a bond-holder and lending at fixed interest. Thus the concentration of all residual claims in the monitor, as in the classical capitalist firm, is likely to exist only where capital requirements are small and monitors are risk neutral.

Contracts which link managerial rewards to profits will only work, of course, if the individual manager's effort is actually capable of influencing the overall performance of the firm. In a 'team' environment where the individual contribution of each manager cannot be identified the 'public good trap' will lead to shirking, and, as was seen in Chapter 4, contracts based upon 'effort' will be instituted. 'Monitoring gambles' and the hier-archical structures associated with them will become important, as described in chapter 6. Eventually, however, the problem must be faced of who monitors the effort of the most senior managers? If shareholdings are dispersed the answer seems to be no one, and the house of cards erected in Chapter 6 falls down as predicted by Adam Smith. By giving senior managers at the apex of the hierarchy compensation packages which depend upon overall performance, however, effort incentives are provided. A manager low down the hierarchical structure will not find the holding of shares a great incentive to effort because the total profit of the enterprise may be imperceptibly affected by his behaviour. Senior managers are like the key stone in an arch, however. Take them away and collapse ensues. In place the whole structure stands. Thus the effort of top managers clearly will influence outcomes, and changes in the intensity of monitoring will permeate through the hierarchical structure. This argument is therefore based upon Alchian and Demsetz's (1972) observation that monitors need an incentive to monitor, but it does not lead to the conclusion that the residual must be completely undiluted and assigned to a single person. All that is required is that incentives to top management are good enough for the joint-stock form with its benefits of risk spreading and large team operations to prevail over alternative available institutional forms.

The remuneration of senior executives is clearly a matter of great importance, and the evidence concerning the incentives built into various payment packages is still in dispute. Early work by Sargant Florence (1961) for the UK and Villarejo (1961) for the US pointed to the small percentage of shares held by directors in very large companies. The median holding was between 1 per cent and 2 per cent in the early 1950s. Managerial shareholding rose during the 1950s and 1960s however, and the combined interest of corporate directors and management is often considerable. Demsetz (1983) reports that in the years 1973–82 the ownership interest of corporate directors and management was 19.3 per cent for the middle ten firms in the 1975 Fortune 500 list. For ten randomly selected firms too small to be included in the Fortune 500, the managerial interest was 32.5 per cent. It was in the very largest size range (the top ten firms), as would be expected, that the percentage interest of managers and directors fell to 2.1 per cent. Thus 'a substantial fraction of outstanding shares is owned by directors and management of corporations in all but the very largest firms' (p. 388).

From the point of view of incentives, neither the combined

shareholding of management nor the *proportionate* holding of senior managers is the most important factor, however. Of greater significance is the nature of the remuneration package of the most senior managers. Work in the early 1960s suggested that management income was more closely related to company size as measured by total sales than to company profits.[11] McGuire *et al.* (1962), for example, reported statistical correlations between executive compensation, profits and sales in a cross-section of firms in the period 1953–9. Their evidence supported a relationship between sales and executive incomes, although they cautiously warned that statistical problems meant that their tests 'do not completely rule out the possibility of a valid relationship between profits and executive incomes too' (p. 760). By the early 1970s, cross-section studies of this nature were subjected to considerable criticism.[12] Given the hierarchical structure of large firms the internal incentive arrangement might be expected to result in a different scale of prizes for the contestants in a big tournament than a smaller one. But this would not permit us to deduce that, for a manager at the top of a *given* firm, an overriding incentive existed to increase the size of that particular hierarchy. A further criticism concerned the measure of executive incomes used. By concentrating on salaries, other important components were overlooked.

Masson (1971) constructed a measure of executive compensation which included deferred compensation such as stock options and retirement benefits as well as stock ownership, salary and bonuses. His sample consisted of the top three to five executives of thirty-nine electronics, aerospace and chemical companies for the years 1947–66. From these data Masson concluded that executives receive a positive reward for increasing stock value, that changes in stock value are more important to the executive than changes in profit earned, and that the hypothesis that executives were paid to expand sales was rejected. Similar conclusions were reported by Lewellen (1969). In a survey of fifty of the largest 500 US firms, Lewellen found that only about one-fifth of the total remuneration of the top executive came from salary. This study was followed by a further enquiry by Lewellen and Huntsman (1970). One of their measures of executive compensation included the 'current income equivalent' of various deferred and contingent pay schemes. In the case of a pension plan, for example, the extra salary necessary to buy equivalent cover from an insurance company was estimated and included as part of the comprehensive measure of managerial compensation. Their results indicated that 'reported company profits appear to have a strong and persistent influence on executive rewards, whereas sales seem to have little, if any, such impact' (p. 918). A surprising aspect of this finding was that it applied to the simpler measure of executive compensation (salary plus bonuses) as well as to the more sophisticated measure. Meeks and Whittington (1975) concluded in contrast that managerial compensation was strongly correlated with sales in cross-section tests. Developing the point mentioned earlier, Meeks and Whittington did not, however, deduce from this that incentives are primarily in the direction of increasing size at the expense of profits. It is simply not open to managers or directors suddenly to choose to be as big as IBM or ICI in order to raise their salary. Although cross-section correlations are strong, large proportionate increases in size would be necessary to have a noticeable effect on a manager's income. In practice the manager does not choose the size of the firm but may have some influence over the rate of growth. When Meeks and Whittington considered the relative influence of higher growth and higher profits on managers' rewards, however, their data suggested that profits were the more important.

Interpretation of data derived from cross-section studies is subject to many pitfalls. Apart from the technical econometric problems which accompany all such work,[13] the direction of 'causation' can always be disputed (do higher profits 'induce' higher remuneration and thus provide incentives, or is it that the price of managerial services rises with its quality and that high-quality management results in higher profits?). These two hypotheses are difficult to disentangle and indeed both could be true simultaneously. From the point of view of the theory of incentive contracts it is merely necessary to note that the hypothesis that good-quality and expensive managers produce high profits requires the existence of a managerial labour market in which managerial services are traded. These services must be thought of as similar to other inputs purchased by the firm and there must be some mechanism for monitoring their quality and punishing poor performance. It was, of course, the assumed total absence of any such mechanism for monitoring the top managers that led us to consider the relationship of remuneration to profits in the first place. The role of the managerial labour market may be more important that we have thus far allowed for, however, and we consider its operation in the next subsection.

(b) The Managerial Labour Market

Let us envisage that managerial services are purchased from specialist suppliers. The nature of the service is highly complex and costly to monitor, but let us further suppose that shareholders through specialist advisors, journalists, independent auditors and other personal contacts are able to form some assessment of the competence and dedication of the management. They have, in the jargon of Chapter 5, some 'informative signal' at their disposal. Incentives could then be given to the top management, not through the direct ownership of shares, but through a type of 'monitoring gamble'. This system has traditionally been regarded as inapplicable to the joint-stock form of enterprise, and it is interesting to consider whether the traditional approach is justified.

(i) In the first place, in a dispersed corporation there is no *single* shareholder in a position to monitor the management in this way and enforce the terms of any monitoring gamble. A penalty for 'shirking' could be imposed only through the mechanism of the shareholders' meeting, and we have already drawn attention to the lack of any incentive for the small individual shareholder to attend, or even to become acquainted with whatever 'informative signal' might be relevant. Further, in the unlikely event of a substantial shareholder revolt, it has usually been assumed that the incumbent management has an advantage because of the system of 'proxy' votes.[14] Uninformed shareholders may simply permit the managers to vote on their behalf. Persuading them from doing this by informing them of the evidence of managerial shirking may be a very costly undertaking, and if any single shareholder or group of shareholders attempted it they would effectively be supplying a public good (information) free of charge to the rest of the shareholding body. Thus, except in the special circumstances of zero costs of acquiring a sufficiently informative signal, and zero participation costs at shareholders' meetings, shareholder monitoring would appear to be of little practical importance. A world of zero information costs is not, however, the world we have been considering in this book.

(ii) There is a further element to this problem of management incentives which requires consideration in the context of the analysis of earlier chapters. If the managerial labour market is to play a part in disciplining managers the mechanism must be through the establishment and protection of 'reputation'. Shirking will be punished through loss of reputation and a lower value on the market. Alchian (1969) argues, for example, that much of the effort of academics in the fields of publication and research is not the result of a desire to enhance the prestige of the institutions which employ them, or to serve the interests of the taxpayer, but derives from attempts to increase the value of the individual in the academic labour market. Similarly, Fama (1980) constructs a model in which a manager's wages fall if he or she is associated with failure and rise if associated with success. Fama argues that managerial labour markets may result in a form of *ex post* 'settling up' whereby shirking is punished by future losses of income equivalent to the resulting shortfall in performance.

For this mechanism to work, it has to be assumed that managers recontract period by period and that they are effectively always selling their services on an external market. The whole of Chapter 6, however, was dedicated to the proposition that incentives required *long-term commitments* and the formation of *internal* labour markets. Further, it was there argued that reputations and 'brand name capital' were more costly for individual managers to establish than for firms. Is it possible to reconcile these points of view? The answer is that incentives based upon hierarchies and internal labour markets will develop in conditions of information asymmetry and task idiosyncracy, but that eventually all such arrangements confront the central problem of this chapter—who monitors the person at the top? To this question there are two possible responses. The first is that the person at the top, whether a dominant shareholder or a manager, has a personal interest in the residual great enough to induce effort and ensure the viability of the organisation. This is the answer provided in subsection 3(a). The second response is that the top managers are constrained by impersonal 'market pressures'. 'The market' will force a penalty for poor performance. This is the answer suggested by Alchian and Fama, and reported in this subsection. Essentially an appeal is made to some *external* force to restrain the behaviour of senior managers, in the case considered above the force of competition in the managerial labour market.

The mechanism by which competition influences behaviour is

still somewhat mysterious, however. We are asked to imagine a world in which a group of elite senior managers take a succession of posts and build up reputations for high-quality service which then become a valuable component of 'human capital'. Intuitively plausible though this may be, there is a difficulty. Managers in a dispersed corporation will be appointed by other managers. If attention to shareholders' interests cannot be assumed on the part of managers promoted internally to the top of the hierarchy, there seems no good reason to assume that in their screening of senior managers from outside they will be any more efficient. Good outside applicants might simply highlight the shortcomings of the established group. If, on the other hand, we assume that internally promoted managers at the top of the tree are by convention moved to positions where their ability to damage the firm is limited, and that all senior appointments are under the control of a mobile manager, it is still not clear that, in choosing a successor, such a manager would have an incentive to pick the best candidate. He might attempt to portray his 'reign' in the best light by picking a poor successor unless the managerial labour market is very sophisticated and penalises failure in this function as surely as failure in internal monitoring. Arguments along these lines therefore appear, at the least, incomplete. Ultimately, they seem to come down to the idea that a mobile manager who contracts on the labour market at frequent intervals will not shirk because he believes that other managers will penalise him later if he does. These other managers penalise him because they believe that if they do not do so they themselves will be penalised by other managers elsewhere who believe.... The joint-stock enterprise survives through the power of shared beliefs, an institutional proof of the existence of collective levitation.

The power of shared beliefs is not to be underestimated, but we might expect these beliefs to be more durable if founded on something more substantial than thin air. If senior managers are constrained by outside forces it is because they know that there are people outside the firm who are alert enough to spot a team operating short of its potential and with an incentive to act on that information. Competition is not an automatic impersonal force, it operates through the activities of the entrepreneur, and it is the entrepreneur with his accompanying threat of unexpected change who provides the managerial incentives. In section 4 it is argued that the importance of the managerial labour market as a device for encouraging profit-orientated behaviour can only be understood *in conjunction with* the possibility of entrepreneurial intervention, and the restructuring of property rights which this brings about.[15]

4. ENTREPRENEURSHIP AND MANAGERIAL INCENTIVES

A joint-stock firm is not by its very nature either concentrated or dispersed in the structure of its shareholdings. No document or consitution exists proclaiming that a particular company's shares will be dispersed widely. The degree of concentration or dispersion is capable of changing over time. It may appear *at any given moment* that shareholdings are dispersed and management has great discretionary power. But financial capital can congeal suddenly and unexpectedly. A dominant interest can emerge which changes the top management and consigns the existing top managers to the labour market. As with the model of Shapiro and Stiglitz (1984), reported in Chapter 6, the penalty involved in being fired will depend on conditions in this market. If all managers were identical the penalty might be a period of unemployment (top managers' salaries are above market clearing levels). Where managers differ in attributes and skills the penalty might be extorted through downward revision of the wage, as suggested by Fama. This will occur because managers, fearing takeover themselves, will have a clear incentive to avoid appointing other managers with a poor record.

Fama (1980), however, explicitly rejects the influence of the takeover or the entrepreneur as necessary ingredients in an explanation of the operation of the labour market. Manne's (1965) description of management discipline as an 'entrepreneurial job' is criticised (p. 295) and the takeover is considered merely a 'discipline of last resort'. Instead Fama prefers to rely on markets in outside directors (p. 294) who 'are in their turn disciplined by the market for their services which prices them according to their performance as referees'. Like a steeplejack gingerly edging further and further up an elaborate tower of indeterminate height, monitor stacked upon monitor, Fama is apparently determined not to look down. The whole argument is reminiscent of debates surrounding the survival of a paper currency. Once the psychology of acceptability has been established no one bothers to present his paper to the issuer and demand the gold or other commodities promised. Yet many would still argue that the *potential* for convertability would be important in maintaining confidence in circumstances where coercive power cannot compel acceptance of the currency. Similarly, in a free society, the survival of the dispersed joint-stock company ultimately depends upon a recognition that it can be turned into something else. The agents of any such transformation are Kirznerian entrepreneurs.

(a) The Takeover

Where the management of a dispersed corporation is judged by an outside entrepreneur to be inefficient, the advantages of establishing a controlling interest are obvious. The gains from closer monitoring may outweigh the disadvantages of less widely spread risks and, if this is so, entrepreneurial rewards are available. To achieve these rewards, however, the entrepreneur must have knowledge which is not widely available to others. As was seen in Chapter 3, the entrepreneur will gain if his judgement is different from that of other people and it proves to be correct. Where information is publicly available and capital markets are efficient in using this information for valuing assets such as equity shares, the scope for entrepreneurial action is much more limited, however. The difficulty is once more the free rider problem.

As Grossman and Hart (1980) point out, if the public good trap and the free rider problem prevent internal monitoring by existing shareholders it seems unreasonable to assume that the same problem would not be faced by outsiders. Specifically, any offer made by an outside bidder for the existing shares will not succeed because it will be in no individual shareholder's interest to accept the price and sell to the raider. Our Kirznerian raider is hoping to gain from the appreciation of the shares which he purchases, but any profit which he makes 'represents a profit shareholders could have made if they had not tendered their shares to the raider' (p. 43). A small shareholder will reason that whether or not they accept the raider's offer will not perceptibly affect the chance of the raid succeeding, and they will refuse in the hope of making capital gains.[16] The problem is similar to that encountered in Chapter 4 by the entrepreneur attempting to purchase communal rights to fish in the island lake. An existing holder of the communal right might 'hold out'[17] for a price which made the whole enterprise profitless (Chapter 4, p. 87).

Differences in information and expectations between raider and shareholders may permit profits to be achieved by the entrepreneur and hence takeovers to take place. However, if the *threat* of takeover is to exercise a disciplinary effect on managers we might argue that efforts to circumvent the free rider problem will be sought by shareholders to encourage entrepreneurial intervention. To overcome free riding it is necessary to exclude non-payers. How can this be achieved? Grossman and Hart suggest that minority shareholders (that is, those who do not tender their shares to a raider and still hold shares in a company following a successful raid) might be excluded from the benefits brought about by the raider. Once a raider has control of 51 per cent of the shares, the assets or output of the company could be sold to another company owned by the raider at a price disadvantageous to minority interests. A constitution which permitted a raider to behave in this way would represent a 'voluntary dilution of (the shareholders') property rights' (p. 43) which was nevertheless 'essential if the takeover bid mechanism is to be effective' (p. 46). Shareholders face a trade-off. The greater the 'dilution' they permit, the more closely are managers constrained by the takeover threat, but the prospect of pecuniary gain arising out of a raid is reduced. The attitude of the law towards post-raid behaviour of the new majority shareholders, and the provisions of corporate constitutions, will therefore play an important part in determining the costs of pursuing a takeover. Managers of a dispersed corporation, if they wish to avoid the managerial labour market, must therefore exert a level of effort which leaves no scope for pure profit on the part of a raider after allowing for the costs which he will incur.

A continuing process of competition between institutional forms, or what Jensen and Meckling call 'ownership structures', can be regarded as taking place through trading in the various claims which make up the firm. In Chapter 4 we saw how, in Jensen and Meckling's model, the agency costs associated with using outside finance (equity or debt) were set against the benefit to the 'peak coordinator' of a less risky portfolio. Here, we are arguing that if, in a dispersed corporation, agency costs rise too far and the market value of the firm falls too low, the potential gain from mitigating the agency problem may outweigh the risk-bearing costs associated with running the firm with a more concentrated share structure, and potential entrepreneurial profits will arise. Conversely, if the top manager is interested in ensuring that no takeover occurs, there is a limit on the non-pecuniary benefits which he can derive from the firm. This limit will depend upon the transactions costs faced by the entrepreneur in effecting a takeover and implementing a new 'ownership structure.'

Evidence on the size of these transactions costs and the general effectiveness of the 'market in corporate control' is notoriously difficult to appraise. Here we merely refer to a few of the better-known studies. Hindley (1970) compares the actual value of a corporation, as measured by the market value of its shares, with the potential value, which he relates to the accounting value of its assets. The ratio of accounting values to stock market price (R) is, in effect, taken as a proxy for 'agency costs' and we might therefore expect raided firms to exhibit a higher value of R than non-raided firms. Hindley tested this proposition on a sample of firms for the years 1958–63 and concluded that a 'market in corporate control does exist' although a rather large discrepancy between actual and potential value' can be reached before takeover becomes probable (p. 209). He also related R to the dispersion of stockholdings, finding that in five out of eight groups tested 'managerial' corporations had higher values of R than 'closely held' corporations (p. 217). This result is, of course, perfectly consistent with the ideas of Jensen and Meckling, who would predict just such a relationship, but without the implication that there is anything necessarily inefficient about a high value of R.

A study directly concerned with the transactions costs of making a tender offer is that of Smiley (1976). Transactions costs included the tender offer premium (i.e. any excess of the offer price over the market price just before the offer), costs of management time, legal expenses, brokers' fees, advertising and so forth. Smiley estimated that the '*ex ante* certainty equivalent costs of tender offers are at least 13 per cent of the market price of the shares after the offer' (p. 30). The management of a corporation, he concluded, had some scope for achieving non-pecuniary benefits before attracting a takeover. Singh (1975) investigated takeovers in the UK during the post-war years, and was also sceptical of their role in maintaining management incentives. In a comparison of acquiring and acquired companies Singh found the former were bigger, more profitable, faster growing, more liquid and more highly geared in the years 1967–70. Although higher profits reduced the chance of being taken over, size was much more important and led Singh to conclude that 'for larger firms the empirical evidence supports the new managerial and behavioural theories of the firm...'(p. 511). It is not clear, however, that this evidence can be taken as support for any particular view of the firm. The 1950s and 1960s coincided with developments in corporate strategy and structure which were reviewed in Chapter 7. Mergers and takeovers are simply ways in which a firm's operations can be extended or widened, and many will therefore take place between firms whose managers have perceived that there are advantages to a close association. There is no *necessary* implication that agency costs are inefficiently high in one of the firms, and the top managers of both firms may retain their respective posts. Disentangling mergers and takeovers designed to achieve mutual benefits from those aimed at unseating an inefficient management is a difficult task.

(b) The Product Market
Competition in the product market is widely considered an incentive to effort. Monopolists are popularly supposed to take much of their profit in the form of a quiet life, while competition is expected to reduce the capacity of managers to indulge in discretionary behaviour. In the case of perfect competition, elementary textbooks imply that all discretion disappears. We do what must be done and survive, or we do something else and perish. This has led many neoclassical economists to assume that, provided product markets are competitive, problems of the division of ownership from control can safely be ignored. Machlup's (1967) view on this matter has already been quoted in section 1.

Behavioural theorists such as Leibenstein, who invented the term 'X' inefficiency to describe the achievement of less than the maximum output technically possible from given inputs, and who has developed his own approach to the internal workings of the firm, also assign a prominent role to competition. In Leibenstein (1979) the incomplete nature of employment contracts and the necessity for monitoring are recognised. A theory of average production costs is then developed. As the effort of workers increases, money costs per unit of output fall. Effort depends on 'pressure' either from peers (horizontal pressure) or from superiors (vertical pressure). The degree of pressure is, in turn, a function of average costs. As costs rise the survival of the firm is threatened and the pressure on the individual to 'pull his weight' is increased. Diagrammatically, Leibenstein's approach is summarised in Figure 8.1. Curve A shows how costs depend on effort. Curve $B(T_1)$ shows how effort increases as costs rise (because of more intensive monitoring or 'pressure'). The equilibrium is at point a with average costs C_1 and effort E_1.

Competition enters Leibenstein's theory in the form of 'environmental tightness', which influences the position of curve B. For any given level of average costs, 'pressure' and hence 'effort' will be lower the more protected is the firm from competition. Conversely, as 'environmental tightness' increases, effort will increase at each level of costs. If 'tightness' increases from T_1 to T_2, the new position of equilibrium will be point b. If effort increases to E_2, costs fall to C_2 and the firm becomes more 'X'-efficient. Leibenstein's approach has been subjected to much criticism by neoclassical economists (Stigler, 1976, De Alessi, 1983). First, they object to the idea that failure to 'maximise' output is in any sense inefficient. As we have seen, the existence of agency costs is perfectly compatible with efficiency if it does not benefit anyone to reduce them.[18] Second, they dislike Leibenstein's behavioural insistence that individual people facing problems of bounded rationality cannot be

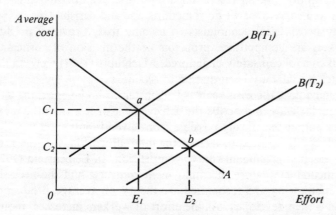

Figure 8.1: Leibenstein's X-efficiency theory of costs

regarded as rational 'utility maximisers'.[19] Third the ability of the theory to produce refutable predictions is questioned.[20]

For our present purposes, however, the relationship between 'environmental tightness' and monitoring 'pressure' is of central interest. The relationship has intuitive appeal but the mechanism is not clearly specified. If many firms in a particular market had dispersed shareholdings, for example, what would impel the managers to greater effort? Just because there are many firms, are we saying that property rights no longer matter, and that twenty nationalised firms in a market will behave like twenty joint-stock firms, or twenty closely held ones? Presumably this cannot be correct. As Jensen and Meckling (1976, p. 330) express it: 'the existence of competition in product and factor markets will not eliminate the agency costs due to managerial control problems.... If my competitors all incur agency costs equal to or greater than mine I will not be eliminated from the market by their competition'. The argument is therefore identical to that used in section 3(b) to question the role of competition in the managerial labour market.

Once more our basic difficulty is caused by attempting to talk about competition without the entrepreneur. Our instinctive feeling that competition does matter requires a more detailed look at the *types* of firm that are involved in a particular market, and the provisions of the contracts offered to managers. This is attempted in a paper by Hart (1983). Hart starts by assuming that managers are extremely risk averse. Their preferences are such that the indifference curves illustrated in Figure 5.2 would be L-shaped. From the analysis of Chapter 5 it is evident that we cannot offer such a manager incentives based upon sharing the risk. If effort is unobservable the best that can be done is to pay the manager a fixed time-rate conditional upon achieving some minimum level of performance (profit). Hart does not intend this to be realistic, but merely convenient for illustrating the working of his model. He then assumes that there are two types of firm: 'entrepreneurial'[21] and 'managerial'. The only difference between these two types is that in the 'entrepreneurial' firm, managerial effort can be monitored. Achieving this monitoring potential is not costless, however, and again for simplicity Hart assumes that there are additional fixed costs incurred in setting up an entrepreneurial relative to a managerial firm.

Where people are able to set up either managerial or entrepreneurial structures, Hart shows that if v is the proportion of entrepreneurial firms, there is a market equilibrium with $v \neq 0$. There will, in other words, be both entrepreneurial and managerial firms in the market. The intuition behind this result is as follows. Suppose that $v = 0$ and only managerial firms exist, then agency costs will be great and considerable managerial shirking will occur. If this is so, however, it may be profitable to set up an entrepreneurial firm and accept the additional fixed costs necessary to reduce managerial shirking. Again the argument is similar to that used to demonstrate the potential benefits from a takeover raid, but here we are allowing for the possibility that instead of changing an existing managerial firm into an entrepreneurial one via a raid, we can simply set up a new firm. As new entrepreneurial firms enter the market, however, industry output increases and the price of the product falls. This makes it more difficult for managers to achieve their minimum profit constraint and their effort level will rise. The rise in managerial effort which accompanies a fall in product price implies that the industry will not necessarily come to be composed entirely of entrepreneurial firms. To see this, consider the case of $v = 1$. Managerial shirking is at a minimum and product price is at its lowest. The entry of a managerial firm might now be profitable since the low market price will ensure high managerial effort and the fixed costs of instituting monitoring devices can be dispensed with. Thus managerial firms will displace entrepreneurial ones until an equilibrium position is reached.

Hart's model implies therefore that 'entrepreneurial firms provide a source of discipline for managerial firms'.[22] The market mechanism can indeed function as an incentive scheme but it does so through the medium of the entry of entrepreneurial firms which affect market price and induce greater effort from managers, who are assumed to have a rather special contract. As Hart points out 'if managerial tastes are less extreme, ordinary salary incentive schemes will become more effective in reducing managerial slack, and competition will become less important' (p. 381). This possibility has already been discussed in section 3(a). Formal economic theory has yet to determine whether competition will reduce managerial slack under more general conditions.

5. INSTITUTIONS WITH NO EXCHANGEABLE RESIDUAL CLAIMS

The discussion of sections 3 and 4 concerns institutions where exchangeable claims to the residual play an important role. As was noted in section 2, however, some institutional forms have no residual claimants or, if they have, the status is not exchangeable. The result is that certain incentive arrangements are ruled out, in particular the granting of stock options and the takeover threat. At first sight this would appear to be a serious handicap and to suggest poor survival qualities in the competitive battle between institutional arrangements. Everything depends, however, upon detailed circumstances, the aims of the people involved, and the contractual possibilities open to them given the costs of monitoring.

Consider once more the non-profit firm and the principal–agent problem of Chapter 5. Easley and O'Hara (1983), following the work of Hansmann (1980), consider the circumstances in which a non-profit organisation 'can be at least partially described as the solution to an optimal contracting problem' (p. 531). In their formulation the consumer becomes the principal and the firm or manager becomes the agent. A profit-making firm faces no constitutional constraints on the payment of executives, production techniques, or profits distributed. Providing the consumer is supplied with the benefits for which he has contracted, the manager of the firm is left to arrange production by any means deemed appropriate. Diagrammatically this is equivalent to the consumer (principal) receiving a definite payoff, and the manager (agent) bearing the entire risk (point ϕ in Figure 5.5). In contrast a non-profit firm is constrained to pay 'reasonable' compensation to its executives and cannot distribute any profits. This might be interpreted as the manager receiving a definite, constant, payoff and the consumer bearing the risk by receiving variable benefits depending upon the state of the world (point θ in Figure 5.5). Assume that consumers can observe neither the effort of managers nor the state of the world, then if consumers are risk averse and managers are risk neutral a first-best position will be achieved with a for-profit institution (at ϕ in Figure 5.6). This approach would suggest that non-profit institutions merely cope with managerial risk aversion, and to the extent that this can be achieved by other methods implies a limited role for the non-profit firm.

There is, however, another possibility that consumers cannot observe the benefits which they hope they are buying. If I buy medical care I may not be in a position to judge whether the services were really delivered or not. This is obvious if my purchase is on behalf of someone else who is not capable of reporting to me, but it might also apply to my own purchases. Whether the treatment I am being offered is really in my best interests or merely serves to increase the profits of the supplier may be very difficult to determine. A profit-maximising agency employed to transport food to the starving would have an incentive to pocket all charitable donations if the actual delivery of food could not be monitored. In circumstances such as these, the ability to control the manager's remuneration may be valuable. Where benefits are completely unobservable, a profit-maximising firm will produce no benefits at all. A non-profit firm will operate at minimum effort, but providing this results in some positive output it may nevertheless permit activities not possible under alternative institutional arrangements.

Complete 'unobservability' of output is an extreme assumption designed merely to illustrate the 'contractual' approach to non-profit institutions. In less extreme conditions a profit-orientated firm would have to worry about the loss of reputation if it cheated its customers, and this may be as effective as a constraint on managerial rent seeking as restricting managerial remuneration. We do not observe non-profit garages, for example, even though customer ignorance may be substantial. The consequences of using a poor garage may be expected to be less severe than a poor hospital, and the discipline of continuous dealings is likely to be more significant. In the case of hospitals a bias in favour of high-quality service for the managerial reasons mentioned by Newhouse (1970) may be precisely the type of bias that customers would prefer.[23]

Cooperative enterprises, like non-profit enterprises, do not involve exchangeable residual claims. The essence of the cooperative form, at least in a society where they arise spontaneously, is that members each have a non-exchangeable claim to the residual, and that capital and managerial services are provided by the members or hired from outside sources (i.e. in the case of capital, borrowed). Thus, in the case of a workers' cooperative, labour collectively hires capital and management rather than the other way round.

From a contractual point of view, the cooperative faces severe problems, and the form is not common. Successful examples exist, however, the most celebrated being the Mondragon cooperatives in Spain.

A major difficulty with the cooperative is the distribution of risk which is implied. As was seen in Chapter 5 the 'implicit' contracts literature suggests that 'insurance' is a component of employment arrangements. A worker generally cannot spread his efforts over many enterprises and typically commits himself to a single team. Capital, in contrast, is capable of being spread more widely. As Meade (1972) argues 'this presumably is a main reason why we (traditionally) find risk-bearing capital hiring labour rather than risk-bearing labour hiring capital' (p. 426). An optimal contract involves risk-neutral suppliers of capital bearing the risk, although, as was seen in Chapter 6, incentives may require labour to be presented with piece rates or 'monitoring gambles'. Reversing this traditional arrangement adds further to the risk assignment problem because of the *form* in which capital is supplied. Hiring capital at fixed interest implies very high gearing and a greater risk of bankruptcy in unfavourable conditions. Relying on capital supplied by members of the cooperative faces the non-exchangeability problem. The returns from a successful investment can be received only for so long as a person is a member of the particular cooperative undertaking it. Thus, workers near retirement, or those who expect to move for other reasons, will clearly be unwilling to contribute unless rates of return are expected to be very high.[24] Circumventing this problem would require membership of the cooperative, with its rights to claim a share in the residual, to be exchangeable.

As was seen at length in Chapter 5, however, the sacrifice of risk-sharing benefits may be perfectly efficient if the incentive effects are sufficiently strong. It is precisely in this field that controversy is most concentrated. The principal advantage of the cooperative enterprise has long been considered the more positive motivation of the workforce and the absence of 'alienation' which is said to afflict workers in joint-stock enterprises. This can be interpreted in different ways. The effect may be sociological in nature, perhaps based upon the ethical responses of the workforce. People may feel an obligation to a group of cooperators which they do not feel to an individual employer or a joint-stock company. Cooperative enterprise then supplies a satisfying 'contractual atmosphere'.[25] Alternatively, we can ignore this possibility and concentrate on a purely individualistic response to the new contractual environment.

Policing of managerial performance by workers presents no more intrinsic difficulties than policing by shareholders in a joint-stock company. However, the larger the cooperative group, the more pronounced the free rider problem in terms both of exercising a collective right to monitor the management, and of the incentive to shirk at work if output is joint to many team members. Further, hierarchical incentive devices discussed in chapter 6 are inconsistent with the 'residual sharing' basis of cooperation. These factors would appear to limit the size and scope of cooperative endeavours. Managerial incentives will be stronger if the managerial labour market represents a serious threat. This suggests that management taken from outside the cooperative may be more effective than management appointed from within. Managers might also be given the right to terminate a person's membership of the cooperative. Arrangements of this nature, however, raise the question of the point at which a cooperative enterprise turns into something different.

Pressure from the product market could act as an incentive device for cooperatives along the lines suggested by Hart (1983), but the absence of exchangeable residual claims rule out the takeover threat. The cooperative cannot therefore enlist the services of the Kirznerian entrepreneur as a policeman, and the diminished scope for entrepreneurship has been noted by Sirc (1979, p. 252) in the context of the Yugoslav system. It would be wrong to conclude that cooperative enterprises are never entrepreneurial in character, however, and it is instructive to consider their role in the transformation of the retail trade in the UK in the nineteenth century.[26]

Until the mid 1860s, middle-class shoppers in London faced a multitude of specialised small establishments offering elaborate service and extended credit. They published no price lists and were widely assumed to charge different prices to different customers. Resentment was widespread. The demand for a new form of retail service was satisfied by the rapid growth of cooperatives which initially catered to particular middle-class groups (Hood and Yamey, 1957). The most successful of these consumer cooperatives was the Army and Navy Cooperative Society Ltd (A and N), which started trading in 1872. Membership was open to army and naval officers and the initial capital consisted of 15,000 shares of £1 each. Those eligible but unwilling to become members could nevertheless shop at the A and N by purchasing an annual 'ticket'. The new societies offered low prices, assurance of quality, and much reduced service. They offered no credit and accepted cash only. They published price lists and distributed them four times per year to members. There were few shop assistants. Shoppers made out their own bill.

So successful were the new cooperatives that their competitors attempted to restrict them 'by political and other coercive action' (Hood and Yamey, p. 318). Given the membership of the cooperatives, these attempts were doomed to failure, and emulation of some of the societies' methods became the only rational response. By the early 1870s the range of products sold by the cooperatives was enormous. 'The societies played a large part in bringing about other changes which have generally been credited to the ordinary department stores (that is, stores not organised on cooperative lines). It is probable that their shops were the first major department stores in England.' (p. 317). Thus it was that admirals and generals (who comprised five out of eight directors of the A and N in 1879) presided over a movement that, *The Times* insisted, 'threatens nothing less than a social revolution'. As time advanced, however, the societies themselves had to meet competition from stores offering low prices but greater services, including Whiteley's and Harrod's. Restrictions on membership were relaxed and the advantages of cooperative status less clear. By the mid 1920s the societies had transformed themselves into joint-stock firms and their premises were open to all customers by 1939.

In the context of the earlier analysis presented in this book, it is interesting to consider why the cooperative form of enterprise proved so attractive in retailing during this period. First we should notice that *consumer* cooperatives suffer less from the risk-sharing disadvantages of *producer* cooperatives. Consumers are able to distribute their expenditure between establishments as they think fit, and the capital requirements of forming a retail cooperative are less of an obstacle. Most fundamentally, the societies provided consumers with information about the wholesale costs of various products and were in a good position to establish a reputation for quality and fair dealing. It is no accident that they started out with a membership taken from fairly closely defined professional groups and that their achievement was to let people know 'what things cost, and what they ought to cost...'.[27] Their very success produced the conditions in which competitors could also build up this kind of reputation by matching the societies' prices and emulating their methods.

When expansion was called for, the restrictive tendencies of cooperative enterprise with respect to capital investment became apparent. A and N shareholders[28] refused to sanction an increase in capital to permit the premises to be extended in 1879. This led to the establishment of the Junior Army and Navy Stores by members of the armed services unable to join the A and N. After the profitability of the new retailing methods had become fully demonstrated, it was the joint-stock enterprise that was best equipped to raise the capital to exploit them. Further, the accumulated profits held by the societies were a constant temptation to 'shareholders' to establish the exchangeability of residual claims and to realise the full present value of their entrepreneurial gains, instead of reducing prices and sharing them period by period with the rapidly expanding body of 'ticket holders'.[29] The history of the cooperatives represents therefore a case study of the continuing process of competition between organisational forms.

6. MANAGERIAL THEORIES OF THE FIRM

In sections 3, 4, and 5 we have concentrated on using the 'nexus of contracts' framework to discuss various institutional arrangements. Our approach amounted to the observation that in a world where people are free to experiment with differing contractual forms, those that survive in a competitive struggle must have something going for them. Many economists would argue, however, that this *ex post* rationalisation of existing institutions is a form of 'story telling' which has little claim to scientific status. True science requires that we can derive hypotheses from our theories which are capable of being refuted by observation.[30] Theories have to yield 'predictions' and not merely persuasive explanations. The importance of confronting theoretical propositions with empirical evidence has been recognised at various points and potentially refutable propositions have been presented.

Thus in Chapter 6 incentive devices such as the tournament were associated with monitoring costs; in Chapter 7 quasi-vertical integration was associated with the size of appropriable quasi rents, and the international corporation with product-specific non-patentable 'know-how'; in Chapter 8 the non-profit firm was associated with the costs of observing 'output'. In each of these instances it is open to researchers to find cases which appear not 'to fit' into the framework of the transactions costs theory and hence to refute that theory.[31]

A major attraction of 'managerial' theories of the firm to many economists is that they adhere to neoclassical traditions of constrained maximisation and produce qualitative comparative static predictions. All managerial theories have the same essential structure. The agency problem is recognised, and it is assumed that managers pursue their own interests subject to certain outside constraints. Thus the managerial approach is capable of producing an enormous variety of particular models depending upon the objectives assumed of the managers and the way that constraints on their behaviour are handled.

The most celebrated managerial models are those of Baumol (1959), Marris (1964) and Williamson (1964). They are distinguished primarily by the assumed objectives of the managers. Baumol suggested that managers maximise revenue from sales, Marris that they maximise growth, and Williamson that they maximise a utility function including 'staff' or 'emoluments'. In each case the existence of monitoring from outside and limits to managerial discretion were recognised. Baumol included a minimum profit constraint in his model, and Marris similarly incorporated a valuation ratio constraint to reflect pressure from shareholders. The valuation ratio is the market value of outstanding equity shares divided by the book value of the assets of a firm. Too low a ratio will involve a risk of takeover 'unacceptable' to the management (Marris, 1963, p. 205).[32]

In the 1970s managerial theory was applied to other areas. Niskanen's (1968) model of bureaucracy is a managerial model, as we have already noted. He assumes that bureaucrats maximise their budget in the ultimate interests of power, status or prestige and are constrained only by the demand curve for the services they provide. The situation is illustrated in Figure 8.2 and is intended to be representative of the managerial approach in general. Curve *MV* is

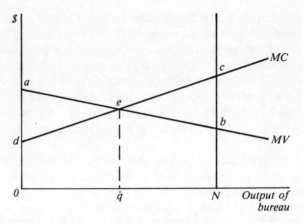

Figure 8.2: Niskanen's model of the budget maximising bureau

the demand curve faced by the bureaucrat. It shows the marginal willingness to pay for output by the bureau's consumers: *MC* is the marginal cost curve. As drawn, bureaucratic output will be *ON* at which point the total benefit derived from the output will be equal to the total costs incurred. The bureaucrat's budget will be given by area *abNO* = *dcNO*. The total willingness to pay for service level *ON* is extorted from the 'consumer' in the manner of a perfectly discriminating monopolist.

Clearly, this is a rather special set of circumstances, and Migué and Belanger (1974) amended Niskanen's approach and presented a more general managerial discretion model. They first calculated 'the margin of discretion enjoyed by the manager' (p. 30) as 'the excess of revenue over minimum cost'. This is the curve *ON* in Figure 8.3(a). They then assume that the manager 'can choose to divide his discretionary profit between only two desired goods: output and a combination of other expenses' (p. 31). The size of the bureau is still important but it is now combined with other possible items yielding managerial satisfaction. The manager's utility function can be represented conventionally as a set of indifference curves, and the final position is at point *m* in Figure 8.3(a).

In many ways Figure 8.3 is absolutely typical of diagrammatic representations of managerial models of the firm. The only major difference between Williamson's managerial firms and Migué and

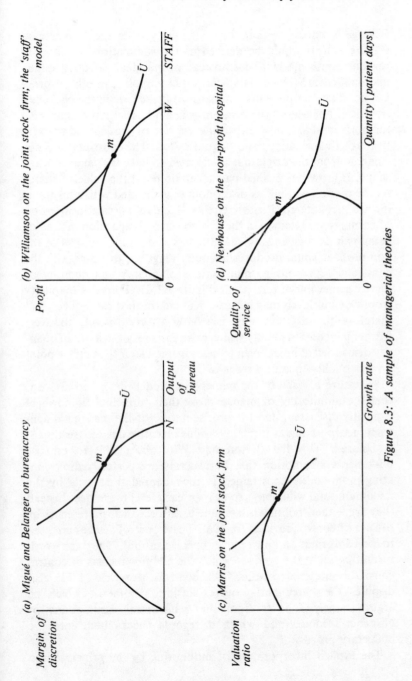

Figure 8.3: A sample of managerial theories

(a) Migué and Belanger on bureaucracy

Margin of discretion

$\bar{U}$

m

0   q   Output of bureau

N

(b) Williamson on the joint stock firm; the 'staff' model

Profit

$\bar{U}$

m

W

0   STAFF

(c) Marris on the joint stock firm

Valuation ratio

$\bar{U}$

m

0   Growth rate

(d) Newhouse on the non-profit hospital

Quality of service

$\bar{U}$

m

0   Quantity [patient days]

Belanger's bureau is that the constraint oW in the former case (Figure 8.3(b)) would be derived as the summation of marginal revenue minus marginal cost instead of marginal valuation minus marginal cost. Williamson's firm is a monopolist, in other words, but not a perfect price discriminator as is the case in the Niskanen tradition. For Marris the diagram is again basically the same with the horizontal axis now measuring the rate of growth and the vertical axis the valuation ratio (Figure 8.3(c)). The constraint will not emanate from the origin but is expected to have the same concave shape. If growth is pushed past a certain point the value of shares on the market will fall as diseconomies associated with staff training are encountered (Penrose effects[33]) and as a greater proportion of earnings are retained in the firm to finance expansion instead of being paid in dividends to shareholders. Newhouse's model of the non-profit hospital produces a similar diagram, this time with the constraint representing combinations of quality and quantity of service achievable at zero profit (Figure 8.3(d)). Increases in quality from very low levels may increase demand for medical services, and therefore quantity also may rise. After a certain point, however, further increases in quality which raise costs result in a fall in quantity demanded at break-even prices. Hospital staff then pick a point on this quality–quantity trade-off.

A feature of each of the managerial models described above is that the monitoring of managers by their 'principal' is nowhere explicitly discussed, and the precise nature of the manager's contract incorporating as it might various incentive devices (section 3) is ignored. This led Breton and Wintrobe (1975) to criticise Niskanen's assumption that bureaucrats are perfectly discriminating monopolists constrained in their depredations only by the maximum total willingness to pay for each level of service. Instead they argue that 'politicians are able to enforce their preferences by the use of control devices' (p. 206). These control devices are used to gain information and reduce 'overexpansion'. They are worth instituting up to the point at which the additional costs of control equal the marginal benefits from control. Musgrave (1981) also disputes the bureaucratic overexpansion hypothesis, which he argues largely follows from the behavioural assumptions of Niskanen's model and which disregards checks built into the budgetary process.

The explicit incorporation of monitoring by the principal into managerial models has been attempted by a number of recent theorists. Lindsay (1976) compares the problem of monitoring a manager of a joint-stock firm with monitoring a manager of government enterprise. Monitoring financial statements will not be appropriate for a government enterprise if output is not marketed or if the manager's job is to modify market outcomes in the interests of social policy. Lindsay concludes that crude 'performance indicators' will be established relating 'output' to total costs. Output is often very difficult to define and measure and may be multidimensional, however, and thus 'the output of government enterprises will, in general, contain fewer of those attributes which are "invisible" to Congress, that is, whose presence and quantity are not measured'. (p. 1066). 'Observable' attributes, on the other hand, will be overproduced, with the result that the average cost of these 'observable' attributes is predicted to appear lower in government enterprises than in proprietary enterprises. Managers in government enterprises, for example Veterans Administration Hospitals, have less incentive to incur staffing costs to produce non-observable benefits such as reassurance to patients, closer attention to personal comfort and so forth, compared with proprietary hospitals.

Monitoring also plays a central part in Eckel and Vining's (1985) approach to the mixed enterprise. A mixed enterprise has a proportion of its equity shares held by the state and a proportion held by private individuals. The form is common in Europe, well-known examples including British Petroleum (39 per cent state owned at present), and Volkswagen in West Germany (40 per cent owned by federal and state government). Many smaller enterprises in the UK received state finance through equity capital provided by the National Enterprise Board (set up in 1975 and merged in 1981 with the National Research Development Corporation to form the British Technology Group). Eckel and Vining suggest that this particular 'mixed' form of enterprise has advantages in certain circumstances over purely public or private forms. Suppose the government wished to ensure that a firm produced a certain 'social output' in addition to its usual 'private output'. Some modification of the firm's activity is required, in other words, in the public interest. The government might regulate the private firm, but this would require the devising of costly monitoring procedures to check performance in the achievement of social goals. Alternatively it might nationalise the firm, but in so doing would leave the managers free of monitoring from stockholders, without the takeover threat, and hence with less effective pressures from the managerial labour market. The 'mixed' enterprise gives the government an influential position and may permit minority or perhaps majority 'control'. But, as Eckel and Vining argue, 'Partial private ownership provides an alternative source of pressure for efficiency, lessening the need for efficiency monitoring by government' (p. 92).

As we saw in sections 3 and 4, the existence of exchangeable residual claims plays an important role in theoretical discussions of managerial incentives. Senior executives can be given incentives based on the performance of the shares, the share price provides concise information to the managerial labour market, and individual monitoring by shareholders is always a possibility. The government itself may be constrained not to push its demands for social output too far because of the effects on the share price and the difficulties that might imply for the raising of further capital. Figure 8.3(b) can be used to illustrate the argument further. Eckel and Vining suggest that in 100 per cent state-owned corporations managerial indifference curves will be very steep. More staff or other managerial perquisites will always be valued highly in terms of willingness to sacrifice profits. Managers will therefore choose a point on the constraint close to W. Indeed if bankruptcy is technically ruled out and governments have to finance losses it is not at all clear why managers should stop at W and do not pick a point below the horizontal axis until dismissal is threatened. The effect of selling equity shares to private buyers is to make managers more 'profit conscious' and hence to flatten their indifference curves. They are prepared to sacrifice less profit than before in pursuit of staff, and the managerial utility-maximising point moves from W towards point m. This approach indicates therefore that achieving a given target level of 'social output' may be accomplished more efficiently by the state buying shares in an enterprise than by outright nationalisation.

7. TESTING THE MANAGERIAL APPROACH TO THE FIRM

Although managerial theories of the firm allow the methods of constrained maximisation to be applied and lead to refutable propositions, the approach yields such a bewildering variety of individual models that it is difficult to assess the contribution of managerialism as a whole. Very often different theorists adopting managerial analysis will come to opposite conclusions. In Niskanen's model of a bureau, for example, the assumption of budget maximisation leads to the conclusion that the actual techniques of production are '*X*-efficient' and that bureaucrats will have an incentive to keep marginal cost as low as possible.[34] Others, for example, De Alessi (1974a) argue that operating costs will be higher in government than in proprietary enterprises, and Peacock (1983) emphasises 'on the job leisure' as an important component of bureaucratic rewards in a European context where senior bureaucrats are tenured. 'Managerial output' may be seen as of higher quality in some instances (Newhouse, 1970) but lower quality in others (De Alessi, 1974a) compared with output produced in profit-orientated enterprises. Managers of dispersed joint-stock companies are expected to adopt more risk-averse strategies than those monitored by majority shareholders (Baumol, 1959) except when they are expected to adopt less risk-averse strategies (Palmer, 1973a). It is not even universally agreed that managerial firms will be less profitable than owner-managed ones since an owner manager may be able and willing to indulge all sorts of personal fads at the expense of profit. McEachern (1978a) for example, distinguishes three control types: owner managed, manager controlled and externally controlled. The owner-manager, he argues, may be as interested in empire building as the manager. Note that this view is not compatible with the type of analysis presented by Jensen and Meckling (1976) who expect the market value of the firm to rise as the proportion of equity held by the manager rises, on the grounds that the personal financial cost of pursuing other objectives increases. McEachern's view is based on the assumption of different preferences rather than different constraints and therefore incorporates psychological factors. Owner-managers often have dominating personalities. Edwards and Townsend (1967), for example, described Lever as a person for whom pride was more important than any financial loss: 'He had a consuming desire to be top dog...and he liked empire building for its own sake' (p. 217).

This variety of possible approaches has not yet been resolved by empirical studies. Space constraints prevent a detailed appraisal

of a growing literature, but the problems of empirical work can
be illustrated by reference to studies of profit rates and 'control'
types, and of comparisons between public and private enterprise.
Monsen, Chiu and Cooley (1968) studied a sample of the largest
firms in the US in the period 1952–63 inclusive. They divided the
sample by control type[35] and found a significantly higher return to
owners' equity in owner- than in management-controlled firms
(12.8 per cent compared with 7.3 per cent). Kamerschen (1968)
using multiple regression techniques, however, could find no such
relationship. The dependent variable (the 'average' rate of return
after tax on year-end equity 1959–64) was regressed on independent variables which included total assets, a measure of barriers to
entry, the industry growth rate and dummy variables indicating
ultimate 'control'. The variable representing *changes* in control was
statistically significant, indicating a higher rate of return if control
type changed between 1929 and 1963, but as most changes were in
the direction of greater managerial control this appeared to contradict the managerial theories of the firm.

Other studies finding significant differences in profitability
between control types include Radice (1971), Palmer (1973), Stano
(1976) (who uses the rate of return on the shareholders' stock as the
dependent variable instead of the more usual return on equity or
net worth) and Bothwell (1980). On the other hand Sorenson (1974)
and Kania and McKean (1976) corroborate the findings of
Kamerschen. McEachern (1978b) criticises Kania and McKean for
drawing their sample of firms 'from industries which appear on
average to be quite competitive' (p. 492). He argues that
managerial hypotheses are only supposed to apply in highly concentrated industries where the opportunities for the exercise of
discretion are greater. To this Kania and McKean reply (pp.
497–99) that they deliberately used a sample which allowed for
considerable variation in concentration and that this was more
interesting than undertaking 'studies which may only prove the
obvious'.

The exchange between McEachern and Kania and McKean is
illustrative of the fundamental problem of managerial theory.
Managerial approaches to the firm are rooted in the agency problem yet, as a general rule, this problem is not specifically
addressed.[36] As a result, in empirical work, the constraints on
managers discussed in sections 3 and 4 are either recognised

implicitly by selecting a sample of firms where they are expected to be very weak; or they are incorporated explicitly in an *'ad hoc'* manner by including variables such as firm size (difficulty of takeover), industry concentration (product market pressure), barriers to entry and so forth. In the latter case the underlying theory being tested is much more general than a strictly 'managerial' theory, and accords more closely with the earlier discussion in this chapter. Hart's (1983) model, outlined in section 4, would suggest, for example, that in competitive markets dispersed corporations would still reveal more 'managerial' behaviour than concentrated corporations, but the effect on profit would be less clear because of the extra monitoring costs experienced by a dominant shareholder.

Studies of public and private enterprise have also attempted to measure the influence of property rights on the performance of firms. This has usually involved comparing public and private firms operating in otherwise 'similar circumstances'. Comparisons, it is argued, should involve firms of roughly similar size (to control for technical economies of scale), producing similar output, operating in similar market structures (to control for monopoly power), and facing the same prices of inputs, but with a different 'ownership structure'. Attention is then focused on factor productivity or costs of production in the different enterprises. The expectation is that managers of public enterprises have greater discretion than those in private enterprises and that costs will be higher because of the absence of shareholder monitoring and the takeover threat.

Evidence is rather mixed. Davies (1971, 1977) compared the performance of competing airlines (one public, one private) in Australia and found the private carrier more efficient in terms of freight tons per employee and passengers carried per employee. Similarly, Pryke (1982) compared the record of British Airways (public) with British Caledonian (private); Sealink (a publicly owned ferry service) with European Ferries; and Gas and Electricity Board Showrooms for the sale of domestic appliances with Currys and Comet (equivalent private-sector companies). Public enterprise, he concluded, 'has performed relatively poorly in terms of its competitive position, has used labour and capital inefficiently and has been less profitable' (p. 70). Other studies supporting this view include Crain and Zardkoohi (1978) for water utilities in the US, Ahlbrandt (1973) for fire services, Bennett and Johnson (1979) for garbage collection, and Frech III (1976) for the processing of medical insurance claims.

Some work runs counter to these findings of public sector inefficiency. Caves and Christensen compare the Canadian National railroad (public) with the Canadian Pacific Railroad (private). They calculate measures of total factor productivity and compare their growth over time and between firms. The public firm appears to have exhibited a lower level of productivity in the early 1960s but to have caught up with Canadian Pacific by 1967. Caves and Christensen therefore conclude that 'public ownership is not inherently less efficient than private ownership' (p. 974) although they accept that the existence of competition between the two railroads might provide an explanation of the performance of Canadian National. Electricity companies in the United States have provided another useful field for comparative institutional analysis. Meyer (1975), Neuberg (1977) and Pescatrice and Trapani (1980) all found lower costs in publicly owned utilities but found interpretation difficult because the private enterprises involved were operating under regulatory constraints on rates of return which could induce private companies to inflate their costs artificially.[37]

An attempt to isolate the influence of competition in the product market is that of Primeaux (1977), again in the context of the electricity supply industry. Primeaux compared a set of municipally owned firms in a monopoly market with a set of municipally owned firms facing some competition from alternative private-sector suppliers. Competing and non-competing municipal firms were then matched together in pairs. Each pair had to be in the same state, with the same primary source of energy, and of approximately equal size. A cost function was then estimated from the entire sample using independent variables such as sales, fuel cost, market density and dummy variables to reflect location and the presence of competition. Primeaux found that average cost in competitive firms was lower at the mean by 10.75 per cent. Further, 'even though scale economies exist, the benefits of X-efficiency outweigh them until very large output levels are reached' (p. 107). Pressure from the product market seems to be established in this case, although there is no attempt to relate this pressure to the detailed provisions of the contracts held by public-sector managers. In addition we should remember that in Hart's (1983) model it is the 'entrepreneurial' firm which disciplines the dispersed corporation, and that therefore 'competition' cannot be regarded as synonymous with some exogenously determined market structure unrelated to the nature of the firms of which the market is comprised. The process of competition is itself dependent upon the ability of entrepreneurs to trade in property rights (section 4), and studies which implicitly accept the possibility of product market competition independent of the structure of existing institutions may therefore be suspect.

8. CONCLUSION

Throughout Part II of this book the enormous variety of firms has been continually emphasised—variety of hierarchical structure, of scope and size, and of 'ownership structure'. An attempt has been made at each stage to link this variety to the transactional problems encountered, and to the process of evolutionary change which accompanies the practice of entrepreneurship. In Chapter 6 the problem was to provide incentives to the workforce, in Chapter 7 to monitor suppliers of other inputs, and in Chapter 8 to consider how motivation of the top managers was to be achieved. Although the static analysis of principal and agent was used extensively, we were careful to note that bounded rationality and continual change made it inadvisable to think in terms of determinate 'solutions' to agency problems. Firms were continually adjusting to new circumstances and required entrepreneurs to assist in this process—to make greater use of 'tacit knowledge' accumulated by workers, to make judgemental decisions about the appropriate responses to economic change, to force through new developments, and to restructure property rights in response to new information.

No institution is ideal for all possible circumstances, and through the competitive process a varied and fascinating system of institutions evolves,[38] often mutually dependent in subtle ways. The ideas surveyed in this book enable us to escape from the constructors of utopian systems. The supporters of big business, the admirers of small-scale enterprise, the advocates of cooperative ventures and the patrons of charitable activities can all find a place in the pattern of interdependent institutions which go to make up the economic system.

NOTES

1. p. 244 A. A. Berle and G. C. Means (1967).
2. A statistical process by which all firms face the same probability of growing or declining by a certain percentage in each period will result, over time, in an increasingly skewed size distribution of firms and a tendency for 'concentration' (or at least inequality as measured by the variance) to rise. This process is associated with Gibrat (1931). Marris and Mueller (1980) are particularly impressed by the implications of this argument: 'The legal and institutional permissions of capitalism imply a self-organizing process leading to persistently increasing concentration in the absence of special legal restrictions on conglomerate growth or in the absence of specific fiscal handicaps...' (p. 50).
3. With the exception of 'minority control' which Larner argued could be achieved with as little as 10 per cent of the shares.
4. A firm is privately controlled if an 'individual, family, or group of business associates' holds more than 80 per cent of the voting shares.
5. *See* Hannah (1976, Ch. 5) for a description of developments in the capital market during this period.
6. For the view that the popular reception was uncritical, and that the lack of influence on professional economists was fully justified, *see* Stigler and Friedland (1983).
7. For a more comprehensive coverage of these developments *see* Pryke (1981), Redwood and Hatch (1982), Redwood (1984).
8. Not to be confused with 'public companies'.
9. Figures from E. A. Doggett (1984), *Economic Trends Annual Supplement* 1985 p. 48, and *UK National Accounts* 1984 Tables 1.2 and 6.1.
10. Important contributions have been made by Ward (1958), Vanek (1970, 1975, 1977), Furubotn and Pejovich (1970), Meade (1972), Chiplin, Coyne and Sirc (1977), Sirc (1979), Moore (1980), among many others.
11. Roberts (1959), Patton (1961), McGuire *et al.* (1962).
12. Notably by Lewellen (1969), Lewellen and Huntsman (1970), Masson (1971).
13. Especially collinearity between variables (such as profits and size, salary and other benefits), and heteroscedasticity.
14. 'The proxy machinery has thus become one of the principal instruments not by which a stockholder exercises power over the management of the enterprise, but by which his power is separated from him.' (Berle and Means, p. 129).
15. It is not denied that the managerial labour market may be influential even in the absence of entrepreneural intervention, but the incentives in this case will be quite different. Alchian's argument that academics strive to increase their market value by research, for example, ignores the point that the research they do will be designed to appeal to other academics or administrators in non-profit institutions who will appoint them. The academic labour market is widely considered effective as an

incentive mechanism. David Lodge's satirical novel, *Small World* is about the stimulating effects of this market and competition for the UNESCO Chair, a post entirely unencumbered with inconvenient responsibilities. But it is also about the importance of the make-up of the selection board.

16. As with the paradox of voting (Chapter 7 note 15) and the paradox of innovation we should note here that a small shareholder could reason that since a raid must fail through lack of support for the raider's offer from others, the best policy will be to accept with alacrity if the price includes any potential gains. Clearly much will depend on the precise mechanism by which the offer is made. Grossman and Hart set up their model so that the only takeovers that occur are *certain* to succeed. This implies that none will take place. Existing shareholders will not tender their shares to a raider who is certain to succeed at any price less than the post-raid price. Any successful raid will therefore be profitless to the raider.

17. Not to be confused with 'hold-up'.

18. It is worth noting, however, that this type of neoclassical reasoning leads to the conclusion that anything which exists must be efficient since it has not paid anyone to change it. From the point of view of normative theory, which we do not discuss in this book, this neoclassical position would appear somewhat inhibiting. *See* Culyer (1984) on these Panglossian issues.

19. We have deliberately avoided methodological disputes. Essentially our approach has been to present the theory of the agency problem in terms of rational expected utility-maximising people, but to view the *process* by which 'solutions' are found as one not of calculation but of entrepreneurial discovery and trial and error.

20. The 'Austrian' theorists would not count this a great deficiency since their subjectivism leads them to question the ability of *any* economic theory to produce truly refutable implications. *See also* note 31.

21. Note throughout this section on Hart (1983) that the word 'entrepreneurial' is used merely to signify the existence of monitoring by shareholders (or a dominant shareholder). Our use of the term in this book has, of course, been quite different. However, the competitive process implied by Hart's model does suggest that it is entrepreneurial in Kirzner's sense.

22. The entrepreneurial firm is responsible for an external effect by reducing shirking in managerial firms. These effects are not considered by the entrepreneur when he makes his entry decision, and it is thus possible to argue, using standard welfare economic theory, that entrepreneurial firms should be encouraged.

23. Non-profit enterprises may be encouraged by tax concessions and the reader should not infer from this section that 'contractual' considerations are all that matter.

24. *See* Vanek (1975) on these problems.

25. Williamson (1975, p. 37) considers the importance of 'supplying a

satisfying exchange relation' though not in the context of cooperatives. *See also* Chapter 6 note 5.

26. The following account relies completely on Hood and Yamey (1957).

27. *The Times* 31 January 1873, quoted in Hood and Yamey (1957), p. 314).

28. Each member had one vote and interest on 'shares' was in practice a steady 5 per cent per annum.

29. Hood and Yamey (1957) indicate that the management of the enterprises resisted the demands of the 'shareholders' and supported 'ticket holders'. In 1874 half the Civil Service Supply Association (CSSA) management resigned in protest when shareholders moved to increase their proprietory rights. They formed another society, the New Civil Service Cooperation Ltd, to maintain the 'spirit of cooperation'. Eventually they were taken over by the CSSA in 1906. *See* Hood and Yamey, footnote 1 p. 320.

30. *See* Blaug (1980) for an extensive discussion of methodological issues in economics.

31. It is possible to argue that transactions costs are, like all costs, subjective (e.g. Buchanan 1967; Coase 1946, 1970) If they cannot be measured 'objectively' by the researcher but are at any given time a matter for entrepreneurial judgement, transactions cost theory becomes tautologically true and can never be refuted. Incorporation of the entrepreneur into economic theory thus leads us into a dangerous methodological bog around which the author has attempted to skirt during the entire development of this book. Generally, neoclassical economists prefer to take their transactions cost theory without the entrepreneur. The more experimental Austrians prefer it with. Yet others limit their indulgence to special occasions.

32. In Marris (1963) the security constraint takes the form of 'a long-run maximum on the leverage ratio and a long-run minimum on the liquid assets ratio' (p. 200).

33. *See* E. T. Penrose (1959) *The Theory of the Growth of the Firm*.

34. This applies only if the bureau is not 'demand constrained'. In terms of Figure 8.2, if the MV curve rotated about e and cut the horizontal axis between $\bar{q}$ and N, costs of production would not exhaust the total budget at 'X'-efficient levels. Thus the bureaucrat would have to 'waste' the budget in some way.

35. Owner control was indicated by a block of 20 per cent of shares, or 10 per cent if the person was on the board of directors. Management control existed if no holding was greater than 5 per cent.

36. We have already drawn attention to exceptions to this observation in section 6 where theoretical models incorporating monitoring costs were mentioned. Empirical work requires measures of these costs to be derived, however, and this has proved extremely difficult.

37. These effects are called Averch–Johnson effects; *see* H. Averch and L. L. Johnson (1962).

38. The evolutionary analogy has been used frequently in this book,

although space constraints have prevented a systematic discussion. Biological analogies have a long history in economics and can be found in Marshall (1925) who compared the life cycle of firms to trees in a forest (pp. 315–16), in Boulding (1950), also a supporter of a life cycle theory, in Alchian (1950), who suggests the evolutionary analogy, and most recently in Nelson and Winter (1982). To consider the economy as similar to a biological system of interdependent organisms, each one adapted to specialised conditions (an ecological system of institutions), is intended to be what Penrose (1952) calls a 'descriptive analogy' rather than an 'exact analogy'. It is not claimed that each component of the theory of evolution or ecology has a precise counterpart in economics.

Bibliography

Adams, J. Stacy (1965) 'Inequity in social exchange' in Berkowitz, L. (ed.) *Advances in Experimental Social Psychology*, Vol. 2, p. 267, Academic Press, New York

Ahlbrandt, R. (1973) 'Efficiency in the provision of fire services', *Public Choice*, Vol. 16, p. 1

Akerlof, G. A. (1970) 'The market for "lemons": qualitative uncertainty and the Market Mechanism', *Quarterly Journal of Economics*, Vol. 84, p. 488

—— (1976) 'The economics of caste and of the rat race and other woeful tales', *Quarterly Journal of Economics*, Vol. 90 p. 599

—— (1982) 'Labor contracts as partial gift exchange', *Quarterly Journal of Economics*, Vol. 97, p. 543

—— (1984) 'Gift exchange and efficiency-wage theory: four views', *American Economic Review*, Vol. 74, p. 79

Alchian, A. A. (1950) 'Uncertainty, evolution and economic theory', *Journal of Political Economy*, Vol. 58, p. 211

—— (1965) 'Some economics of property rights', *Il Politico*, Vol. 30 p. 816

—— (1969) 'Corporate management and property rights' in Manne, H. (ed.) *Economic Policy and the Regulation of Corporate Securities*, American Enterprise Institute

—— (1969) 'Information costs, pricing, and resource unemployment', *Economic Inquiry*, Journal of the Western Economic Association, Vol. 17, p. 109

—— and Demsetz, H. (1972) 'Production, information costs, and economic organization' *American Economic Review*, Vol. 62, p. 777

—— (1977) 'Why money?' *Journal of Money, Credit and Banking*, Vol. 9, p. 133

—— (1977) *Economic Forces at Work*, Liberty Press, Indianapolis

Alonso, W. (1964) 'Location theory', in Alonso, W. and Friedman, J. (eds) *Regional Development and Planning*, MIT Press, Cambridge, Mass.

Archibald, G. C. (ed.) (1971) *The Theory of the Firm*, Penguin, Harmondsworth

Armour, H. O. and Teece, D. J. (1978) 'Organizational structure and economic performance: a test of the multidivisional hypothesis', *Bell Journal of Economics*, Vol. 9, p. 106

—— (1980) 'Vertical integration and technological innovation' *Review of Economics and Statistics*, Vol. 62, p 470

Arrow, K. J. (1962) 'Economic welfare and the allocation of resources for invention in *The Rate and Direction of Economic Activity: Economic and Social Factors* (NBER) p. 609, Princeton University Press, Princeton

—— (1969) 'The organization of economic activity' in Joint Economic Committee, 91st Cong, 1st Sess. *The Analysis and Evaluation of Public Expenditure: The PPB System*, p. 59

—— (1973) 'Higher education as a filter', *Journal of Public Economics*, Vol. 2, p. 193

—— (1974) *The Limits of Organization*, W. W. Norton and Co., New York

—— (1975) 'Vertical integration and communication', *Bell Journal of Economics*, 6, p. 173

Auster, R. (1978) 'Shirking in the theory of the firm' *Southern Economic Journal*, Vol. 45, p. 867

Auster, R. D. and Silver, M. (1979) *The State as a Firm: Economic Forces in Political Development*, Martinus Nihoff, The Hague

Averch, H. and Johnson, L. L. (1962) 'Behavior of the firm Under regulatory constraint', *American Economic Review*, Vol. 52, p. 1052

Azariadis, C. and Stiglitz, J. E. (1983) 'Implicit contracts and fixed price equilibria', *Quarterly Journal of Economics*, Vol. 98, Supplement p. 1

Bacharach. M. (1976) *Economics ant the Theory of Games*, Macmillan, London

Baily, Martin, N. (1974) 'Wages and unemployment under uncertain demand', *Review of Economic Studies*, Vol. 41, pp. 37–50

Bannock, G. (1981) *The Economics of Small Firms: Return from the Wilderness*, Basil Blackwell, Oxford

Baumol, W. J. (1959) *Business Behavior, Value and Growth*, Macmillan, New York

—— (1962) 'On the theory of expansion of the firm', *American Economic Review*, reprinted in Archibald, G. C. (ed.) (1971), op. cit.

—— (1965) *Welfare Economics and the Theory of the State,* G. Bell and Sons Ltd., London

Becker, G. S. (1965) 'A theory of the allocation of time', *Economic Journal*, Vol. 75, p. 493

—— (1964) *Human Capital*, NBER, New York

Becker, G. S. and Stigler, G. J. (1974) 'Law enforcement, malfeasance, and compensation of enforcers', *Journal of Legal Studies* Vol. 3, p. 1

Bell, D. and Kristol, I. (eds) (1981) *The Crisis in Economic Theory*, Basic Books, New York

Bennett, J. T. and Johnson, M. H. (1979) 'Public versus private provision of collective goods and services: garbage collection revisited', *Public Choice*, Vol. 34, p. 55

Berle, A. A. and Means, G. C. (1932) Revised Edition (1967) *The Modern Corporation and Private Property*, Harcourt, Brace and World, Inc., New York

Binks, Martin and Coyne, John (1983) *The Birth of Enterprise: An Analytical and Empirical Study of the Growth of Small Firms*, Hobart Paper 98, Institute of Economic Affairs

Blaug, M. (1980) *The Methodology of Economics: or How Economists Explain*, Cambridge University Press, Cambridge

Bolton, J. E. (1971) *Small Firms Report of the Committee of Inquiry On Small Firms*, Cmnd 4811, HMSO

Bothwell, J. L. (1980) 'Profitability, risk and the separation of ownership from control', *Journal of Industrial Economics*, Vol. 28, p. 303

Boulding, K. E. (1950) *A Reconstruction of Economics*, Wiley and Sons, New York

Breton, A. and Wintrobe, R. (1975) 'The equilibrium size of a budget maximizing bureau' *Journal of Political Economy*, Vol. 83, p. 195

Buchanan, J. M. and Tullock, G. (1952) *The Calculus of Consent*, University of Michigan Press, Ann Arbor

Buchanan, J. M. (ed.) (1967) *L. S. E. Essays on Costs*, Weidenfeld and Nicolson, London

Buchanan, J. M. (1980) 'Rent seeking and profit seeking' in J. M. Buchanan *et al.* (eds) *Towards a Theory of The Rent Seeking Society* p. 3, Texas A and M University Press, College Station, Texas

Buchanan, J. M., Tollison, R. D. and Tullock, G. (eds) (1980) *Toward a Theory of the Rent Seeking Society*, Texas A and M University Press, College Station, Texas

Buckley, P. J. and Casson, M. (1976) *The Future of Multinational Enterprise*, Macmillan, London

Calvo, G. A. and Wellisz, S. (1978) 'Supervision, loss of control, and the optimum size of the firm' *Journal of Political Economy*, Vol. 86, p. 943
—— (1979) 'Hierarchy, ability, and income distribution', *Journal of Political Economy*, Vol. 87, p. 991

Casson, Mark (1982) *The Entrepreneur: An Economic Theory*, Martin Robertson, Oxford
—— (1984) 'The theory of vertical integration: a survey and synthesis', *Journal of Economic Studies*, Vol. 2, p. 3

Caves, D. W. and Christensen, L. R. (1980) 'The relative efficiency of

public and private firms in a competitive environment: the case of the
Canadian railroads', *Journal of Political Economy*, Vol. 88, p 958

Caves, R. E. (1980) 'Industrial organization, corporate strategy and
structure' *Journal of Economic Literature*, Vol. 18, p. 64

—— (1982) *Multinational Enterprise and Economic Analysis*, Cambridge
University Press, London

Chandler, A. D. (1977) *The Visible Hand: The Managerial Revolution in
American Business*, Harvard University Press, Cambridge, Mass

—— (1980) 'The transnational industrial firm in the United States and the
United Kingdom: a comparative analysis', *Economic History Review*,
Vol. 33, p. 396

Channon, D. F. (1973) *The Strategy and Structure of British Enterprise*,
Harvard University, Boston

Chiplin, B., Coyne, J. and Sirc, L. (1977) *Can Workers Manage?*, Hobart
Paper 77, Institute of Economic Affairs

Christaller, W. (1933) *Die Zentralen Orte in Suddeutschland*, Gustav
Fischer, Jena

Clapham, J. H. (1922) 'Of empty economic boxes', *Economic Journal*,
Vol. 32, p. 305

Clark, R. C. (1983) 'Agency costs versus fiduciary duties' in Pratt, J. W.
and Zeckhauser, R. J. (eds) (1985) *Principals and Agents: The Structure
of Business* p. 55, Harvard Business School, Boston

Coase, R. H. (1937) 'The nature of the firm', *Economica*, Vol 4, p. 386

—— (1946) 'The marginal cost controversy', *Economica*, Vol. 13, p. 169

—— (1960) 'The problem of social cost', *Journal of Law and Economics*,
Vol. 3 p. 1

—— (1970) 'The theory of public utility pricing and its application' *Bell
Journal of Economics and Management Science*, Vol. 1, p. 113

Crain, W. M. and Zardkoohi, A. (1978) 'A test of the property rights
theory of the firm: water utilities in the United States', *Journal of Law
and Economics*, Vol. 40, p. 395

Culyer, A. J. (1984) 'The quest for efficiency in the public sector:
economists versus Dr Pangloss' in Hanusch, H. (ed.) *Public Finance and
the Quest for Efficiency*, p. 39, Proceedings of the 38th Congress of the
International Institute of Public Finance, Copenhagen, 1982

Cyert, R. M. and March, J. G. (1963) *A Behavioral Theory of the Firm*,
Prentice Hall, New York

Davies, D. G. (1971) 'The efficiency of public versus private firms: the case
of Australia's two airlines, *Journal of Law and Economics*, Vol 14,
p. 149

—— (1977) 'Property rights and economic efficiency—the Australian
airlines revisited', *Journal of Law and Economics*, Vol. 20, p 223

Davis, O. A. and Whinston, A. B. (1961) 'The Economics of urban
renewal', *Law and Contemporary Problems*, Vol. 26, p. 105

De Alessi, L. (1969) 'Implications of property rights for government investment choice', *American Economic Review*, Vol. 59, p. 13
—— (1974a) 'An economic analysis of government ownership and regulation theory and the evidence from the electric power industry', *Public Choice*, Vol 19, p. 1
—— (1974b) 'Managerial tenure under private and government ownership in the electric power industry', *Journal of Political Economy*, Vol. 82, p. 645
—— (1980) 'The economics of property rights: a review of the evidence', *Research in Law and Economics* 2, p. 1
—— (1983) 'Property rights, transactions costs and x-efficiency', *American Economic Review*, Vol. 73, p. 69
Demsetz, H. (1964) 'The exchange and enforcement of property rights' *Journal of Law and Economics*, Vol. 7, p. 11
—— (1967) 'Toward a theory of property rights', *American Economic Review*, Vol. 57, p. 347
—— (1968) 'The cost of transacting', *Quarterly Journal of Economics*, 82, p. 33
—— (1969) 'Information and efficiency: another viewpoint', *Journal of Law and Economics*, Vol. 12, p. 1
—— (1970) 'The private production of public goods', *Journal of Law and Economics*, Vol. 13, p. 293
—— (1979) 'Ethics and efficiency in property rights systems', in Rizzo, Mario, J. (ed.), op. cit. p. 97
—— (1983) 'The structure of ownership and the theory of the firm', *Journal of Law and Economics*, Vol. 26, p. 375
Doeringer, P. and Piore, M. (1971) *Internal Labor Markets and Manpower Analysis*, D. C. Heath and Co. Boston.
Dunning, J. H. (1973) 'The determinants of international production', *Oxford Economic Papers*, Vol. 25, p. 289
—— (ed) (1974), *Economic Analysis and the Multinational Enterprise*, Allen and Unwin; London
—— (1981) *International Production and the Multinational Enterprise*, Allen and Unwin, London

Easley, D. and O'Hara, M. (1983) 'The economic role of the non-profit firm', *Bell Journal of Economics*, Vol. 14, p. 531
Eckel, Catherine, C., and Vining, Aidan, R. (1985) 'Elements of a theory of mixed enterprise', *Scottish Journal of Political Economy*, Vol. 32, p. 82
Edgeworth, F. Y. (1925) *Papers Relating to Political Economy*, Macmillan, London
Edwards, R. S. and Townsend, H. (1967) *Business Enterprise*, Macmillan, London

Ekelund, R. B. and Higgins, R. S. (1982) 'Capital fixity, innovations, and long-term contracting: an intertemporal economic theory of regulation', *American Economic Review*, Vol. 72, p. 32

Ekelund, R. B. Jr. and Tollison, R. D. (1980) 'Mercantilist origins of the corporation', *Bell Journal of Economics*, Vol. 11, p. 715

Etgar, M. (1978) 'The effects of forward vertical integration on service performance of a distributive industry', *Journal of Industrial Economics*, Vol. 26, p. 249

Fama, E. F. (1980) 'Agency problems and the theory of the firm' *Journal of Political Economy*, Vol. 88, p. 288

Fama, E. F. and Jensen, M. C. (1983a) 'Separation of ownership and control' *Journal of Law and Economics*, Vol. 26, p. 301

—— (1983b) 'Agency problems and residual claims', *Journal of Law and Economics*, Vol. 26, p. 327

Flanagan, R. J. (1984) 'Implicit contracts, explicit contracts, and wages', *American Economic Review*, Vol. 74, p. 345

Forester, T. (1978) 'Asians in businesss', New Society, Feb 23

Forsyth, P. J. and Hocking, R. D. (1980) 'Property rights and efficiency in a regulated environment: the case of Australian airlines', *Economic Record*, p. 182

Frech, III, H. E. (1976) 'The property rights theory of the firm: empirical results from a natural experiment,' *Journal of Political Economy*, Vol. 84, p. 143

Friedrich, C. J. (1929) (*Translation*) *Alfred Weber's Theory of the Location of Industries*, University of Chicago Press, Chicago

Furubotn, E. and Pejovich, S. (1970) 'Property rights and the behavior of the firms in a socialist state: the example of Yugoslavia' in Furubotn, E. and Pejovich, S. (eds) (1974), op. cit. p. 227

—— (1971) 'Towards a general theory of property rights' in Furubotn, E. and Pejovich, S. (eds) (1974), op. cit. p. 341

—— (1972) 'Property rights and economic theory: a survey of recent literature' *Journal of Economic Literature*, Vol. 10, p. 1137

Furubotn, E. and Pejovich, S. (eds) (1974) *The Economics of Property Rights*, Ballinger, Cambridge, Mass.

Galbraith, J. K. (1952) *American Capitalism: The Concept of Countervailing Power*, Houghton Mifflin, Boston

—— (1967) *The New Industrial State*, Hamish Hamilton, London

—— (1973) *Economics and the Public Purpose*, Houghton Mifflin, Boston

George, D. A. R. (1982) 'Worker participation and self-management', *Scottish Journal of Political Economy*, Vol. 29, p. 310

Gibrat, R. (1931) *Les Inequalités Économiques*, Paris

288   Bibliography

Goetz, C. J. (1984) *Law and Economics: Cases and Materials*, American Casebook Series West Publishing Co., St. Paul, Minn.

Goldberg, V. P. (1976) 'Regulation and administered contracts' *Bell Journal of Economics*, Vol. 7, pp. 426

—— (1976) 'Toward an expanded economic theory of contract', *Journal of Economic Issues*, Vol. 10, p. 45

Gordon, R. A. (1940) 'Ownership and compensation as incentives to corporate executives', *Quarterly Journal of Economics*, Vol. 54, p. 455

Gravelle, H. and Rees, R. (1981) *Microeconomics*, Longman, London

Grossman, S. J. and Hart, O. D. (1980) 'Takeover bids, the free rider problem, and the theory of the corporation', *Bell Journal of Economics*, Vol. 11, p. 42

Hannah, L. and Kay, J. A. (1976) *Concentration in Modern Industry: Theory, Measurement and the U.K. Experience*, Macmillan, London

Hannah, L. (1983) *The Rise of the Corporate Economy*, 2nd Edition, Methuen, London and New York

—— (1983) 'Entrepreneurs and the social sciences' An Inaugural Lecture, London School of Economics and Political Science

Hannon, T. H. and Mavinga, F. (1980) 'Expense preference and managerial control: the case of the banking firm' *Bell Journal of Economics*, Vol. 11, p. 671

Hansmann, H. B. (1980) 'The role of non-profit enterprise' *Yale Law Journal*, Vol. 89, p. 835

Harris, M. and Raviv, A. (1978) 'Some results on incentive contracts with applications to education and employment, health insurance and law enforcement', *American Economic Review*, Vol. 68, p. 20

Hart, O. D. (1983) 'The market mechanism as an incentive scheme', *Bell Journal of Economics*, Vol. 14, p. 366

Hay, D. A. and Morris, D. J. (1979) *Industrial Economics: Theory and Evidence*, Oxford University Press, Oxford

Hayek, F. A. (1937) 'Economics and knowledge', *Economica*, Vol. 4, p. 33

—— (1945) 'The use of knowledge in society', *American Economic Review*, Vol. 35, p. 519–30, reprinted in Townsend, H. (ed.) (1971), *Price Theory*, Penguin Modern Economics Readings, p. 17

—— (1978) 'Competition as a discovery procedure', in *New Studies in Philosophy Politics and the History of Ideas*, p. 179, Routledge and Kegan Paul, London

Hill, C. W. L. (1984) 'Organisational structure, the development of the firm and business behaviour' in Pickering, J. F. and Cockerill, T. A. J. (eds), (1984), op cit., p. 52

Hindley, B. (1970) 'The division of ownership from control in the modern corporation', *Journal of Law and Economics*, Vol. 13, p. 185

Hirshleifer, J. (1983) 'From weakest link to best shot: the voluntary provision of public goods', *Public Choice*, Vol. 41, p. 371

Holmström, B. (1979) 'Moral hazard and observability', *Bell Journal of Economics*, Vol. 10, p. 74

Holtmann, A. G. (1983) 'A theory of non-profit firms', *Economica*, Vol. 50, p. 439

Hood, J. and Yamey, B. S. (1957) 'The middle-class co-operative retailing societies in london, 1864–1900', *Oxford Economic Papers*, N.S. Vol. 9, p. 309

Hume, D. (1978) *Treatise of Human Nature* P. H. Nidditch (ed), Clarendon Press, Oxford First published 1740

Hymer, S. H. (1976) *The International Operations of National Firms: A Study of Foreign Direct Investment*, MIT Press, Cambridge, Mass.

Jackson, P. (1983) *The Political Economy of Bureaucracy*, Philip Allen, London

Jensen, C. M. and Meckling, W. H. (1976) 'Theory of the firm: managerial behavior agency costs and ownership structure', *J. Financial Economics*, Vol. 3, p. 305

Jewkes, J. (1948) *Ordeal by Planning*, Macmillan, London

Jewkes, J., Sawyers, D., and Stillerman, R. (1958) *The Sources of Invention*, Macmillan, London

Kamerschen, D. (1968) 'The influence of ownership and control on profit rates', *American Economic Review*, Vol. 58, p. 432

Kania, J. and McKean, J. R. (1976) 'Ownership, control, and the contemporary corporation: a general behaviour analysis', *Kyklos*, Vol. 29, No. 2, pp. 272–91

Kay, N. M. (1979) *The Innovating Firm: A Behavioural Theory of Corporate R and D*, Macmillan, London

—— (1982) *The Evolving Firm*, Macmillan, London

—— (1983) *The Emergent Firm: The role of Bounded Rationality in Economic Organisation*, Macmillan, London

Kim, Jae-Cheol (1985) 'The market for "lemons" reconsidered: a model of the used car market with asymmetric information', *American Economic Review*, Vol. 75, p. 836

Kirzner, I. M. (1973) *Competition and Entrepreneurship*, University of Chicago Press, Chicago

—— (1976) *The Economic Point of View: An Essay in the History of Economic Thought*, Sheed and Ward Inc., Kansas City

—— (1979) *Perception, Opportunity and Profit*, University of Chicago Press, Chicago

—— (1980) 'The primacy of entrepreneurial discovery' in Seldon, A. (ed.) *Prime Mover of Progress: The Entrepreneur in Capitalism and Socialism*, p. 5, Institute of Economic Affairs Readings 23

—— (ed) (1982) *Method, Process and Austrian Economics Essays in Honor of Ludwig Von Mises*, Lexington Books, Lexington

Klein, B., Crawford, R. G. and Alchian, A. A. (1978) 'Vertical integration, appropriable rents, and competitive contracting process', *Journal of Law and Economics*, Vol. 21, p. 297

Klein, B. (1984) 'Contract costs and administered prices: an economic theory of rigid wages,' *American Economic Review*, Vol. 74, p. 332.

Knight, F. H. (1921) *Risk, Uncertainty and Profit*, Houghton Mifflin, Boston

Lancaster, K. J. (1966) 'A new approach to consumer theory, *Journal of Political Economy*, Vol. 74, p. 132

Larner, R. J. (1966) 'Ownership and control in the 200 largest non-financial corporations, 1929 and 1963', *American Economic Review*, Vol. 56, p. 777

Lazear, E. P. (1979) 'Why is there mandatory retirement?' *Journal of Political Economy*, Vol. 87, p. 1261

—— 'Agency, earnings profiles, productivity and hours restrictions', *American Economic Review*, Vol. 71, p. 606

Lazear, E. and Rosen, S. (1981) 'Rank order tournaments as optimal labour contracts', *Journal of Political Economy*, Vol. 89, p. 841

Lazear, E. P. (1984) 'Incentives and wage rigidity', *American Economic Review*, Vol. 74, p. 339

Leibenstein, H. (1966) 'Allocative efficiency v. x-efficiency', *American Economic Review*, Vol. 56, p. 392

—— (1975) 'Aspects of the x-efficiency theory of the firm', *Bell Journal of Economics*, 6, p. 580

—— (1976) *Beyond Economic Man: A New Foundation for Microeconomics*, Harvard University Press, Cambridge, Mass

—— (1978) *General X-efficiency Theory and Economic Development*, Oxford University Press, New York

—— (1978) 'X-inefficiency xists-reply to an xorcist', *American Economic Review*, Vol. 68, p. 203

—— (1979) 'A branch of economics is missing: micro-micro theory' *Journal of Economic Literature*, Vol. 17, p. 477

Lewellen, W. G. (1969) 'Management and ownership in the large firm', *Journal of Finance*, Vol. 24, p. 299

Lewellen, W. G. and Huntsman, B. (1970) 'Managerial pay and corporate performance', *American Economic Review*, Vol. 60, p. 710

Lewellen, W. G. (1971) *The Ownership Income of Management*, Columbia University Press, New York

Lindsay, Cotton, M. (1976) 'A theory of government enterprise', *Journal of Political Economy*, Vol. 84, p. 1061

Littlechild, S. C. (1979) 'Controlling the nationalised industries: quis custodiet ipsos custodes?', Series B Discussion Paper No. 56, University of Birmingham

—— (1979) Comment on Shackle's 'Imagination, formalism and choice': Radical subjectivism or radical subversion?' in Rizzo, M. J. (ed.) *Time Uncertainty and Disequilibrium* pp. 32–49, Lexington Books D. C. Heath, Lexington

—— (1982) 'Equilibrium and the market process' in Kirzner, I. M. (ed), *Method, Process, and Austrian Economics, Essay in Honor of Ludwig Von Mises* p. 85, Lexington Books, Lexington

Loasby, B. J. (1976) *Choice, Complexity and Ignorance*, Cambridge University Press, Cambridge

—— (1982) 'The entrepreneur in economic theory', *Scottish Journal of Political Economy*, Vol. 29, p. 235

—— (1982) 'Economics of dispersed and incomplete information' in Kirzner, I. M., (ed) *Method, Process and Austrian Economics Essays in Honor of Ludwig Von Mises*, p. 111, Lexington Books

—— (1984) 'Entrepreneurs and organisation', *Journal of Economic Studies*, Vol. 11, p. 75

Losch, A. (1954) *The Economics of Location*, translated by Waglam and Stolper, Yale University Press, New Haven

Luce, R. D. and Raiffa, H. (1957) *Games and Decisions*, John Wiley and Sons Inc., New York

Machlup, F. (1967) 'Theories of the firm: marginalist, behavioral, managerial' *American Economic Review*, Vol. 62, p. 1

Macrae, N. (1976) 'The coming entrepreneurial revolution: a survey', *The Economist*, 25th Dec, p. 42

Malcolmson, J. M. (1981) 'Unemployment and the efficiency wage hypothesis', *Economic Journal*, Vol. 91, p. 848

—— (1982) 'Trade Unions and economic efficiency" *Conference Papers* (*Supplement to the Economic Journal*), Conference of the Royal Economic Society and the Association of University Teachers of Economics, I. S. E. R. Reprint No. 360, University of York

—— (1984) 'Work incentives, Hierarchy, and internal labor markets' *Journal of Political Economy*, Vol. 92, No. 3. p. 486

Manne, H. G. (1965) 'Mergers and the market for corporate control', *Journal of Political Economy*, Vol. 75, p. 110

Mansfield, E. (*et al.*) 1971 *Research and Innovation in the Modern Corporation,* Norton, New York

Marris, R. (1963) 'A model of the managerial enterprise', *Quarterly Journal of Economics*, Vol. 77, p. 185

Marris, R. L. (1964) *The Economic Theory of Managerial Capitalism*, Macmillan, London

Marris, R. L. and Wood, A. (eds) (1971) *The Corporate Economy*, Macmillan, London

Marris, R. L. (1971) 'An introduction to theories of corporate growth' in

Marris, R. L. and Wood, A. J. B. (eds) *The Corporate Economy*, Macmillan, London

Marris, R. and Mueller, D. C. 'The corporation, competition and the invisible hand', *Journal of Economic Literature*, March, Vol. 18, p. 32

Marshall, A. (1925) *Principles of Economics*, 8th Edition, Macmillan, London

Masson, R. T. (1971) 'Executive motivation, earnings and consequent equity performance', *Journal of Political Economy*, Vol. 79, p. 1278

Meade, J. (1972) 'The theory of labour-managed firms and of profit sharing' *Economic Journal*, Vol. 82, p. 402.

Meeks, G. and Whittington, G. (1975) 'Directors pay, growth and profitability' *Journal of Industrial Economics*, Vol. 24, p. 1

Meiners, R., Mofsky, J., and Tollison, R. (1979) 'Piercing the veil of limited liability', *Delaware Journal of Corporation Law*, Vol. 4, p. 351

Menger, Carl (1950) *Principles of Economics*, translated and edited by Dingwall, Jones, and Hoselitz, Bert. F., Free Press, Glencoe, Ill.

Meyer, R. A. (1975) 'Publicly owned versus privately owned utilities: a policy choice', *Review of Economics and Statistics*, Vol. 57, p. 391

Migué, J. and Bélanger, G. (1974) 'Toward a general theory of managerial discretion', *Public Choice*, Vol. 17, p. 27

Mill, J. S. (1898) *Principles of Political Economy with some of their applications to Social Philosophy*, People's Edition, Longmans, Green, and Co. London. First published 1848

Millward, R. (1978) 'Public ownership, the theory of property rights and the public corporation in the U.K.', Salford Papers in Economics, 78-1

Mirrlees, J. A. (1976) 'The optimal structure of incentives and authority within an organization', *Bell Journal of Economics*, Vol. 7, p. 105

Von Mises, Ludwig (1945) *Bureaucracy*, William Hodge and Co., London

—— (1949) *Human Action*, William Hodge and Co., London

Monsen, R. J. Jr., Chiu, J. S. and Cooley, D. E. (1968) 'The effect of separation of ownership and control on the performance of the large firm', *Quarterly Journal of Economics*, Vol. 82, p. 435

Monteverde, K. and Teece, D. J. (1982a) 'Supplier switching costs and vertical integration in the automobile industry', *Bell Journal of Economics*, Vol. 13, p. 206

—— (1982b) 'Appropriable rents and quasi-vertical integration', *Journal of Law and Economics*, Vol. 25, p. 321

Moore, J. H. (1980) *Growth with self-Management: Yugoslav Industrialization 1952–1979*, Hoover Institution Press, Stanford

McEachern, W. A. (1978a) 'Corporate control and growth: an alternative approach' *Journal of Industrial Economics*, Vol. 26, p. 257

—— (1978b) 'Ownership, control and the contemporary corporation: a comment', *Kyklos*, Vol. 31, p. 491

McGuire, J. W., Chiu, J. S. Y., and Elbing, A. O. (1962) 'Executive incomes, sales and profits', *American Economic Review*, Vol. 52, p. 753

Nelson, R. (1959) 'The simple economics of basic scientific research, *Journal of Political Economy*, Vol. 67, p. 297

Nelson, R. R. and Winter, S. C. (1982) *An Evolutionary Theory of Economic Change*, Harvard University Press, Cambridge, Mass.

Neuberg, L. G. (1977) 'Two issues in the municipal ownership of electric power distribution systems' *Bell Journal of Economics*, Vol. 8, p. 303

Von Neumann, J. and Morgenstern, O. (1944) *Economics and the Theory of Games*, Macmillan, London

Newhouse, J. (1970) 'Toward a theory of non-profit institutions: an economic model of a hospital', *American Economic Review*, Vol. 60, p. 64

Nicols, A. (1967) 'Stock versus mutual savings and loan associations: some evidence of differences in behavior', *American Economic Review*, Vol. 57, p. 337

Niskanen, W. (1978) 'Non-market decision making: the peculiar economics of bureaucracy', *American Economic Review*, Vol. 58, p. 293

—— (1971) *Bureaucracy and Representative Government*, Aldine, Chicago

—— (1973) *Bureaucracy: Servant or Master?*, Hobart Paperback 5, IEA, London

—— (1975) 'Bureaucrats and politicians', *Journal of Law and Economics*, Vol. 18, p. 617

Okun, Arthur, M. (1981) *Prices and Quantities: A Macroeconomic Analysis*, Basil Blackwell, Oxford

Owen, G. and Grofman, B. (1984) 'To vote or not to vote: the paradox of nonvoting', *Public Choice*, Vol. 42, No. 3, pp. 311–325

Palmer, J. (1973a) 'The profit variability effects of the management enterprise', *Western Economic Journal*, Vol. 2, p. 228

Palmer, J. (1973b) 'The profit performance effects of the separation of ownership from control in large U.S. industrial corporations', *Bell Journal of Economics and Management Science*, Vol. 4, p. 293

Patton, A. (1961) *Men, money, and Motivation*, New York

Pauly, M. V. (1968) 'The economics of moral hazard', *American Economic Review*, Vol. 58, p. 531

Peacock, A. T. (1983) 'Public x-inefficiency: informational and institutional constraints', in H. Hanusch (ed.), *Anatomy of Government Deficiencies*, Springer Verlag, Heidelberg

Peltzman, S. (1971) 'Pricing in public and private enterprises: electric utilities in the United States', *Journal of Law and Economics*, Vol. 14, p. 109

Pelzman, S. (1976) 'Toward a more general theory of regulation', *Journal of Law and Economics*, Vol. 19, p. 211

Penrose, E. T. (1952) 'Biological analogies in the theory of the firm', *American Economic Review*, Vol. 42, p. 804

Penrose, E. T. (1959) *The Theory of the Growth of the Firm*, Basil Blackwell, Oxford

Perry, M. K. (1980) 'Forward integration by Alcoa: 1888–1930', *Journal of Industrial Economics*, Vol. 29, p. 37

Pescatrice, D. R. and Trapani, J. M. III (1980) 'The Performance and objectives of public and private utilities operating in the U.S.', *Journal of Public Economic*, Vol. 13, p. 259

Pickering, J. F. and Cockerill, T. A. (eds) (1984) *The Economics Management of the Firm*, Philip Allen, London

Pigou, A. C. (1949) *The Veil of Money*, Macmillan, London

Pinchot, G. III (1985) *Intrapreneuring: Why you Don't Have to Leave the Corporation to Become an Entrepreneur*, Harper and Row, New York

Polanyi, M. (1958) *Personal Knowledge*, Routledge and Kegan Paul, London

Polanyi, M. (1967) *The Tacit Dimension*, Doubleday Anchor, Garden City New York

Prais, S. J. (1976) *The Evolution of Giant Firms in Britain*, Cambridge University Press, London

Pratt, J. W. and Zeckhauser, R. J. (eds) (1985) *Principals and Agents: The Structure of Business*, Harvard Business School Research Colloquium, Boston

Primeaux, W. J. (1977) 'An assessment of 'x'-efficiency gained through competition', *Review of Economics and Statistics*, Vol. 59, p. 105

Pryke, R. (1982) 'The comparative performance of public and private enterprise' *Fiscal Studies*, July, p. 68

Radice, H. K. (1971) 'Control type, profitability and growth in large firms: an empirical study', *Economic Journal*, Vol. 81, p. 547

Radner, R. (1981) 'Monitoring cooperative agreements in a repeated principal-agent relationship', *Econometrica*, Vol. 49, p. 1127

Redwood, J. and Hatch, J. (1982) *Controlling Public Industries*, Basil Blackwell, Oxford

Redwood, J. (1984) *Going for Broke...Gambling with Taxpayers' Money*, Basil Blackwell, Oxford

Rees, R. (1980) 'The principal-agent relationship and control of public enterprise' Paper presented to seminar on Regulation at the Centre for SocioLegal Studies, Wolfson College, Oxford, March

Ricardo, D. (1891) in Gonner, E. C. K. (ed.) *Principles of Political Economy and Taxation*, George Bell and Sons, London. First published 1817

Richardson, G. B. (1956) 'Demand and supply reconsidered', *Oxford Economic Papers*, Vol. 8 (New Series), p. 113

—— (1959) 'Equilibrium, expectations and information', *Economic Journal*, Vol. 69, p. 223

—— (1960) *Information and Investment*, Oxford University Press, Oxford

—— (1972) 'The organisation of industry', *Economic Journal*, Vol. 82, p. 883

Rizzo, Mario, J. (ed.) (1979) *Time, Uncertainty, and Disequilibrium Exploration of Austrian Themes*, Lexington Books, D. C. Heath, Lexington Toronto

Robbins, L. (1935) *An Essay on the Nature and Significance of Economic Science*, Macmillan, London

Roberts, D. R. (1959) *Executive Compensation*, Free Press, Glencoe, Ill.

Robertson, D. H. and Dennison, S. R. (1960) *The Control of Industry*, Cambridge Economic Handbook, Nisbet, Cambridge University Press, Cambridge

Ross, S. A. (1973) 'The economic theory of agency: the principal's problem', *American Economic Review*, Proceedings Vol. 63, p. 134

Rowley, C. and Elgin, R. (1985) 'Towards a theory of bureaucratic behaviour' in Shaw, G. K. and Greenaway, D. (eds) *Public Choice, Public finance and Public Policy, Essays in Honour of Alan Peacock*, p. 31, Basil Blackwell, Oxford

Rubin, P. H. (1978) 'The theory of the firm and the structure of the franchise contract', *Journal of Law and Economics*, Vol. 21, p. 223

Rugman, A. M. (1980) 'Internationalisation as a general theory of foreign direct investment: a reappraisal of the literature' *Weltwirtschaftliches Archiv*, III, p. 365

Rumelt, R. (1974) *Strategy, Structure and Economic Performance*, Harvard University Press, Cambridge, Mass.

Salop, S. (1979) 'A model of the natural rate of unemployment,' *American Economic Review*, Vol. 69, p. 117

Sargant, Florence, P. (1933) *Logic of Industrial Organisation*, Trench, Trubner & Co., London

—— (1961) *Ownership, Control and Success of Large Companies*, Sweet and Maxwell, London

Schelling, T. C. (1960) *The Strategy of Conflict*, Harvard University Press, Cambridge, Mass.

Scherer, F. M. (1980) *Industrial Market Structure and Performance*, 2nd edition, Rand McNally, Chicago

Schmalensee, R. (1973) 'A note on the theory of vertical integration' *Journal of Political Economy*, Vol. 81, p. 442

Schumpeter, J. A. (1936) *The Theory of Economic Development*, Harvard University Press, Cambridge, Mass.

—— (1943) *Capitalism, Socialism and Democracy*, Unwin University Books, London

—— (1954) *History of Economic Analysis*, Allen and Unwin, London

Shackle, G. L. S. (1961) 2nd edition (1969) *Decision, Order and Time in Human Affairs*, Cambridge University Press, Cambridge

—— (1966) *The Nature of Economic Thought. Selected Papers 1955–1964*, Cambridge University Press, Cambridge

—— (1970) *Expectation, Enterprise and Profit: The Theory of the Firm*, Allen and Unwin, London

—— (1972) *Epistemics and Economics: A Critique of Economic Doctrines*, Cambridge University Press, Cambridge

—— (1979) *Imagination and the Nature of Choice*, Edinburgh University Press, Edinburgh

—— (1979) 'Imagination, formalism, and choice', in Rizzo, Mario, J. (ed.), op. cit. p. 19

—— (1982) 'Means and meaning in economic theory' *Scottish Journal of Political Economy*, Vol. 29, p. 223

Shannon, H. A. (1931) 'The coming of general limited liability', *Economic History*, Vol. II, p. 267

Shapiro, C. and Stiglitz, J. E. (1984) 'Equilibrium unemployment as a worker discipline device', *American economic Review*, Vol. 74, p. 433

Shavell, S. (1979) 'Risk sharing and incentives in the principal and agent relationship', *Bell Journal of Economics*, Vol. 10, p. 55

Silver, M. and Auster, R. (1969) 'Entrepreneurship, profit, and the limits on firm size', *Journal of Business*, University of Chicago, Vol. 42, p. 277. Reprinted in Auster, R. D. and Silver, M. (1979) *The State as a Firm*, op. cit. p. 111

Silver, M. (1984) *Enterprise and the Scope of the Firm*, Martin Robertson, Oxford

Simon, H. A. (1957) *Models of Man*, John Wiley and Sons, New York

—— (1964) 'On the concept of organizational goal', *Administrative Science Quarterly*, Vol. 9, p. 1

—— (1969) *The Sciences of the Artificial*, M.I.T. Press, Cambridge, Mass.

—— (1976) *Adminstrative Behavior: A Study of Decision Making Processes in Administrative Organization*, 3rd edition New York Free Press, New York

—— (1976) 'From substantive to procedural rationality', in Latsis S. J. (ed.), *Method and Appraisal in Economics*, Cambridge University Press, Cambridge

—— (1978) 'Rationality as process and as product of thought', *American Economic Review*, Papers and Proceedings, p. 1

—— (1979) 'Rational decision making in business organizations', *American Economic Review*, Vol. 69, p. 493

Singh, A. (1971) *Take Overs*, Cambridge University Press, Cambridge

Singh, A. (1975) 'Takeovers, economic natural selection and the theory of the firm: evidence from the post-war U.K. experience', *Economic Journal*, Vol. 85, p. 497

Sirc, L. (1979) *The Yugoslav Economy Under Self-Management*, Macmillan, London

Sisk, D. E. (1985) 'Rent seeking, noncompensated transfers, and laws of succession: a property rights view', *Public Choice*, Vol. 46, p. 95

Slater, M. (1980) 'The managerial limitation to the growth of firms', *Economic Journal*, Vol. 90, p. 520

Smiley, R. (1976) 'Tender offers, transactions costs and the theory of the firm, *Review of Economics and Statistics*, Vol. 58, p. 22

Smith, Adam (1925) *The Wealth of Nations*, 4th edition, Edwin Cannan (ed.), Methuen and Co, London. First published 1776

Sorenson, R. (1974) 'The separation of ownership from control and firm performance: an empirical analysis', *Southern Economic Journal*, Vol. 40, p. 145

Spence, M. A. (1975) 'The Economics of internal organization: an introduction', *Bell Journal of Economics*, Vol. 6, p. 163

Stano, M. (1976) 'Monopoly power, ownership control, and corporate performance', *Bell Journal of Economics*, Vol. 7, p. 672

Steer, P. and Cable, J. (1978) 'Internal organization and profit: an empirical analysis of large U.K. companies', *Journal of Industrial Economics*, Vol. 27, p. 13

Stigler, G. J. (1951) 'The division of labour is limited by the extent of the market', *Journal of Political Economy*, Vol. 59, p. 190

—— (1961) 'The economics of information', *Journal of Political Economy*, Vol. 69, p. 213

—— (1964) 'A theory of oligopoly', *Journal of Political Economy*, Vol. 72, p. 44

—— (1976) 'The xistence of x-efficiency', *American Economic review*, Vol. 66, p. 213

Stigler, G. J. and Friedland, C. (1983) 'The literature of economics: the case of Berle and Means', *Journal of Law and Economics*, Vol. 26, p. 237

Stiglitz, J. E. (1975) 'Incentives, risk, and information: notes towards a theory of hierarchy', *Bell Journal of Economics*, Vol. 6, p. 552

Storey, D. J. (1982) *Entrepreneurship and the New Firm*, Croom Helm, London

Taylor, F. W. (1911) *The Principles of Scientific Management*, Harper and Row, New York

Teece, D. J. (1981) 'Internal organisation and economic performance: an empirical analysis of the profitability of principal firms', *Journal of Industrial Economics*, Vol. 30, p. 173

Thompson, R. S. (1981) 'Internal organisation and profit: a note', *Journal of Industrial Economics*, Vol. 30. p. 201

Thünen, J. H. Von, (1966), translated by C. M. Wartenberg, *Von Thünen's Isolated State*, ed. P. Hall. First volume of original published 1826, second part 1850

Titmus, R. M. (1970) *The Gift Relationship*, Allen and Unwin, London

Tullock, G. (1965) *The Politics of Bureaucracy*, Public Affairs Press, Washington

—— (1980a) 'Rent seeking as a negative sum game', in Buchanan, J. M. *et al.* (eds) *Toward a Theory of the Rent Seeking Society*, p. 16, Texas A and M University Press, College Station

—— (1980b) 'Efficient rent seeking' in Buchanan, J. M. *et al.* (eds) *Toward a Theory of the Rent Seeking Society*, p. 97, Texas A and M University Press, College Station

—— (1980c) 'The welfare costs of tariffs, monopolies, and theft' in Buchanan, J. M. *et al.* (eds) *Toward a Theory of the Rent Seeking Society*, p. 39, Texas A and M University Press, College Station

Urwick, L. F. (1943) *The Elements of Administration*, Harper and Row, New York

Utton, M. A. (1982) *The Political Economy of Big Business*, Martin Robertson, Oxford

Vanek, J. (1970) *The General Theory of Labour-Managed Market Economies*, Cornell University Press, Ithaca

Vanek, J. (ed) (1975) *Penguin Modern Economics Readings in Self-Management*, Penguin, Harmondsworth

Vanek, J. (1977) *The Labour Managed Economy*, Cornell University Press, Ithaca

Vaupel, J. W. (1971) 'Characteristics and motivations of the U.S. corporations which manufacture abroad', Paper presented to Atlantic Institute, Paris, June 1971

Vernon, J. M., and Graham, D. A. (1971) 'Profitability of monopolization by vertical integration', *Journal of Political Economy*, Vol. 79, p. 924

Villarejo, D. (1961) 'Stock ownership and the control of the corporation', *New University Thought*, Chicago

Walras, L. (1954) *Elements of Pure Economics*, translated by William Jaffé, Allen and Unwin, London

Ward, B. (1958) 'The firm in Illyria: market syndicalism', *American Economic Review*, Vol. 48, p. 566

Weber, M. (1947) *The Theory of Social and Economic Organization*, Free Press, New York

Weiss, L. W. (1983) 'The extent and effects of aggregate concentration', *Journal of Law and Economics*, Vol. 26, p. 429

Whynes, D. K., and Bowles, R. A. (1981) *The Economic Theory of the State*, Martin Robertson, Oxford

Williamson, O. E. (1963) 'Managerial discretion and business behavior', in Furubotn, E. and Pejovich, S. (eds) (1974), op. cit. p. 109

—— (1964) *The Economics of Discretionary Behavior Managerial Objectives in a Theory of the Firm*, Prentice-Hall, Englewood Cliffs, N.J.

—— (1967) 'Hierarchical control and optimum firm size', *Journal of Political Economy*, Vol. 75, p. 123

—— (1970) *Corporate Control and Business Behavior*, Prentice-Hall, Englewood Cliffs, N.J.

—— (1975) *Markets and Hierarchies: Analysis and Antitrust Implications A Study in the Economics of Internal Organization*, The Free Press, Collier Macmillan, London and New York

Williamson, O. E., Wachter, M. L. and Harris, J. E. (1975) 'Understanding the employment relation: the analysis of idiosyncratic exchange', *Bell Journal of Economics*, Vol. 6, p. 250

Williamson, O. E. (1979) 'Transaction-cost economics: the governance of contractual relations', *Journal of Law and Economics*, Vol. 22, p. 233

Williamson, O. E. (1981) 'The modern corporation: origins, evolution, attributes', *Journal of Economic Literature*, Vol. 19, p. 1537

Williamson, O. E. (1983) 'Organization form, residual claimants, and corporate control', *Journal of Law and Economics*, Vol. 26, p. 351

Wolf, B. M. (1977) 'Industrial diversification and internationalisation: some empirical evidence', *Journal of Industrial Economics*, Vol. 26, p. 177

Yellen, J. L. (1984) 'Efficiency wage models of unemployment', *American Economic Review*, Papers and Proceedings Vol. 74, p. 200

Yunker, J. A. (1975) 'Economic performance of public and private enterprise: the case of U.S. electric utilities', *Journal of Economics and Business*, Vol. 28, p. 60

Index of Names Cited

Subject Index

Adverse selection 26–7, 42–3, 159–61, 162, 163–4, 203, 214–16

Agency cost 106, 257

Agency relation 40–1, 94, 95; and incentive contracts 115–50, 154–8; applied to joint-stock company 240–1; applied to managerial incentives in joint stock company 246–50; applied to other institutions 261–4; and managerial theories of the firm 274–5

Austrian theory xi, 20, 55, 64, 66, 67, 68, 71, 76–7, 279, 280

Bounded rationality 17, 30, 36, 185, 200

Bureaucracy 242–3, 267–71

Chicken game 108, 110

Conglomerate diversification 193–4; and the use of information 212; as response to uncertainty 213–14

Co-operatives 262–6

Corporate structure 194–202

Division of ownership from control 103–4, 239–77

Efficiency wage 161–4, 188

Employment relation 39–40

Entrepreneur: classical view of 45–7; as bearer of uncertainty 47–9; as intermediary 49–54; as innovator 58–63; as specialist coordinator 65–71; and equilibrium 58–63; and subjectivism 63–5; and knowledge 54–5; place within the firm 71–3; and access to capital 54, 62–3, 67, 75, 210; and entrepreneurial profit 53, 85; and corporate strategy, 205, 210, 225, 228–31; and managerial incentives 253–60; contrasted with neoclassical searcher 55–8; contrasted with rent seeker 177–81;

Equilibrium: Walrasian 16–17, 50; Hayekian 47; and entrepreneurship 58–61, 70–1

Exchange : bargaining and the core of the exchange game 6–13; and the tatonnement process 13–16; and the equilibrium method 16–17;

Externalities xi, 86–90

Firm: as production function 151, 207; as nexus of contracts 3–4, 19, 72, 144, 147, 240; as policing device 90–3, 158–66, 214–25; as response to uncertainty 17–20, 48, 206–14; as vehicle for innovation 225–31; as governance structure 185–7, 204; boundaries of 146, 147, 193, 202–6; embodying differing property rights structures, 93–107, 239–45

Franchise contracts 146–7, 189

Hierarchies 151–90
Hold out 87
Hold up 185, 190, 220–3
Horizontal integration 207–9

Idiosyncratic exchange 39, 175–7
Implicit contracts 138, 165, 240, 263
Incentive contracts: in insurance markets 135–6; in law enforcement 136–7; in employment 137–8; and the firm 143–8; piece rates and time rates 154–8
Information: asymmetry of 26–9, 36, 144; property rights in 180, 183, 210; Austrian approach to 51–5, 58; neoclassical approach to 55–8; Arrow's paradox and 210, 232; value of 131–5; and integration 210–20
Internal capital market 200, 210–14
Internal Labour market 182–5, 200

Joint stock company 101–7, 234–9, 246–60

Knowledge: tacit knowledge 59, 76–7, 176; of time and place 59, 176, 182; and entrepreneurship 54–8; *see also* Information

Labour managed firms 245

Managerial labour market 250–3
Managerial theories of firm 266–77
Mixed enterprise 271–2
Money 31–5
Monitoring 91–2, 96–9, 120, 131–5, 139–43, 158–64, 214–20, 247, 250, 251, 270

Moral hazard 27–9, 91, 93, 94, 95, 98, 99, 135, 159, 161–6, 175, 203
Multinational integration 194, 211; and conventional trade theory 211; and use of firm specific resources 212, 227; and research and development 227

Nationalised firms 241–2, 275–7
Non-profit enterprise, 243–4, 261–2

Opportunism 40, 91, 99, 110, 144, 164–5, 176, 177–87, 200, 220–3; *see also* Rent seeking

Partnership 96–101
Piece rates 154–8
Principal-agent relation *see* Agency relation
Prisoners dilemma 111
Property Rights: private 80–1; communal 81; collective 81–2; enforcement of 84–5; evolution of 85–90; exchangeability of 82–4; and the proprietorship 94–6; and the partnership 96–101; and the joint stock enterprise 101–7, 246–60; and bureaucracy 242–3; and non-profit firms 243–4, 261–2; and nationalised firms 241–2, 271; and mixed enterprises 271–2; and labour-managed firms 245; and cooperatives 262–6
Proprietorship 90–3, 94–6
Public goods 35–6, 91

Quasi-rents 220–3
Quasi vertical integration 204–5, 222–3

Rank-order tournament 166–75
Rent-seeking 177–81, 188–9, 239
Reservation price 57
Risk Sharing: and the proprietorship 95; and the